Making history

CW00953309

Making History begins with a puzzle. In 1976 the inhabitants of Pukapuka, a Polynesian island in the South Pacific, revived a traditional form of social organization that several authoritative Pukapukan informants claimed to have experienced previously in their youth. Yet five professional anthropologists, who conducted research on the island prior to 1976, do not mention it in any of their writings. Had the Pukapukans "invented" a new tradition? Or had the anthropologists collectively erred in not recording an old one?

In unraveling this puzzle, Robert Borofsky compares two different ways of "making history," two different ways of constructing knowledge about the past. He examines the dynamic nature of Pukapukan knowledge focusing on how Pukapukans, in the process of learning and validating their traditions, continually change them. He also shows how anthropologists, in the process of writing about such traditions for Western audiences, often overstructure them, emphasizing uniformity at the expense of diversity, stasis at the expense of change.

As well as being of interest for what it reveals about Pukapukan (and more generally Polynesian) culture, *Making History* helps clarify important strengths and limitations of the anthropological approach. It provides valuable insights into both the anthropological construction of knowledge and the nature of anthropological understanding.

Robert Borofsky is Assistant Professor of Anthropology at Hawaii Loa College, Oahu.

Making history

Pukapukan and anthropological constructions of knowledge

ROBERT BOROFSKY
Hawaii Loa College

Drawings by David Friedman

CAMBRIDGE
UNIVERSITY PRESS

Published by the Press Syndicate of the University of Cambridge
The Pitt Building, Trumpington Street, Cambridge CB2 1RP
40 West 20th Street, New York, NY 10011-4211 USA
10 Stamford Road, Oakleigh, Melbourne 3166, Australia

First published 1987
Reprinted 1989
First paperback edition 1990
Reprinted 1996

Library of Congress Cataloging-in-Publication Data

Borofsky, Robert, 1944–
Making history.
Bibliography: p.
Includes index.
1. Ethnology – Cook Islands – Pukapuka Atoll.
2. Pukapuka Atoll (Cook Islands) – Social life and
customs. 3. Knowledge, Theory of. 4. Education,
Primitive – Cook Islands – Pukapuka Atoll. 5. Ethnology –
Methodology. I. Title.
GN671.C6B67   1987   306'.0996'23   86–26381

British Library Cataloguing in Publication Data

Borofsky, Robert
Making history : Pukapukan and
anthropological constructions of knowledge.
1. Ethnology – Cook Islands
2. Cook Islands – Social life and
customs
I. Title
305.8'994   GN671.T77

ISBN 0-521-30520-9 hardback
ISBN 0-521-39648-4 paperback

Transferred to digital printing 1999

To Nancy, Amelia, and Robyn,
who shared in the making of this book

We are concerned to write the anthropology and the history of those moments when native and intruding cultures are conjoined. Neither can be known independently of that moment.

Greg Dening
Islands and Beaches

Contents

Illustrations

Maps

Figures

Drawings

Photographs of selected informants

ix

Foreword

As in many of the best ethnographies, *Making History* begins by presenting the reader with a puzzle. How is it possible that a basic feature of traditional social organization could be overlooked by well-trained anthropologists specifically concerned with social organization? When Rob Borofsky, his wife Nancy, and their young daughter Amelia arrived on the Polynesian atoll of Pukapuka in November 1977, they found the island in the midst of a cultural revival. In place of the regular three-part village system, the 'Council of Important People' had established the *Akatawa* which divided the island into two parts. The mystery was that Pukapukans insisted the *Akatawa* was traditional and described earlier experiences with it in concrete historical terms; yet several highly competent anthropologists who had worked on the atoll in the past, as well as a number of other observers, had failed to record its existence. What could account for this anomaly?

In order to unravel the mystery Borofsky had to delve into the nature of Pukapukan knowledge: how this knowledge is constructed, learned, and used in a variety of contexts. It also led him to question the nature of anthropological knowledge – how it *too* is constructed, learned, and used. The problem forced him to examine critically the work of his anthropological predecessors, especially the contexts surrounding the research of Ernest and Pearl Beaglehole and Julia Hecht, so he could understand how such competent fieldworkers could miss a fundamental feature of social structure. He went beyond published sources, poring over the Beagleholes' field notes and engaging in extensive discussions with Hecht. The result is a fascinating case of anthropological reflexivity. Although self-reflection has become commonplace in recent years, Borofsky's treatment is refreshing in its lack of self-indulgence, in the way that it illuminates central questions of ethnography.

What Borofsky confronts, ultimately, are the strengths and weaknesses of anthropological ways of constructing knowledge. He delineates important limitations regarding the construction of anthropological accounts, but he also emphasizes the real strengths of anthropology as well. The discipline's concern with comparison and the analysis of different perspectives, Borofsky points out, fosters cumulative knowledge over time. One moves from accounts of simplicity that attempt to capture the broader structures at the sacrifice of the real texture of Polynesian life to an understanding that comes closer to an appreciation of the complexities of that texture.

Along with Borofsky, I believe that our cumulative understanding of Polynesian cultures has been advanced to a considerable extent in recent years by the application of more appropriate theories. Earlier perspectives were based on a somewhat static view that resulted in traitlike descriptions that failed to take note of ambiguous features of social organization in favor of those that could be easily categorized. As Borofsky insightfully points out, some parts of social organization are easier to describe than others; if one is striving for a neat, coherent description, it is tempting to ignore the ambiguities. Societies were categorized as patrilineal, patrilocal, and so forth, depending on statistical counts, ideology, or some combination of the two, but without due consideration for the inevitable anomalies. The historical past was also often merged with the "ethnographic present" in the interest of generating a coherent structural-functional account. The results, though enlightening in some ways, often failed to capture the essence of Polynesian culture which, as Marshall Sahlins has recently indicated, involves a constant interplay between structures and process.

Because of the lengthy period Borofsky spent in the field, more than forty months, and aided by a fluency in the Pukapukan language, he was able to gain an appreciation of processes often missed by those who stay for shorter times on Polynesian islands. In his writing, both the pragmatic nature of Pukapukan approaches to knowing and acting and the willingness of Pukapukans to experiment with structural forms come alive. Among other things, we come to appreciate better than ever a quality of atoll life pointed out by Marshall Sahlins in his *Social Stratification in Polynesia*: the commitment to cross-cutting ties based on communal activities. The Pukapukan experiment with the *Akatawa*, along with comparable experiments with patrilines and matrilines, vividly illuminates Sahlins's point.

Borofsky's account also makes important contributions to two other areas that have fascinated students of Polynesian culture. One is the study of socialization; the other is the dynamics of status rivalry, which was posed provocatively by Irving Goldman in *Ancient Polynesian Society*. The study of socialization has come a long way since Mead, especially in the work of the Beagleholes and Ritchies in New Zealand, Levy's work in Tahiti, and, if I may be immodest, my own work with Ron Gallimore in Hawaii. All of this research was undertaken with the aim of comprehending adult character and behavior in terms of socialization experiences. Borofsky, however, has a complementary interest. He is concerned with how individuals learn about the construction and manipulation of knowledge. Thus the processes may sound familiar, but their implications are extended in new and illuminating ways. It is similar with Borofsky's treatment of status rivalry. Whereas Goldman's analysis of status rivalry focuses on contention between chiefs and on political maneuvering in the more stratified Polynesian societies, Borofsky demonstrates its effect on the formation of knowledge in the relatively egalitarian setting of an atoll. Here we see rivalry softened by humor, in contrast with its harsh expression among ambitious chiefs in hierarchical societies. The result is a new appreciation of the implications of status rivalry in Polynesia, one that goes well beyond the dynamics of political intrigue.

Finally, Borofsky makes a valuable point about the nature of cultural traditions. Whereas others have discussed the "invention of tradition," he examines in detail the specific processes by which this comes about. We read specific case studies of Pukapukans reformulating their traditions, and we perceive both anthropologists and Pukapukans adjusting aspects of the past to suit present-day needs.

As I read Borofsky's analysis, I could not help compare and contrast it with Derek Freeman's recent critique of Margaret Mead. There are some interesting parallels between Borofsky and Freeman. Both spent considerably longer periods on location than their predecessors and enjoyed greater linguistic competence. Both were struck by anomalies between their observations and those reported by prior workers. And both have been concerned with the implications of these discrepancies for the construction of anthropological theory. But the differences are more dramatic. Whereas Freeman is intent on attacking the credibility of Mead as a fieldworker and attempts to "prove" that he is right and she wrong by amassing data, Borofsky is more concerned with understanding how the inevitable biases of ethnographers influence the results they achieve. Borofsky is engaged in what might be termed the archaeology of ethnography. By examining the residues of ethnographic research (the publications, field notes, manuscripts, and memories), he believes we can develop a more sensitive understanding not only of the peoples we study but of our own constructions about them. Rather than placing his stock in disconfirmation, as Freeman does, he emphasizes the value of understanding how and why people develop differing perspectives.

Borofsky, of course, has his own biases and his research, like his predecessors', is bounded by certain contexts. His prior position as a grade school teacher, his studies at the University of Hawaii, and his affiliation with the East-West Center's Communication Institute, the fact that his wife and daughter were with him, that an Australian teacher-friend's stay on the atoll overlapped with theirs – all these circumstances shaped his research and this book. But perhaps even more important is the nature of the interaction between Borofsky, the ethnographer, and Pukapukans, the subjects of study. He is candid about the ways in which his goals differed from theirs and how these differences affected the conclusions each drew in their discussions with one another. So we are able to juxtapose the construction of anthropological knowledge with the construction of Pukapukan knowledge in significant ways. The comparison makes us seem much more like Pukapukans – much more subject to pragmatic as well as cultural contingencies than we have sometimes been comfortable admitting. It makes both Pukapukan and anthropologist, from my perspective, seem more human.

Alan Howard
Professor of Anthropology
University of Hawaii

Preface

A variety of factors influenced the making of this book and the doctoral dissertation that preceded it (Borofsky 1982). Because I was a participant in the East-West Center's Communication Institute while a doctoral candidate at the University of Hawaii, my research plans initially called for investigating the effects of Western media on the distribution and preservation of traditional knowledge. Eventually I expanded this to include a general concern with the transmission, construction, and validation of traditional knowledge. I chose Pukapuka because of the availability of the Beagleholes' field notes in the Bishop Museum and because of the atoll's healthy environment (which meant my family could accompany me).

Fieldwork[1]

Research on the atoll lasted for forty-one months – from November 1977 to April 1981. During that time, I made two brief sojourns to Samoa (for medical treatment and supplies) involving a total absence of approximately four weeks. No other off-island travel occurred. While awaiting transportation to Pukapuka, I spent approximately one month microfilming documents pertinent to the atoll in the Rarotongan government archives. This book is based on the approximately ten thousand pages of field notes and more than three thousand microfilm exposures collected.

My interactions with Pukapukans covered a wide range of activities and contexts. It is important to note that my wife Nancy and daughter Amelia (who was one year old at the time of our arrival) accompanied me throughout the fieldwork. We lived as a family among families on the atoll.

I utilized a variety of research strategies. As in most anthropological research, I relied extensively on participant observation. In addition, I systematically surveyed Pukapukans' knowledge of their traditions across a breadth of subjects: social organization, legends, fish names, fishing techniques, material culture, place names, cooking recipes, and wind names and directions. The first four surveys involved stratified samples of eighty informants ranging in age from ten to approximately eighty; the last four surveys, samples of thirty informants over sixty-three years of age.[2] I frequently followed up these broad surveys with in-depth interviews of selected individuals. Five to six knowledgeable informants also subsequently discussed a number of these issues with me in a series of group meetings.

In addition, I carried out numerous informal interviews, casually asking people certain questions whenever the opportunity arose. I did not simply listen to what Pukapukans told me. I discussed, I argued with them – so I could better understand what they meant (cf. Stocking 1983a:99). Finally, I systematically gathered data on a variety of special topics. I examined, for example, people's exposure to Western media, and while gathering genealogies, mapped thirty-nine sections of land and sixteen taro swamps, mostly in Yato village. Maps 3, 5, and 6 in the text derive from this work. (Additional details regarding fieldwork – especially concerning field assistants, language skills, and Pukapukan phonetics – are elaborated in Borofsky 1982.)

Rather than focus on abstract discussions and theoretical reviews, I consciously emphasize individual informants and the role they played in the construction of this book. People cited in the Pukapukan acknowledgments include informants interviewed at some length. The eighteen people listed in the seventh paragraph of the Pukapukan acknowledgments constitute what might be termed key informants, individuals interviewed in particular depth. The 210 informants cited in the eighth paragraph were primarily involved in various surveys and/or special projects.

For clarity, I have separated informants cited in the text into two main groups, named and unnamed. The named informants (such as Molingi and Petelo) convey a sense of how specific individuals both illustrate and diverge from the broader themes discussed. (Their sexes and approximate ages are listed in the notes.)[3]

Readers should know that the data presented in Chapters 3 and 4 are not derived from my observations alone. They represent the observations of three "outsiders." I paid close attention to my wife Nancy's observations as well as to those of Ron Vetter, an Australian Volunteers Abroad teacher whose time in Pukapuka overlapped with ours for almost two and a half years. The three of us did not always agree in our analyses, but we did concur on the general ideas described below. Agreements were far more common than disagreements. Nancy's investigations did much to lessen male biases in the research. I have cited Ron Vetter's observations at some length because he possessed a sensitive, in-depth understanding of the high school students with whom he worked. I could have as well drawn from my own field notes since I studied Pukapukans slightly younger and slightly older than Ron's students, but is is important for readers to grasp that different Westerners, with different backgrounds and different experiences, frequently perceived Pukapukans in the same way. (In line with Ron's request, I have cited him in the text simply as the Australian teacher.) I alone should be held responsible for the analysis of the *Akatawa*, Pukapukan social organization, and the broader themes stressed throughout the book.

The construction of this text

Following my fieldwork, in conversations with Alan Howard and Greg Dening and in reflecting on ideas in the writings of Mannheim, G. H. Mead, and Gadamer, I gradually developed the perspective that forms the core of this book – how Pukapukans and anthropologists come to possess different "ways of knowing," different ways of constructing accounts of the atoll's traditions. Readers should realize that my own ideas developed within a broader context, which both framed and influenced them. Chief among these were the present interpretative paradigm in the social sciences; a sense of self-consciousness within anthropology as an earlier generation writes their autobiographies and have histories written about them; the process of decolonization and the politics of knowledge that go with it; and reflections on the ethnographic process stimulated by hermeneutic concerns and the recent Freeman-Mead controversy.[4] But beyond these statements, I feel hesitant to contextualize my work in the same manner as I do for the Beagleholes and Hecht. There is something self-serving and incongruous, it seems to me, in presuming to explain one's biases to others - in acting as both author and subject of an ethnography. A dialogue with reviewers is more productive and, in this respect, I refer readers to various reviews of the book.

Unless otherwise indicated, all quotes are verbatim transcriptions of taped conversations and all translations are my own. The anecdotes are paraphrased material drawn from field notes.[5] The book is presented as a puzzle in line with a theme developed years ago by Archibald MacLeish in *Ars Poetica*. I have tried to draw readers into both the analysis *and* experience of making history.

Acknowledgments

Ko te puka nei ko te toe tuanga wakamaalama tenei o taku yanga kimi kite i lunga o to kotou wenua, ko Te Ulu-o-te-Watu. Ka wakamaalama atu te leila i naa mea aaku na kite, me kole, na talaina mai kiaku, i loto o te lauwaa malama na noo ai au ma toku ngutuale i lunga o Pukapuka, mai te matawiti 1977 ki te matawiti 1981. Aulaka laa te puka nei e meaina e, na pau te wii mea ki loto, me kole, ko tano tikaai te wii mea i loto.

Te tayi, e wainga aku mea naa wakaputuputu e kiai laa na tukua ki loto. Mei te mea ka akatai mai au i naa toe wakamaalamaanga no naa toe yanga o Wale naa, ka loaangalele atu pa te puka nei. Ka tala te puka nei i te wakatukeenga a te tangata i na yanga o te vaaia mua, peia oki ma naa yanga e wakaemaema tikaai e kotou i te vaaia nei. Ko te puka nei, na taataaina tikaai na naa anthropologists, e wolo i leila te mea i loto e ye puapinga loa ki naa tangata o Pukapuka, ka puapinga laa kia latou wua.

Te lua, ko te puka nei, ka tala mai iaana i naa wakamaalamanga ma naa manako o naa tangata o Wale, no lunga o naa toe akonoanga (yanga) tupuna ma naa toe akonoanga i te vaaia nei. No naa mea na taaikua i te puka nei, penei e ye aaliki te toe kau i naa mea na taataaina nei. Ka veveia tikaai au ke taataa mai e tangata no naa takayala na ana kitea i loto o te puka nei. I leila ka akatau au i tona manako ki naa manako o te toe kau, penei ka maua i leila te apiianga puapinga no maua. Me ka taataa mai kotou, taataa kia Robert Borofsky, Anthropology Department, Hawaii Loa College, Kaneohe, Hawaii 96744 United States.

Noatu e kooku na taataaina te puka, e ye tano loa pa ke akameitaki wua kooku no lunga o naa mea na taataaina ki loto, yaula na te wii tangata o Pukapuka na tuku mai kiaku. Enei wua taku yanga, ko te onoono, tilotilo wakalelei, uwiuwi uwianga, ma te wakapaapu i naa wii tika na tukua mai.

Ka wano katoa taku akaatawai ki te kau na tautulua au ma toku ngutuale i te vaaia naa noonoo ai matou i Wale naa. E tolu tu tautulu ka winangalo au ke tala takitaiina.

Te tayi, kia Tukia Mataola ma Paleula Katoa. Ko laaua na waka-mataina e te wakaoo ma te alataki i toku manako ki naa toe yanga wenua o Pukapuka, penei oki ma te wuliwuli manako tautulu kiaku, ma te wakatano i oku takayala, ke taungalulu taku yanga. Na lilo tikaai ta laaua tautulu wai mea puapinga na oko ai ma taku yanga ulu kite ki te openga.

Te lua, e wainga oki te tangata ko latou na talaina mai aku mea naa winangalo ke iloa. Enei o latou ingoa (na wakapapa au mai te leta "A" ki te leta "Y"): Akima, Apela, Kililua, Loumanu, Mataola Tutai, Mol-ingi, Ngalau, Ngutu, Paani, Paleula, Petelo, Vailoa wolo, Vavetuki, Walemaki wolo, Wuatai wolo, Yala, Yingonge, ma Yolo. Ko te tangata ko mina ai au no tona tu mataola, ata talatala, maawutu, e ye ekoko au e te tala atu, ko Molingi. Kaaleka laa, ko te kau taakatoa i lunga nei e wolo tikaai a latou mea na tautulu mai.

Kale ai oki ko te kau wua i lunga nei, e wolo oki naa mea na meaina mai e te toe kau: Akailo, Akakino, Akatu, Aketa, Alalua, Alama, Amota, Andrew, Ane, Ape, Apitai, Ataela, Atela, Atiau, Aumatangi, Auola, Avili, Don, Elati, Elikana, Ene, Etuena, George, Ielemia, Iel-uta, Ilo, Inapa, Ine, Ipo, Isalaela, Iva, Ka, Kaatia, Kaila, Kailua, Kain-ana, Kaitala, Kalito, Kaututu, Kikau, Kilianu, Kino, Kinolongo, Kita wolo, Kitea, Kiti, Koia, Koyi lewu, Kumala, Kupa, Lakela, Lakii, Lak-ini, Lalua, Langiuila, Latalo, Latea, Lautana, Lavalua, Leleau, Lelei-mua, Lemuna, Letai, Limapeni, Lipene, Litawa, Lito, Lotoua, Luaine, Lualau wolo, Lulutangi, Lupena lewu, Lutonga, Lutu, Maina, Makonia, Mala, Male, Malo, Maloti, Malu lewu, Malu wolo, Malua, Maluu, Ma-moe, Manava, Manea, Mani, Manila, Manulele, Mataola Apolo, Maua, Melota, Metua, Metua lewu, Miimetua, Mikala, Moapii, Mou, Mouauli, Moukite, Moukole, Naomi, Nelia, Ngalupe, Nimeti, Okotai, Olani, Ono, Paala, Paito, Palau, Pana, Paniani, Papaa, Papino, Pateteepa, Paulo, Paunu, Pelepele wolo, Peli, Pelia wolo, Pilato, Pitia, Poilua, Potai, Punavai, Punga wolo, Samuela, Taakave, Taakele, Taakelepo lewu, Taakelepo wolo, Taapaki, Taapeta wolo, Taavini, Tai, Taiiki, Takitengutu, Tala lewu, Tala wolo, Talai, Talakaka, Taleima, Tama, Tamali wolo, Tanetoa, Tangiula, Tango, Tatai, Taumaina, Tealaika, Teatu, Telai, Tele, Telema lewu, Telema wolo, Teleni, Teleolo, Teluia, Temanaki, Temela, Temoana, Tengele, Tenua, Teopenga lewu, Teo-penga wolo, Tepa, Tiaaki, Tiaki, Tiava, Tilipa, Timi, Tinga, Tinokula,

Tinomana, Tioni, Tipapa, Toa, Toia, Tolu, Toolua, Tuakana, Tuiloa, Tuiva, Tumu, Tupou, Tutai, Tutoka, Ulaula, Unukimua, Vailoa lewu, Vailoa wolo, Vakaula, Vaotiale, Vavalu, Viday, Vigo, Viliamu, Waleeu, Walemaki lewu, Walevaka, Walewaoa, Witivaka, Woetai, Wualelei wolo, Wuliia, Yaewua, Yeia, Yikiatua, ma te toe kau.

Te tolu, ko te kau naa tautuluina au ma taku wawine, ko Nancy, ma taku tamaawine, ko Amelia, no o latou tu lelei na tauyala wua ai to matou olaanga i Wale naa. E mea tautonu lava ke waapiki mai au i te wii tangata o Pukapuka, no te mea koi ai naa konga na tautulu mai ai te toe, ma te toe ia matou.

Ka winangalo katoa oki au e te vavae wua i taku akaatawai no Tipuia Tiro, no te mea e tautulu wolo tana mea. Ka wakateniteni au i tona tu maawutu ma te lelei e te ilinakiina.

Ki te kau naa wakatau noonoo matou i Pukapuka, ko pono iaku e, na kite kotou e, na veveia tikaai matou ia tatou noonoonga i lunga o to kotou wenua. E wenua motoilele, e wainga oki te wii yanga wenua (peu tupuna). Na lilo tikaai a tatou noonoonga akatai ia wai akakii i o matou ngaakau ki a kotou wii yanga (lelei), e ye ngalopoaina loa ia matou. Na timata matou e te wakaali atu i to matou veveia la loto o te talatala, peia oki la loto o a matou yanga lelei no kotou. Enei te akalaanga, na timata au e te wakaemaema i ta kotou peu tupuna la loto i taku tautulu i te toe kau puapii e taataa i te Pukapukan-English Dictionary, peia oki te waainganga makomako ma te waiwai na wakatupua eku. Na timata i leila au ma toku ngutuale e te wakaali atu e ko wakaemaema matou i a kotou wii yanga wenua, ko ye maka laa oki matou i a matou peu ma a matou yanga (papaa). No leila e ye pau to matou veveia ma ta matou wakaatawai e te wakaali atu la loto o a matou wainga muna ma a matou wainga yanga naa lave atu. Enei wua ta matou muna ka mea atu, atawai wolo, atawai wolo ye maneke mai loto o matou watumanava.

In addition to the above-mentioned Pukapukans, numerous other people contributed in significant ways to the success of my research in Pukapuka and/or to this book. Ron Vetter very much enriched our stay on the atoll through his friendship. Father Marinus, Dr. Tingika Tele and his wife Tungane, and Dr. Harry Taripo and his wife Kula were also helpful neighbors.

In Rarotonga, the Honorable Sir Tom Davis, the late Honorable Albert Henry, and the Honorable Inatio Akalulu kindly approved our lengthy stay on the atoll. Stuart and Tereapii Kingan contributed to the research in a variety of ways too numerous to mention here (see Borofsky 1982:xi). Several other people provided valuable assistance for which I express my gratitude: George Baniania, Tealiki Jacobs, Joe

Moosman, Gordon Sawtell, Jimmy Tamaiva, Carmen Temata, and the Cook Islands Library and Museum Association.

I would like to acknowledge the assistance and support of my doctoral committee at the University of Hawaii, especially in preparing my dissertation: Richard Lieban, chairman, Andrew Arno, Stephen Boggs, Godwin Chu, and Alan Howard. Douglas Oliver, before his retirement, played a key role in helping to formulate the research project and select an appropriate locale. Jack Bilmes and Richard Gould also provided advice in this respect. At the Communication Institute of the East-West Center, Godwin Chu, Meg White, Mary Bitterman, and Jack Lyle provided valuable assistance. Fieldwork was funded by an East-West Center Participant Award (in the Communication Institute); the final preparation of this book by an East-West Center Fellowship (in the Institute of Culture and Communication). At the Bishop Museum, Roger Rose allowed me to photograph various artifacts and answered numerous questions; Cynthia Timberlake, Marguerite Ashford, Janet Ness, and Janet Short made the Beagleholes' unpublished field notes available for examination; and Anita Manning allowed me to examine materials in the museum's archives.

I appreciate the assistance Julia Hecht provided on a number of occasions, not only in discussing various Pukapukan matters but in reading and commenting on portions of the manuscript, especially Chapter 2. (She also provided the photograph of Petelo that appears in this book.) David Friedman brought sensitivity and skill to the book's drawings. I acknowledge as well the help provided in Hawaii by Jackie D'Orazio, Lynette Furuhashi, April Kam, Karen Peacock, Rick Stanfield, and Iris Wiley. Particularly noteworthy was the assistance provided by Renee Heyum of the University of Hawaii's Pacific Collection and John and Bernida Turpin of Hawaii Microfilm.

Several other people assisted in the writing of this book, and I would like to express my appreciation to them. Alan Howard, Greg Dening, Bradd Shore, Robert Levy, and Judith Huntsman in particular provided suggestions that I have incorporated into this book. Pearl Beaglehole, Fred Eggan, and John Whiting kindly consented to my taping interviews with them. Betsy Brenner, Jim Clifford, Alan Howard, Dorothy Holland, John Kirkpatrick, Jean Lave, Paula Levin, George Marcus, Jim and Jane Ritchie, Buck Schieffelin, Bradd Shore, and Andrew Vayda made available unpublished materials that proved quite helpful. This book took much of its present shape as a result of interchanges with a variety of people who commented on earlier drafts: Sue Allen-Mills, Betsy Brenner, Jim Clifford, Greg Dening, Wimal Dissanayake, Ruth Finnegan, Raymond Firth, Ward Goodenough, Dorothy Holland, Alan Howard, Judith Huntsman, Ed Hutchins, John Kirkpatrick, Jean Lave,

xxii   *Acknowledgments*

Robert Levy, George Marcus, Douglas Oliver, Jim and Jane Ritchie, Renato Rosaldo, Sylvia Scribner, Bradd Shore, and Geoffrey White. I have noted in the text, when possible, specific suggestions each provided. Sue Allen-Mills, my editor at Cambridge University Press, offered support and displayed patience during the revision process. The following in one way or another also assisted and I would like to record my appreciation to them: Ruth Borofsky, Jerry Borofsky, Richard Borofsky, Sandra Chung, Chris Fried, Paul Kurtz, Mary Nevader, Sophia Prybylski, Robert Ravven, and Malcolm Willison.

Finally, I want to express my appreciation to my wife, Nancy Schildt, and my two daughters, Amelia Hokule'a Borofsky and Robyn Wakalua Borofsky, who shared in the making of this book. It is dedicated to them.

1

Differing accounts of the past

In February 1976 the 'Council of Important People' on Pukapuka, a small Polynesian atoll in the South Pacific, revived what it believed to be a traditional form of social organization. For decades the island's three villages had formed the basis for allocating the atoll's main resources. But in 1976 this arrangement was temporarily set aside and a form of social organization known as the *Akatawa* was established in its place — with new land boundaries, new social alignments, and a new means of allocating the island's main resources. The atoll, in brief, seemingly underwent a significant change in social organization. Leaving aside details of how the *Akatawa* functioned, for we shall discuss these at length in the next chapter, the question I want to raise here is whether the *Akatawa* was indeed traditional.

My own ethnographic investigations, lasting from 1977 to 1981, suggested that it was. Elderly informants affirmed in numerous conversations with me that it had definitely occurred in the past. Several described the operation of former *Akatawa*. Some, recognized as authorities on traditional matters, recalled having lived through an *Akatawa* in their youth. Further investigation, moreover, indicated that these assertions did not constitute some historical fabrication, some "mythical charter," to lend credence to the council's decision. Informants who attended the 1976 meeting made clear that knowledgeable elders knew about the *Akatawa* long before the council's meeting ever took place. In fact, it was these people's appreciation of the *Akatawa*'s traditional significance, some informants implied, that precipitated the council's decision to revive it.

But here is the problem. Data collected by various Westerners visiting the island over a period of several decades suggest that the *Akatawa* probably never existed before 1976 and certainly never occurred at the

1

time claimed by some knowledgeable Pukapukans. Five well-qualified anthropologists carried out research on the island between 1934 and 1974, three specifically on traditional Pukapukan social organization. None of them mention anything in their reports about the *Akatawa*. The same holds true for numerous government officials, missionaries, and other outsiders visiting the island from 1908 onward. None of them make any reference to the *Akatawa* – even though some were on the atoll when informants claim the *Akatawa* was in operation.

It might seem, at first glance, that these Western reports must therefore be in error. True, one researcher who visited the island for three days did misinterpret aspects of the traditional culture (see MacGregor 1935). Also, as the recent Freeman-Mead debate indicates, a researcher may develop a theme that another, studying the same culture, downplays, ignores, or simply interprets differently (Freeman 1983; Gartrell 1979; Heider 1983; Hooper 1981; M. Mead 1928). But whatever the reader's skepticism concerning these Western reports, it must be tempered by their sheer number and quality. Again and again various people write about particular forms of traditional Pukapukan social organization. Again and again each source reinforces certain impressions gained from the others. But none of them ever mentions the *Akatawa*.

How did such differing accounts of the Pukapukan past come about? Answering this question draws us into a set of important anthropological concerns. What is at stake, we shall see, is not a matter of one group being right and another wrong about a particular event. The existence of the *Akatawa* in the past, especially in precontact times, is impossible to prove or disprove. The data are too limited in this respect. What is at issue is something of broader significance: How different people construct different versions of the atoll's past. In unraveling the problem, we perceive the dynamic nature of Pukapukan knowledge regarding the past, how Pukapukans, in the process of learning and validating their traditions, continually change them. And we see how anthropologists, in the process of writing about these traditions for Western audiences, overstructure them, how they emphasize uniformity at the expense of diversity, stasis at the expense of change.

Juxtaposing these two "ways of knowing" the past, these two ways of "making history," we shall see, helps clarify important strengths and limitations of ethnographic accounts in general. Perceiving how Pukapukans construct knowledge provides valuable insights into both the anthropological construction of knowledge and the nature of anthropological understanding.

But I am getting ahead of myself here. To grasp the book's central themes, one must first understand the differing accounts of the past in greater depth to ascertain that no sleight of hand, no writer's artifice, has constructed a problem where none exists. Perhaps it is best to begin with a brief description of the island itself – where it is and what it is like – to place the whole issue within a broader context.

Pukapuka

Pukapuka is one of fifteen scattered islands within the Cook Islands, an internally self-governing state with strong political and economic ties to New Zealand. Geographically, the country is divided into two halves: a southern group comprising mostly high or volcanic islands and a northern group of low coral atolls. Pukapuka belongs to the latter group. The island itself is located at 165°50' west longitude by 11°55' south latitude. That makes it approximately 390 miles northeast of Samoa and 715 miles northwest of Rarotonga. Its nearest neighbors are Nassau, 42 miles to the southeast, and Manihiki, 286 miles to the northeast (see Map 1).

Since a fairly large literature already exists on Pukapuka, the following description need only be brief.[1] The first thing to note about the coral atoll is that it is stunningly beautiful. Describing his first glimpse of Pukapuka the anthropologist Ernest Beaglehole, who along with his wife conducted research on the island in 1934–5, waxes poetic:

White clouds flecked the sky overhead, the sea below us was a tangle of shadowy blues and foaming wave crests, the sun had a caressing warmth about it . . . we could distinguish the vivid belt of green coconut and pandanus trees poised in the air above beaches of glittering whiteness . . . coming nearer still, we could make out little coconut-thatched native houses growing as if out of the sandy beach itself. (1944:6)

The American writer Robert Frisbie, who lived there for several years, also describes the island:

[It] comprises three small islets threaded on a reef six or seven miles in circumference, which encloses a lagoon so beautifully clear that one can see the strange forests of coral to a depth of ten fathoms. The islets are little more than banks of sand and bleached coral where coconut palms and pandanus and puka trees break momentarily the steady sweep of the trade wind. (1928a:1)

There is some dispute as to the island's actual size. The Beagleholes (1938:17) estimated the acreage at 1,250; James Gosselin and Paleula Katoa at approximately 1,800 (Hecht 1976a:24; 1977:184). A question also exists as to the island's height:

The height of these islets is stated in the New Zealand Year Book to be 150 feet above high water mark. The Royal New Zealand Air Force have stated the height as 80 feet above sea level. The impression is gained that at no point is the land higher than 20 feet above high water, and a considerable area must be lower than this. (Department of Health n.d.:1)

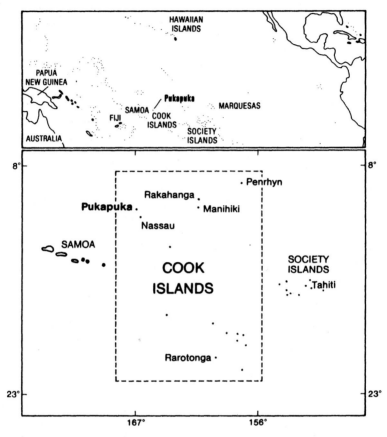

Map 1. Location of Pukapuka.

On the basis of my own investigations, I lean toward the Beagleholes' estimate of the acreage and toward Hecht's (1976a:24) forty-foot estimate of its height. But whatever the precise details, the island is neither very large nor very high.

It has a tropical climate. The average mean temperature based on records from 1930 to 1974 is 27.9 degrees centigrade. The rainfall averages 2,841 millimeters with a standard deviation of 527 millimeters. Technically, the island lies outside the "hurricane belt," but twice during the past seventy years hurricanes have ravaged the island, causing acute food shortages (Beckett 1964:413). (Further details regarding the atoll's climate are presented in Beaglehole and Beaglehole 1938; Borofsky 1982; and New Zealand Meteorological Service.)

According to the Cook Islands Census (1977), the population of Pukapuka was 785 in 1976. The most significant fact about the population is that it is still growing – unlike that of Manihiki, Rakahanga, and Penrhyn, three other atolls in the northern Cooks. Pukapuka also has a proportionately larger number of residents in the fifteen to sixty-four age bracket than these other atolls, indicating that fewer people in this age range emigrate (Borofsky 1982; Turner 1978).

On the main island (or Wale), the atoll's three villages run in a continuous line along the edge of the lagoon. The Cook Islands Census (1977:73) indicates that, in 1976, there were 219 people living within the geographic boundaries of Ngake, 274 within Loto, and 292 within Yato. (In 1971, the figures were 206, 276, and 250, respectively; in 1966, they were 177, 252, and 255.)

Physically, the population falls within the Polynesian "physical type," though stature, perhaps because of dietary problems, is comparatively short (Department of Health n.d.; Shapiro 1942). Davies (1956a, 1956b), Department of Health (n.d.), Hecht (1985), I. Prior (1971, 1974), Prior, Davidson, Salman, and Czochanska (1981), Prior, Harvey, Neave, and Davidson (1966), and Turner (1978) summarize material on Pukapukan health and education.

Pukapuka was discovered by Europeans on August 20, 1595, when Mendana and Quiros passed by the island on their way west (J. Beaglehole 1966:68; Kloosterman 1976:37; Maude 1968:64–6). Commodore Byron made the next recorded European sighting of the atoll on June 21, 1765. Because rocks and breakers discouraged a landing, he called the three islets of Pukapuka "Islands of Danger" (E. Beaglehole 1944; J. Beaglehole 1966:198). From this the atoll acquired the name Danger Island, a name still used on certain maps today. Interestingly, no clear account exists of how the island came to possess the name Pukapuka. The traditional precontact name, Te Ulu-o-te-Watu (or 'the head of the rock'), derives from an indigenous origin myth (see Beaglehole and Beaglehole 1938:375–7), but as the Beagleholes note, "the word Pukapuka has no meaning" today in Pukapukan (1938:17).

Native missionaries from the London Missionary Society landed on Pukapuka in 1857 (Lovett 1899, Vol. 2:372; see also Gunson 1978:358–60). The Seventh Day Adventists started a mission there in 1919 and the Roman Catholics in about 1929 (Beaglehole and Beaglehole 1938:5). Today, according to the Cook Islands Census (1977), 596 Pukapukans are Cook Islands Congregationalists (the former London Missionary Society), 113 are Catholics, and 76 are Seventh Day Adventists. E. Beaglehole (1944:112–17) and Beckett (1964:418–20, 425–7) provide brief overviews of religion on Pukapuka. Both emphasize the generally conservative, traditional orientation of the Christian practices.

Pukapuka became a British protectorate on June 2, 1892, and in 1901

New Zealand took over its administration (Kloosterman 1976:38). But only in 1914 did a government "resident agent" begin living on the atoll (Beaglehole and Beaglehole 1938:5).

The island of Rarotonga dominates the Cook Islands politically, economically, and culturally. Rarotongan, for example, is the country's national language. In everyday affairs, Pukapukans speak a mixture of Rarotongan and Pukapukan (see Beaglehole and Beaglehole 1938:6; Hecht 1981:56).

Pukapukans keep some written records, especially genealogies, but one should realize that, in respect to cultural traditions, Pukapuka still essentially constitutes a preliterate society. Except for what various anthropologists, government officials, missionaries, and other outsiders have noted, Pukapukans possess few written records regarding their cultural past. They basically preserve their traditions through memory and oral transmission.

Pukapukan knowledge regarding the *Akatawa*

Several interesting points come to light when we explore Pukapukan knowledge of the *Akatawa*, the form of social organization revived in 1976. The *Akatawa* has, for example, what some interpret as its own origin myth:

Te Vaopupu [the wife of Mataaliki, the first Pukapukan] became pregnant. She gave birth to a child, the child was born, a male child, Tumulivaka was his name. She swelled again, gave birth also, a girl child; Te Matakiate was her name. She was a younger sister of Tumulivaka.
The group of four lived on. They lived on with Tumulivaka watching the doings of Mata[a]liki. He was gathering the many gods at his side.
Tumulivaka watched, Mata[a]liki was going to give the island to the many gods. Tumulivaka got angry. He stamped on the island; it broke in two.
Mata[a]liki and Te Vaopupu moved to the western side. Tumulivaka and Te Matakiate moved to the eastern side of the island. That was over.
(Beaglehole and Beaglehole 1938:377)

Tumulivaka's action divided Loto village's reserve (named Motu Uta) into two sections of land: Tawa Lalo ('western side') and Tawa Ngake ('eastern side'). Significantly, the *Akatawa*'s two subunits possess the same names as these two land sections. Whether the land sections gave their names to the *Akatawa*'s subunits or the subunits to the land sections is uncertain, but a close relationship clearly exists between them.

Another important point to note in discussing the *Akatawa* is that the word itself contains a mixture of Rarotongan and Pukapukan elements. It consists of two morphemes. *Aka* is a causative prefix. "The general sense of the prefix *aka* is . . . to make . . . to cause something to be done" (Savage 1962:13). It indicates becoming the state mentioned in a noun or approaching (or causing of) the state indicated in a verb. It derives from Rarotongan. The proper Pukapukan prefix would be *waka*. Though Pukapukans certainly use *waka* in a variety of Pukapukan words today – such as *wakalelei, wakamaa, wakaaloa* – I never heard *waka* used by Pukapukans in this context. It was always *Akatawa*.[2]

Tawa, in contrast, is clearly Pukapukan. The letter *w* does not exist in the Rarotongan alphabet. *Tawa* has three meanings: (1) 'side' or 'part,' (2) 'edge of the reef,' and (3) slang for 'money' (Mataola et al. 1981). The first meaning concerns us here. *Ka wakamata te tutaka a te taote mai te tawa ki lalo ia*, 'The doctor's inspection will begin from the westward side [of the island].' Essentially, then, *Akatawa* refers to 'becoming sides' or, for our purposes, 'dividing the island in half.'

Turning to details of informant knowledge regarding the *Akatawa*, it is apparent that Pukapukan understandings do not fit into a single, uniform pattern. Although some core agreement existed in what people told me, there was also considerable variety. The material below raises important questions regarding the organization of Pukapukan knowledge. To what degree, for example, can one say that Pukapukan understandings of the *Akatawa* are shared? In what manner does the knowledge of reputed experts on the subject exceed that of their less informed colleagues?

In examining the traditions surrounding the 1976 *Akatawa* and its antecedents, I interviewed thirty elderly informants, or approximately 54 percent of the Pukapukan population sixty-four years of age and over. (See note 2 of the Preface for further details.) One of the most interesting facts uncovered in these interviews was that seven Pukapukans claimed to have lived through a period of the *Akatawa* in their youth: Molingi, Lemuna, Taavini, Petelo, Apela, Paani, and Walemaki. The first three are women; the last four men.

It is important to note that three of these informants were respected authorities on matters of traditions during my fieldwork. In a 1978 survey (involving ninety-one Pukapukans more than fifty years of age), 84 percent cited Molingi as extremely knowledgeable about traditional matters. Seventy-nine percent mentioned Petelo and 70 percent Apela. (Only 45 percent cited the fourth ranked person.) Thus when these three informants discussed experiencing an earlier Akatawa, they spoke as authorities, as recognized experts, on such matters.

Of the seven informants, Apela claimed to have experienced the *Akatawa* twice before, once around 1913 and then again around 1940. The rest simply claimed to have experienced it once. Of the latter group, only Petelo specifically mentioned a date to me in our individual interviews. He recalled the *Akatawa* occurring shortly after the 1914 hurricane, probably around 1915.

Comparing Molingi's, Petelo's, and Apela's knowledge of the *Aka-tawa* with that of their remaining peers in the sample of thirty helps to place their views in perspective. Seventy-three percent of the sample viewed the 1976 *Akatawa* as similar to previous ones. Ten percent viewed them as different in character and 17 percent (including Molingi) expressed uncertainty on the matter. The emphasis on the 1976 *Akatawa*'s similarity to previous ones fits, of course, with its image as a cultural revival. But I must add that not everyone agreed on what the similarities actually were between the *Akatawa*. Seven of the twenty-two who emphasized similarities referred to the island being again split in half. Three emphasized that the *Akatawa* worked well in all cases; no critical conflicts arose. Five (including Petelo) asserted that *Akatawa* must, by nature, be similar. They belonged to an enduring tradition – one passed down unchanged from generation to generation. Four (one of whom was Apela) gave a variety of other answers. Three gave no clarification at all.

Those who emphasized the differences between the 1976 *Akatawa* and previous ones also did not agree about the nature of the differences. One claimed that previous *Akatawa* had lasted for a shorter period of time, for only months, rather than years as in the present case. Another said that, unlike today, no troubles existed in the past. Finally, one stated that, unlike today, there *had* been troubles in the past.

As to when the *Akatawa* first arose on the island, opinions again differed. Twenty-three percent believed the *Akatawa* was a relatively recent innovation, having originated certainly after the time of Tumulivaka and also after the great hurricane that had reputedly devastated the island roughly four hundred years ago (*te mate o Wanguna*; see Beaglehole and Beaglehole (1938:386).[3] Thirty percent (among them Petelo) thought the *Akatawa* might have originated with Tumulivaka and that it clearly predated the devastating hurricane. Ten percent, though not stating when it arose, stressed that the *Akatawa* did not constitute the island's response to the hurricane's devastation. Another 37 percent (including Molingi and Apela) pleaded ignorance on the issue.

Thus although many Pukapukans knew that Tumulivaka had split the island in half sometime in the past, not all of them viewed his actions as the genesis of the *Akatawa*. What seemed like an origin myth to some Pukapukans did not appear so to others.

As one might expect in a nonliterate society such as Pukapuka, no one could provide a precise figure regarding the number of times *Aka-tawa* had occurred in the past. Seven percent (including Petelo) mentioned that they had been occurring repeatedly from the time of Tumulivaka to the present. Another 20 percent provided vague answers

Celebrating during the *Akatawa*'s revival

affirming its occurrence in the past. Twenty-three percent tended to sidestep the direct question, preferring instead to discuss former *Akatawa* of which they specifically knew. Five (including Molingi and Apela) mentioned their own personal experiences. Two others mentioned experiences people had told them about. Finally, 40 percent expressed ignorance on the matter. (Ten percent of the people dodged the question completely.)

Widespread opinions also existed as to the reasons for former *Akatawa*. Seventeen percent (including Petelo and Apela) emphasized that they had previously occurred to encourage the perpetuation of Pukapukan traditions. This explanation fits with the one generally offered by people today for the *Akatawa*'s revival: to preserve knowledge of the past. Thirteen percent (among them Molingi) thought that earlier *Akatawa* had been "trial runs" so to speak – initiated so that it could be seen how they worked as a form of social organization. Seven percent gave vague miscellaneous answers; 53 percent openly pleaded ignorance; and 10 percent did not really answer the question.

Only 23 percent of the sample gave specific answers regarding the length of previous *Akatawa*. One said one month, another three months, another approximately a year. Apela said one to two years; Petelo three to four years. Another suggested ninety years and one simply stated a long time. Clearly no consensus existed. Another 10 percent (including Molingi) mentioned that the length varied, depending on whether or not trouble arose. Forty-three percent admitted they did not know. And 23 percent either were not asked the question (because of their previous responses) or did not really answer the question.

Likewise, no general agreement existed as to why the previous *Akatawa* had ended. Thirteen percent (among them Molingi, Apela, and Petelo) asserted that Loto villagers had· created problems by being greedy. (All three informants, one should note, belong to Ngake village.) Ten percent vaguely mentioned that problems had developed, though exactly what these were was never clarified. Three percent believed that the island temporarily set the *Akatawa* aside, for revival at a later date. And another three percent suspected its agreed-upon time had come to an end. Forty percent pleaded ignorance as to the correct answer. (Thirty percent were not asked the question because of their previous responses.)

Clearly, then, people disagreed on several significant points in their private interviews. But, interestingly, when I interviewed a group of knowledgeable informants together, a consensus quickly developed on these matters. Molingi, Petelo, and Apela as well as Kililua, Paani, and Ngalau – three other informants Pukapukans viewed as knowledgeable in traditional matters – all agreed, for example, that the modern *Akatawa* paralleled earlier ones. (One of the informants, in his private interview, had insisted they differed.) Likewise, everyone in the group concurred with Petelo's assertion that the *Akatawa* dated back to Tumulivaka's time. And they all agreed that it had been revived several times since then.

In regard to the earlier *Akatawa* some had lived through in their youth, the whole group agreed with Molingi's suggestion that it arose as a result of a decision by the island's chiefs (*aliki*). (The group never clarified the exact reasons for the decision, though presumably they involved some of the factors previously mentioned in people's separate interviews.) All concurred with Petelo's and Molingi's suggestion that this *Akatawa* had lasted for approximately two years. Also, the group agreed with a suggestion, again voiced by Molingi and Petelo, that the earlier *Akatawa* had collapsed as a result of the greediness of the Loto villagers in Tawa Ngake. (As described in Chapter 2, the *Akatawa*'s Tawa Ngake includes all of Ngake and half of Loto village.) Because members of Loto reputedly did not share their property with Ngake villagers to the same degree that Ngake villagers shared with them, considerable resentment arose. The resentment grew so intense, in fact, that eventually the people of Ngake forced the island to terminate the *Akatawa*. Apakuka, a member of Ngake village, supposedly spurred the movement on, insisting (to quote Petelo), "*Langi motu, langi lele,*" 'Break [the *Akatawa*] apart all the way from the earth to the sky.'

In response to my probing, the group also expressed agreement about the date of the earlier *Akatawa* some had lived through. They agreed with Petelo's suggestion that it had been around 1914 or 1915, just after the 1914 hurricane. People in the group were so consensus-minded, in fact, that Ngalau – who was older than three of the participants and who previously had not claimed to have lived through the earlier *Akatawa* – now changed his mind. He, too, recalled having experienced it in his youth.

It should be noted that there is an implicit reasonableness to the 1914–15 date for many Pukapukans. Most adults knew that hurricanes caused great damage to their island and that Pukapukans in times past had had to cope with the devastation in a variety of ways, including altering aspects of their social organization. Many knew, for example, that their island had temporarily taken on a different form of social organization after a hurricane had reputedly depopulated the island approximately four hundred years ago (see Beaglehole and Beaglehole 1938:386–90). Given the occurrence of a hurricane in 1914, the 1914–15 date for the *Akatawa* made considerable sense. It represented a cultural construct in which, to quote Schieffelin, "a particular set of events could be narratively ordered and meaningfully understood" (1982:23).

The absence of Western knowledge regarding the *Akatawa*

Between 1934 and 1974, five professionally trained anthropologists conducted ethnographic investigations on Pukapuka: Ernest and Pearl Beaglehole (1934–5), Andrew Vayda (1957), Jeremy Beckett (1964), and Julia Hecht (1972–4). Collectively, they have produced a fairly large corpus of material: Ernest Beaglehole (1937b, 1944), Ernest and Pearl Beaglehole (1938, 1939, 1941, ms. a, ms. b), Vayda (1957, 1958, 1959), Beckett (1964), and Hecht (1976a, 1976b, 1977, 1978, 1981, 1985). The Beagleholes, Vayda, Beckett, and Hecht all discuss three distinct forms of social organization: villages (*lulu*), patrilineages (*po*), and matri-moieties (*wua*). In addition, Hecht elaborates on cognatic descent categories (*wuanga* or *maelenga*). But nowhere in the extensive literature is any reference made to the *Akatawa*.

How could such highly trained anthropologists miss something so many Pukapukans willingly and spontaneously discussed with me? The evening I sat around with a group of informants discussing the *Akatawa*, I asked them why neither the Beagleholes nor any other anthropologist had ever written about *Akatawa*. Molingi, who had been one of the Beagleholes' key informants, provided an interesting answer. "They did not ask. Ernest [Beaglehole] did not ask about this matter." Though the Beagleholes may not have specifically asked about the *Akatawa*, an analysis of their field notes clearly indicates that they raised numerous questions involving related matters. If I had asked such questions during my fieldwork, informants would certainly have mentioned the *Akatawa*. Apparently they did not do so with the Beagleholes.

Both the Beagleholes' published reports and unpublished field notes make clear that they sought to investigate the island's traditions thoroughly. Their Pukapukan informants were committed participants in this research:

[Veeti] once told me that he was going to live until he saw in his hands a copy of the book we were going to write about Pukapuka. . . . It was typical of his attitude, . . . and that of all his friends, this overwhelming pride in, and affection for, [the] past. . . .

We had shown him scientific books about other Polynesian groups. He was thrilled by words he could not understand and by plates and drawings that he could. When he could see the book on Pukapuka in his hands, he at last would have certitude that some of the past would never be lost to the younger generations about him. It was the same enthusiasm to record the past that brought Pau, the ablest scholar on Pukapuka [to stay with us at Motu Ko for a day or two each week]. (E. Beaglehole 1944:126–7)

The Beagleholes' published and unpublished material indicates that they systematically raised questions regarding different forms of traditional social organization, in terms of both general patterns and the specific structuring of food divisions and games (in which the *Akatawa* clearly differs from other forms of organization). A set of the Beagleholes' unpublished field notes, for example, is labeled "Organizations for Food Division and Games etc." It consists of four sheets of typescript. Two deal with the Yolongo (*sic*), or patrilineal organizational principle, one with the Wua, or matrilineal organizational principle, and one with the Matoyinga, or village organizational principle. Subsequent sheets elaborate on each of these principles in depth. Other material refers to the names and reasons for various feasts. Both the Beagleholes' published ethnography and unpublished field notes mention feasts organized by villages, feasts organized by patrilineages, and feasts organized by matrilineages (or matrimoieties). But there is no mention of feasts organized by *Akatawa*.

One gets the impression that it was not from want of trying that the Beagleholes never discovered anything about *Akatawa*. They asked their major informants all sorts of questions about topics that would have brought the *Akatawa* to the fore if I had asked them of my informants. Could the Beagleholes' informants have been less informed regarding the past than the informants I dealt with? No one I talked to during my forty-one-month stay ever suggested such a thing. People unanimously agreed that the Beagleholes' informants had possessed a considerable fund of knowledge and that, collectively, they knew far more about Pukapukan traditions than the people I interviewed. Certainly if the *Akatawa* had occurred just twenty years before the Beagleholes' research, their informants should have remembered it. When I interviewed people sixty-five years later, they still recalled having lived through it.

The only anthropological mention of the *Akatawa* by an anthropologist comes from Hecht, who conducted research on traditional Pukapukan social organization in Rarotonga and Pukapuka from 1972 to 1974 (1976a:ii). None of her publicly available material (1976a, 1976b, 1977, 1981, 1985) mentions the *Akatawa*. But in an informal conversation I had with her in 1982, she stated that she vaguely remembered someone discussing something during her fieldwork about dividing the island in half, into *Akatawa*, sometime in the past. As to when, how, or why, she could not say. The reference was so vague, she added, she was not even sure what to make of it or what to do with it.

Anthropologists were not alone in omitting any mention of the *Akatawa*. Other visitors to the island, who also recorded information, omitted it as well. No mention of the *Akatawa* exists in any of the government archival material dating from 1908 onward. This is noteworthy since at least one of the island's many visitors might be expected to have recorded something, given the *Akatawa*'s unusual form of organization and its presumed lengthy duration. The evidence, moreover, involves more than simply the absence of citations regarding the *Akatawa*. As the next chapter indicates, village units cease to exist during an *Akatawa*. Mention in the records of the island's three villages and especially of Yato or Loto (which lack named social identities under the *Akatawa*) casts considerable doubt on the *Akatawa*'s existence during the time discussed.

In a report to the government in Rarotonga dated June 26, 1908, the LMS minister Tau discusses the population's plans for cleaning up Pukapuka: "Here is how it will be done. Pilato and the people of his village (*oire*) will go to their reserve (*motu*), Luka and the people of his village will go to their reserve, Pani and his village to their reserve." (Related materials make it clear that these individuals were the leaders of Loto, Yato, and Ngake villages respectively, at the time.)

The next set of reports comes from Johnstone Dyer, the first government resident agent to take up residence on Pukapuka. In an entry entitled "Conduct of People of Pukapuka, September 4 to December 31, 1914" he states, "Roto excellent, Ato excellent, Ngake excellent. No complaints everybody peaceful." The fact that two of the village names are slightly misspelled is of minor concern. Dyer was simply using the Rarotongan spellings. (Pukapukans themselves often use such forms today in referring to the villages.) In a related entry dealing with the conduct of the people in Pukapuka for the year 1915, he states, "Roto ariki settlement excellent. Ato, *Kavana* [Rarotongan coin word for governor] Luka, excellent. Ngake unsettled. At present everything peaceful." A report dated June 24, 1915, includes references to "Luka, Kavana of Ato . . . Pani, Kavana of Ngake and of Motu Ko . . . [and] Tukia Kavana of Roto." A report to H. H. G. Ralfe, Esq., dated June 21, 1915, dealing with the condition of the island after the hurricane mentions Roto and Ngake villages. There is no mention of the *Akatawa*.

A report by the Reverend Koteka dated June 24, 1915, concerns the *kopu ariki* (or family of a high chief; Savage 1962:114) in Roto and Ngake. A report by Dyer dated September 22, 1915, and related to the formation of an island council refers to the Kavanas of Ato, Roto, and Ngake. Sometime during 1916, J. H. Robertson, the collector of customs at Apia, visited the island. In the report on his trip to "Remote Islands of the Pacific" he notes in regard to Pukapuka, "The island on which we landed is the principal island of the three [i.e., Wale]. On it stands the village, or rather three villages all close together."

H. Brian Morris was the next government resident agent to permanently live on the island. In his report regarding the state of the island between November 13, 1917; and March 31, 1918, to the resident commissioner in Rarotonga, Morris observes that "the three villages have worked eagerly to make their villages clean and sanitary." The report contains specific references to Loto and Yato villages. In another report, dated January 29, 1918, Morris describes a group meeting called "to determine the manner in which suspension of the Raui [or prohibition on entering the village reserves] was to be carried out. . . . On former occasions the *mataiapos* [i.e., minor chiefs] of the three villages performed [the duty], but to, it was stated, the sole advantage of Ngake and Ato and the detriment of Roto."

Minutes of the Island Council dated February 13, 1918, contain references not only to three villages but also to the erection of each village's copra house. In the minutes of the Island Council meeting of April 12, 1918, it is reported that Ngake produced 15.5 tons of copra, Loto 12.5, and Ato 13. Numerous other entries in Morris's reports contain similar references to Ato, Roto, and Ngake.

An acting resident agent, R. S. Trotter, in summarizing an Island Council meeting of September 10, 1918, mentions the existence of three settlements as well as the names Ngake, Roto, and Ato. In a later undated entry, which consists of instructions to Ula (the native Pukapukan who subsequently took over as acting resident agent), Trotter urges him to look after the people in the three villages, again mentioning Ngake, Roto, and Ato. Repeatedly in reports written by Ula from 1919 to 1925 there are references to the same three villages (*oire*): Ngake, Roto, and Ato. In his report to the resident commissioner in Rarotonga on October 6, 1919, for example, Ula indicates that Ngake, Ato, and Roto *each* contributed more than a ton of copra to the war fund.

When the resident commissioner, Ayson, visited Pukapuka in June 1924, he wrote a report regarding the atoll's social organization (dated September 22, 1924, to the secretary of the Cook Islands Administration in Wellington). He stated, "Pukapuka consists of three good Islands named Ware [i.e., Wale] (the main Island, on which are the villages of Ato, Roto, or Loto, and Ngake), Ko (presumed to belong to the people of the village of Ngake), and Kotawa or Kotao, which is presumed to belong to the people of Ato."

The American writer Robert Frisbie began living on the island in August 1924. In numerous fictionalized accounts of the Pukapukan way of life, he repeatedly described the three villages, but nowhere, in the material that I have examined, did he ever write about *Akatawa* (R. Frisbie 1928a, 1928b, 1929a, 1929b, 1929c, 1930, 1935, 1939; see also F. Frisbie 1948; J. Frisbie 1959).

We are thus left with differing accounts of the Pukapukan past. Did or did not the *Akatawa* occur before its "revival" in 1976? Pukapukans espouse one opinion; outsiders imply another. How does one resolve the matter? An obvious answer is to assume that my informants made an error. Given the oral nature of their traditions, they may have misjudged the date or duration of the *Akatawa*'s occurrence. Perhaps it existed before 1908 (the earliest date of my records) or lasted only a matter of days (and went unrecorded by outsiders). Unfortunately, we do not know. The data are too limited to determine with any certainty the prior existence or nonexistence of the *Akatawa*.

At this point we might simply let the matter rest, but good reasons exist for not doing so. By asking further questions, by trying to pin down more details, we learn a great deal about how both Pukapukans and anthropologists construct knowledge of the Pukapukan past. We learn a great deal about their respective ways of knowing.

Perhaps the best way to begin our explorations is by examining the *Akatawa*'s match, or mismatch, with Pukapukan social organization. If the *Akatawa* is indigenous and not some alien creation, then logically it should fit within the atoll's basic principles of organization. If anthropologists have stressed anything during the past several decades, they have emphasized that cultures possess elements of coherence. Things do not fit perfectly together, but elements of integration usually occur at some level of analysis.

Before we explore this matter further in Chapter 2, however, a brief comment is in order regarding certain theories of truth. For philosophers of knowledge, there is more than one perspective on truth, and it is important for readers to realize this when evaluating assertions by anthropologists and Pukapukans concerning the atoll's past. For brevity's sake, we shall mention only three.

The first, and perhaps most famous, is the correspondence theory. Truth, according to Russell, "consists in some form of correspondence between belief and fact" (cited in A. Prior 1967:223). Various philosophers, from Aristotle and Aquinas to Moore, have taken this position. Though there are variations in their views, most would agree with a point made by Moore. "To say that [a] belief is true is to say that there is in the Universe *a* fact to which it corresponds. . . . [And furthermore,] to say that it is false is to say that there is *not* in the Universe any fact to which it corresponds" (1953:277).

The second theory emphasizes coherence:

According to the coherence theory [of truth], to say that a statement (usually called a judgment) is true or false is to say that it coheres or fails to cohere with a system of other statements; that it is a member of a system whose elements are related to each other by ties of logical implication as the elements in a system of pure mathematics are related. (White 1967:130)

Bradley, Joachim, and Blanshard are modern representatives of this perspective. (It can also be found in the works of Plato and Locke.) Bradley suggests that coherence is the only criterion for truth one can apply to the past. We cannot compare, for instance, the assertion that

Caesar crossed the Rubicon in 49 B.C. with some external fact of the world because none now exists. What we can do is compare what various documents and history books state to see how they agree or disagree.

The third theory, the pragmatic theory of truth, focuses not on what exists in the world or what coheres but on what works, on what problems are resolved by a particular knowledge claim (see Ezorsky 1967). For James, "true ideas [are] those which 'work' ... which give various kinds of satisfaction, and which bring about various kinds of successes" (Earle 1967:247; see also James 1975:34). For Dewey, truth is what removes doubt and perplexity.

"Warranted assertion" is the term for Dewey's version of the truth. Inquiry is initiated in conditions of doubt; it terminates in the establishment of conditions in which doubt is no longer needed or felt. It is this settling of conditions of doubt, a settlement produced and warranted by inquiry, which distinguishes the warranted assertion. (Thayer 1967:434)

We thus have at least three different senses of truth. One focuses on what does or does not exist in (or correspond to) the external world as people know it. A second examines the fit (or coherence) of one set of facts with another. And a third focuses on what works, on what is successful, at solving problems. As readers proceed through the following chapters, unraveling ambiguities and contradictions in what people say, they might well ponder in what sense (or senses) various people's assertions about the past are true, and in what way (or ways) they are false.

2

Pukapukan social organization
A perspective on anthropological ways of knowing

More than twenty-five years ago, Sahlins (1958) enunciated a theme that most scholars have come to accept regarding the social organization of Polynesian atolls. Social groupings on atolls, such as Pukapuka, often possess a complex set of cross-cutting ties within a comparatively egalitarian framework. The pattern facilitates a sharing of the island's limited resources while at the same time dampening disruptive intergroup conflicts. On Pukapuka today, two alternative organizational patterns exist for handling these pressures: villages and *koputangata*.

Modern Pukapukan social organization

Village organization

Three distinct villages (*lulu* in Pukapukan, *oire* in Rarotongan) exist on the island: Yato, Loto, and Ngake. (Given that few major differences exist among them, we can speak of a generalized form of organization.) Villages constitute clearly demarcated corporate groups. They play a major role in the atoll's organization.

Membership in a village is exclusive. Although a person can change membership near the beginning of each calendar year, he or she can belong to one, and only one, village at any particular time. Village membership has a patrilineal bias as a result of two factors. First, patrilineal ties play a role in determining household residence. Sixty-five percent of the 137 households on the island (at the time I conducted a census in 1978) emphasized virilocal and patrilocal ties in explaining why they reside where they do. Second, though people living within the geographical confines of a particular village may join whatever village organization they wish, a majority belong to the organization of the

18

village within whose boundaries they reside. For the village of Loto, for example, 69 percent of the forty-nine household heads dwelling within the village's geographical boundaries belonged to (or *tau*'d in) that village's organization in 1980. For Ngake the figure was 95 percent of forty; for Yato 58 percent of forty-eight.

But indicating the existence of a pro-patrilineal bias in village membership is not the same as stating that villages constitute patrilineal groupings. The difference, though subtle, is important. Early anthropologists tended to confuse the two. While acknowledging the optative nature of Polynesian social groups, many asserted, in Burrow's words, that "the larger, more permanent kinship groups were almost invariably based on common descent from an ancestor in the male line" (1939:1). Recently anthropologists have shown the situation to be more complex than originally depicted. A patrilineal bias in social groupings does not necessitate formal patrilineages or clans. In fact, a patrilineal bias can coexist with cognatic descent groups and bilateral patterns of affiliation (see Howard and Kirkpatrick 1989).

In Pukapuka, for example, the bias toward patrilineality exists within a broader system of bilateral ties. This becomes evident when we take a closer look at the previous data. Of the 137 households discussed above, 20 percent possess what might be better termed virimatrilocal residence (or ties through one's husband's mother) versus 26 percent with viripatrilocal residence (or ties through one's husband's father). An additional 14 percent possess uxoripatrilocal ties (ties through one's wife's father). In fact, if we temporarily set aside ambiguous cases (leaving their clarification to the note),[1] we can state that only 26 percent of the households possess a strictly patrilineal pattern, whereas 34 percent emphasize a more bilateral pattern.

These data on cross-cutting patterns of kin affiliation fit well with material on cross-cutting patterns of village affiliation. Whereas forty household heads live within the confines of Ngake village, sixty household heads belong to that village's organization. Fifteen of the sixty household heads dwell in Loto, seven in Yato.[2] And though forty-eight household heads live in Yato itself, only twenty-eight actually belong to that village's organization. Thirteen belong to Loto. The bias toward patrilineality in village membership, in other words, exists within a more general system of cross-cutting ties and bilateral affiliations.

Each village owns a large public reserve (*motu*) of land and taro swamps. Collectively the villages control through these reserves perhaps three-fourths of the atoll's total landmass and somewhat less than half of its taro swamps (cf. Beckett 1964:417; Vayda 1959:128). Ngake village owns Motu Ko, Loto village Motu Uta, and Yato village Motu Kotawa and Motu Niua (see Map 2). Entrance into a village reserve is generally

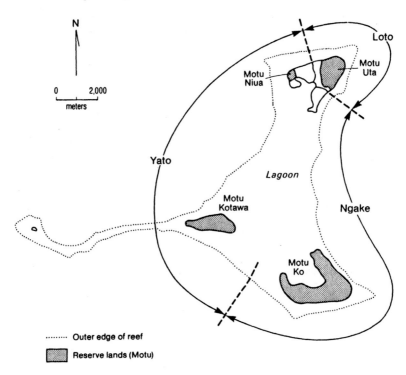

Map 2. Pukapuka's three villages. Unless it is copra season, the atoll's inhabitants live in the nonreserve (or unshaded) sections on the northernmost island (called Wale).[3]

restricted to members of that village's organization. Not all taro swamps within a village's reserve actually belong to that village. Some swamps in Motu Uta and on Motu Ko belong to the cognatic descent groups (or *koputangata*) discussed below. But since free access to such swamps necessitates village membership, the swamps' primary users (or their children) generally belong to that village.

The public reserves contain the vast majority of the atoll's coconut trees. These trees are the principal source of copra for export, the basic supply of coconuts for household consumption during the copra-producing season, and a supplemental source of coconuts at other times of the year. Technically, all village members can collect coconuts from any portion of the reserve, but a general tendency exists in Motu Uta and on Motu Ko for particular households to use specific strips of land (or *kawa*) within these reserves. Village members do not collectively cultivate the village-owned taro swamps. Rather, the swamps are divided into smaller sections, which individual households cultivate. The taro produced from these plots is an important part of each household's diet.

All adult members of a village possess equal access to village re-sources, a fact that both illustrates and buttresses the atoll's egalitarian orientation. Village-owned taro plots, for example, are redistributed once per year so that all members, whether new or old, possess equal shares. Produce collectively gathered by village members is also shared equally among adult members (though slight variations exist in what each sex obtains). Take, for example, the collection of food held by Yato village on February 4, 1981. Before that date all the men of the village went out one evening to fish *talaao* (a type of rock grouper; see Beaglehole and Beaglehole 1938:29). On another night, they all caught coconut crabs (*kaveu*) at their reserve on Motu Kotawa. The village, in addition, decided that all adults must provide the village with certain food: each woman a minimum of six *taataa* (or cooked taro; Beaglehole and Beaglehole 1938:102) and each man four drinking nuts. Through their combined efforts, village members collected approximately 600 *taataa*, 240 coconuts, 370 *talaao*, and 210 coconut crabs.

The village then divided this food among its members. Every man received four *taataa*, every woman three, and every child two. The *talaao* were divided so that each woman got three, each man two, and each child one. Every woman obtained a whole coconut crab, whereas each man and child obtained a half. Each woman received two coconuts; every man and child one.

These divisions of food are based on *tuanga kai*, or village food-sharing units. Ngake has ten such units, Loto eight, and Yato six. Whereas Loto village uses names to describe its units, Ngake and Yato simply refer to them by numbers. It is critical for what follows to note that the Loto units can readily be associated with certain strips of land (*kawa*) in the village reserve of Motu Uta (cf. Beaglehole and Beaglehole 1938:42). Four of these food-sharing units belong to the side of Motu Uta called Tawa Lalo (Te Paa, Taikaiana, Te Welo i te Kilikili, and Te Keonga Lewu) and four to the side called Tawa Ngake (Te Keonga Wolo, Wala Kakala, Te Welo, and Te Utuu). Today, the units in the other villages correspond only roughly to such strips of land. Though older informants generally concur that food-sharing units were once directly related to land strips in these villages, they often disagree on specific details of the relationship (cf. Hecht 1976a:61–2).

The number of members of any particular food-sharing unit varies considerably. In Yato, for example, unit 1 had eight adult men, fourteen adult women, and twenty-one children in 1981. Unit 6 had only four men, four women, and six children. A person may belong to one and only one food-sharing unit at any given time. To a limited extent, families and households coalesce around food-sharing units. Usually families have established genealogical ties to a particular unit, often with a patrilineal emphasis, dating back one or more generations (cf. Hecht 1976a:61–2). Husband and wife have the same food-sharing unit, but a few of their children, while still living at home, may belong (as *tuanga tau*) to other units, either in their own village or in other villages. The "farming out" of these children to other food-sharing units helps cement ties with cognatic relatives, obtain foods for the household available only at certain reserves, and/or strengthen inheritance claims to particular pieces of property (cf. Hecht 1976a:98–9).

These *tuanga tau* children constitute a set of cross-cutting ties among separate food-sharing units both within and between villages. Of the sixty household heads belonging to (or *tau*ing in) Ngake village in 1980, for example, 28 percent had household members in food-sharing units other than their own. In Loto, with forty-eight household heads in its organization, the figure went up to 56 percent and in Yato, with twenty-nine household heads, to 62 percent. The lower figure for Ngake suggests that alternative means exist for establishing ties among households in different villages and/or food-sharing units. Of the three villages, Ngake had the highest number of nonresident members in its village organization in 1980 – 37 percent versus 29 percent for Loto and only 4 percent for Yato. While those belonging to Ngake village thus tend to establish cross-cutting ties through extravillage residence, members of Loto and Yato place greater stress on establishing these ties through *tuanga tau* children.

Though changes in village membership allow for the adjustment of population/resource imbalances, the amount of reserve land any particular village owns is generally set. Only twice in Pukapukan history have villages reputedly altered their reserve boundaries. Once, after a devastating hurricane struck the island, reserve boundaries were set aside and then renegotiated. Generations later, Loto village exchanged land it owned on Motu Ko for land Ngake owned at Motu Uta (see Beaglehole and Beaglehole 1938:34).

Villages have significant political functions. Not only do they play a key role in the organization of islandwide authority but they possess the right to regulate behaviors of their members according to laws they themselves draw up. Each village selects by secret ballot two members to represent the village on the Island Council, the primary body for deciding matters of islandwide concern. The Island Council acts (along with the island's elected representative to the national legislature) as the legal intermediary between the atoll's population and the national government in Rarotonga. A second islandwide council, the *Kau Wowolo* (or 'Council of Important People') includes chiefs from certain patrilineal descent lines in each village. Though it is not as formal village-based as the Island Council, a clear sense exists that some chiefs represent Yato whereas others represent Loto. The Kau Wowolo's meetings in principle need include only chiefs. Generally, however, members of the Island Council also actively participate in them. The Kau Wowolo decides on minor laws for regulating lands outside village reserves, the allocation of rights within the island-owned taro swamps, and matters that affect the preservation of the island's traditions. It may also adjudicate land disputes (though the parties involved are not obligated to accept its decisions). It was the Kau Wowolo that revived the *Akatawa* in February 1976.

Village subunits called *pule* constitute each village's police force. *Pule* enforce village decisions, guard reserve lands against trespassers, and impose fines on individuals for various infractions. The number of *pule* vary with the village: Loto, for example, has six *pule*, Ngake and Yato four (cf. Beaglehole and Beaglehole 1938:35–6). All adults must belong to and participate in one of their village's *pule*. No adult member is exempted.

Each *pule* within a village usually serves a two-week term of office before passing its responsibilities to another *pule* within the same village. At the end of the two weeks, the *pule* holds a meeting (*uwingapule*) to publicize its actions and allow others to comment on them (cf. Beaglehole and Beaglehole 1938:36–7). At these meetings, additional village matters are usually brought up and decided upon. All members have the right to speak either for or against any topic raised. General consensus, more than the formal counting of votes, is the usual basis for reaching decisions at these meetings. Whereas individual *pule* handle minor infractions of village laws, serious crimes are brought before the village as a whole. A village's most severe punishment, reducing an adult to a child's status (*wakatamaliki*), commands serious respect.

Organized competitions, especially among villages, are extremely popular on Pukapuka. One can gain a sense of Pukapukan priorities from the fact that almost three months of every year are taken up with practicing for and competing in the annual New Year's games. A series of cricket games may go on for several weeks at a time as each village defers the production of copra until it can take revenge for some previous loss at the hands of another village. Examined in broader perspective, these competitive games constitute a ceremonial means of publicly affirming village solidarity as well as one's own status vis-à-vis others. Villagers demonstrate their strength, their vitality, through success in such competitions. Though few Pukapukans use the term *mana* in discussing these competitions, the underlying logic shows a striking parallel to the status rivalries of Polynesian chiefs on other islands at other times (see Goldman 1970:10–13). The competitions also help ritualize and channel intergroup conflicts into certain controlled arenas. Games usually end with semihumorous, semiinsulting speeches in which the victors deprecate the losers' inability to win.

Three points require emphasis in this brief overview of village organization. First, the villages are exclusive corporate groups in control of the island's main resources and possess clear political functions. Though membership has a patrilineal bias, the villages are cognatic in character. Second, a strong egalitarian ethos pervades village affairs. All adults participate equally in village activities and, with a few exceptions, all equally reap the rewards of this participation. Important decisions are generally reached through consensus, with all adult members possessing the right to express themselves on issues of significance. Third, a complex system of cross-cutting ties exists among the three villages. The allocation of *tuanga tau* children to other food-sharing units, the only partial correspondence to residence with village membership, and the fluctuation in membership rolls over time all help to redistribute valued resources throughout the island's population.

Koputangata

In contrast to village organization, the most apparent aspect of the *koputangata* is its studied ambiguity. Pukapukans often disagree, sometimes vehemently, concerning who does or does not belong to a specific *koputangata*. The term takes on different connotations in different contexts. It has both an ancestor-oriented and an ego-oriented focus and can refer to abstract categories or actual groupings of people. Given the need for elaboration of the concept – both because of its social significance and because of its relevance to subsequent themes in this book – some structuring of this ambiguity is necessary. What follows is an oversystematized description of an admittedly flexible indigenous concept.

The term *koputangata* is not of Pukapukan origin. It derives from Rarotongan and refers to kinsmen (see Savage 1962:115). *Kopu* denotes 'womb,' 'belly,' or 'stomach'; *tangata* 'person'.[4] One should remember throughout the following discussion that, collectively, *koputangata* control only a limited portion of the atoll.   The heated debates, the recitation of extensive genealogies, that accompany discussions of *koputangata* involve perhaps one-fourth of the island's landmass and less than half of its taro swamps. They concern only nonreserve land and swamps plus the privately held swamps in Motu Uta and Motu Ko.

Koputangata, especially in their ancestor-oriented focus, are structured by and around certain key cultural constructs.[5] These constructs, though imparting a sense of order to Pukapukan social organization, contain numerous ambiguities – facilitating the negotiation and adjustment of genealogical relations to the actual needs of individual households. The following five constructs are particularly salient.[6]

In justifying rights to a particular piece of property – to build a house, plant trees and taro, or simply collect coconuts – knowledgeable Pukapukans almost invariably assert a genealogical link to some earlier ancestor, generally to a *pu mua* who lived four or five generations ago. The *pu mua* is an apical ancestor – or more precisely an 'earlier boss' or 'owner' – in charge of the land. In discussing these ancestors and their living descendants, we must keep in mind two important facts that Pukapukans frequently stress in their conversations (and arguments) regarding land tenure. First, Pukapukans assert that each apical ancestor at one time possessed sole ownership of a particular property. Such ownership, they imply, often derived from a land division among a group of ancestral kin, especially a group of siblings. As a result of the land division, individuals who might conceivably have laid claim to a sibling's property forfeited all rights to it upon receiving a fair share of land elsewhere on the island. Second, Pukapukans generally accept that all cognatic descendants of a particular apical ancestor possess a legitimate claim to that ancestor's property. (Which type of claim and for what duration are usually matters of negotiation.) What is critical here is that, unlike village membership, property rights are not restricted or exclusive. In principle, a person may claim rights to as many pieces of land as he or she can cognatically trace a link back to the property's original owner. The only limiting criterion is that the person be descended from the property's apical ancestor, not his or her kin. The kin long ago forfeited rights to the ancestor's property when they accepted land elsewhere.

Another important cultural construct suggests that in former times men controlled land (*lungaa wenua*), whereas women controlled taro swamps (*loto uwi*). Kililua expressed the general Pukapukan perspective well one afternoon during a discussion on traditional Pukapukan social organization:

In regard to the control (*akateleanga*) of the taro swamps. . . . the right (*mana*) is with the woman, but the right up on the land (*wenua*) is with the man. Up on the land is the male child; he controls (*wakayaele*) up on the land. In the taro swamp, the right is with the female child.

Implicit in the construct is the fact that each gender has its own spheres of labor and control (see Beaglehole and Beaglehole 1938:46; Hecht 1976a:38 ff.). Illustrative of women's work in taro swamps, for instance, is the fact that they had to bring cooked taro (in the form of *taataa*) to the February 4, 1981, Yato food collection. Likewise, because men work up on the land, they had to bring coconuts. That women subsequently got more coconuts than men in the distribution and men more taro than women emphasizes the complementarity of the sexes. They provide food for each other.

From this construct follows the assertion that in earlier times women usually inherited taro swamps whereas men inherited portions of non-swamp or what Hecht (1976a:36) calls dry land. In its most common phrasing, the construct implies the division of property between brothers and sisters, with sisters inheriting swamps and brothers dry land. Exactly how this inheritance worked out in generations after the original division among siblings is ambiguous at best, but the implication is that taro swamps somehow stayed with women and dry land with men. Implicitly, then, there is a sense that swamps were traditionally transmitted from women to women, dry land from men to men.[7]

Another cultural construct stresses the importance of seniority. Older brothers, particularly the oldest, often possess slightly more authority than their siblings. One should be careful, however, in equating this construct with general Polynesian notions of primogeniture. Seniority in Pukapuka is tempered by the atoll's egalitarian ethos. Older brothers essentially watch out for the interests of their siblings. Being older, they are more experienced and more capable of standing up for the group's interests. On Pukapuka, all siblings within a particular generation ideally should inherit equal shares of any property. Pukapukans, I might add, rarely stressed precise birth order in their genealogical discussions with me when I did not emphasize it myself (cf. Hecht 1977:196, 202). Where seniority has its greatest significance is between generations. Usually the oldest living generation within each descent line represents that descent line's interests vis-à-vis others.

A different cultural construct concerns the reconstruction of apical ancestors for pieces of land where, as often occurs, doubt exists as to the original owner's identity. On the basis of what people know about a section's present owners, many use their genealogical knowledge to construct the property's presumed apical ancestor. Take, for example, the case of Nowua. For a long time, Nowua confided to me in 1981, he assumed a section of land in Yaalongo *kawa* derived from the *pu mua* Amona. He based this on the fact that mainly descendants of Amona claimed the land today. But recently, after much reflection regarding who had lived there over the years, he had decided that Uwitai must be the section's apical ancestor. It made more sense, he noted, when one traced out the genealogical relationships.

A final cultural construct deals with the rationale Pukapukans cite for limiting various relatives' claims to property – especially property used by oneself. As readers might suspect given the cognatic nature of modern

Working in the taro fields

Pukapukan descent, this construct touches some of the central ambiguities surrounding *koputangata*. On the one hand, the sharing of food and land constitutes the very essence of kinship for Pukapukans, as it does in a variety of other Polynesian cultures (see, e.g., Howard and Kirkpatrick 1989; Huntsman 1971). On the other hand, a moment of kindness can turn into years of irritation as needy relatives and their kin make increasing demands on one's own limited resources.

A Pukapukan's main defense against excessive claims by relatives on the property he or she uses is to assert that the relatives possess sufficient land elsewhere. Referring to a sense of fair play as well as to the atoll's egalitarian ethos, Pukapukans imply that it is improper for one's relatives to accumulate an excessive amount of land at a kin's expense. An analogy to the land division that gave the apical ancestor sole ownership of certain property is often implicit in the emotionally laden statements surrounding these discussions. Just as the apical ancestor's relatives lost rights to certain property long ago when they gained land elsewhere, so too should one's relatives today utilize property elsewhere on the atoll.

All of these cultural constructs have a reasonable logic that I, as an outsider, can appreciate. Moreover, they fit very well with general Polynesian notions regarding descent and gender as well as with the atoll's specific egalitarian ethos and its cross-cutting ties. They are quite effective for explicating subtle and complex matters, especially since they offer considerable room for negotiation and manipulation.

But certain problems are associated with them. Take, for example, the first construct regarding the ancient land division in which an apical ancestor, or *pu mua*, gained some sections of land and his or her kin others. On a small island such as Pukapuka, where numerous intermarriages of distantly related kin occur (see Hecht 1976a, 1976b), an individual involved in a dispute quite conceivably can trace cognatic ties to *both* the apical ancestor and his or her related kin. Under these circumstances, different people can emphasize different ties for a particular individual, depending on whether they want to support or deny the individual's claim to the property in question.

The cultural construct relating to gender makes sense to both Pukapukans and to myself, but as Figures 1, 2, and 3 indicate, genealogical data collected from informants for specific taro swamps and dry land contradict its premise. The transmission of rights to taro swamps and dry land is far more complicated than implied by the construct. Swamps are not simply transmitted from women to women, nor dry land from men to men. Figure 1 concerns Puwatu, a taro swamp the Beagleholes' informants stated belonged to members of the Kava submatrilineage residing in Yato village. As can readily be seen, male links play a significant role in the transmission process. Figure 2 deals with the taro

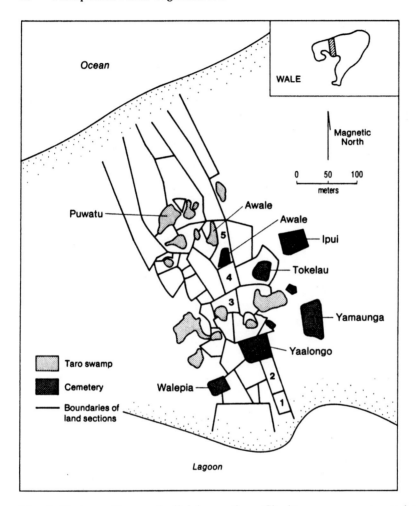

Map 3. Yaalongo Kawa and adjoining sections. Cited taro swamps, cemeteries, and numbered land sections relate to topics discussed in this and later chapters.

swamp Awale, a swamp the Beagleholes' field notes indicate belonged to the Awale branch of the Yaalongo patrilineage. Again male links constitute an important element in the transmission process. A man, moreover, is the apical ancestor for one of the swamp's two major sections. Figure 3 involves the same pattern, but in reverse. The five sections of nonswamp (or dry land), according to the gender construct, should all be traced through men. Yet clearly women have played a role in the transmission of sections over time. The two apical ancestors

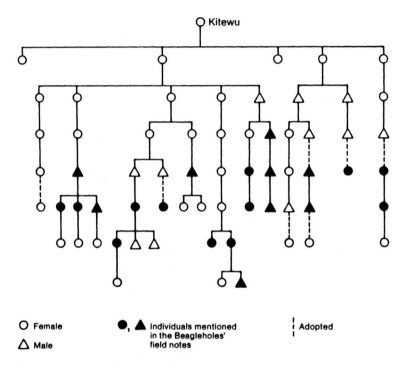

Figure 1. Puwatu taro swamp. Genealogical connections traced from the swamp's reputed apical ancestor, Kitewu, to current cultivators.[8] (References to individuals mentioned in the Beagleholes' field notes relate to material presented later in the chapter.)

for the sections of land presented in Figure 3 are the same apical ancestors described for Awale swamp in Figure 2. Men as well as women, we can see, have played key roles in the transmission of dry land *and* taro swamps.

As one might suspect given the atoll's limited landmass, the construct relating to the exclusion of cognatic relatives from one's own property is extremely difficult to pin down in practice. Several Pukapukans know, for example, that Lakini is the apical ancestor for sections of land in both Yato and Loto villages. When cognatic descendants of Lakini lay claim to land in Yato, their relatives there pointedly suggest that their kin investigate claims in Loto and vice versa. But none of the people, at least with whom I talked, had a real understanding of the details by which some people came to claim property in Yato and others in Loto. Many possessed an understanding of the genealogical ties involved in certain claims as a result of their own reconstructions. But, essentially,

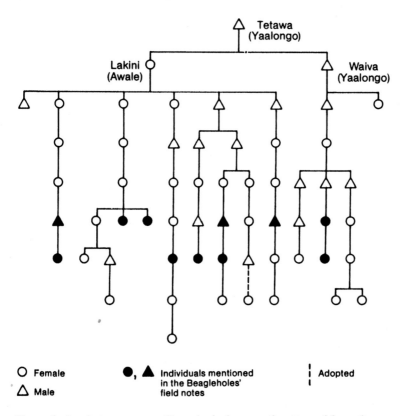

Figure 2. Awale taro swamp. Genealogical connections traced from the swamp's reputed apical ancestor, Tetawa, to current cultivators.[9] (References to the burial sites of Tetawa, Lakini, and Waiva, in parentheses, relate to material presented later in the chapter.)

individuals in each section simply presumed that their relatives had rights to land elsewhere – an assumption that weakened, of course, these relatives' claims to the property the individuals themselves utilized.

The whole sloughing off process in which some people retain claims to certain lands whereas others lose them is full of ambiguities and manipulations. Few individuals trace out their claims in public, except during heated property disputes, for fear that some distant cognatic relative will lay claim to the property. Likewise, Pukapukans may casually hunt around to see if they have claims to property their cognatic relatives never disclosed to them. As Pukapukans are well aware, a diligent person can in principle lay claim to a considerable amount of

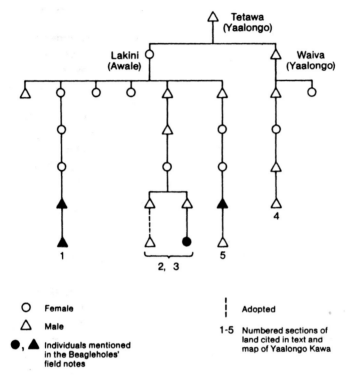

Figure 3. Owners of numbered land sections in Map 3[10]

land. Many people provided me with genealogies on the condition that important details not be shown to relatives. Readers can thus appreciate the reason for all the vague references and impersonal symbols in Figures 1 through 3. It is not simply a matter of giving the diagrams an impersonal aura, a distancing from the present (see Fabian 1983). To give more personal details might create serious difficulties for Pukapukan informants.

These cultural constructs should not be mistaken for "reality" in a correspondence sense of truth, for a set of objective facts that all can perceive and agree on. The ambiguities, manipulations, and deceptions surrounding property claims make it doubtful that individuals fully grasp all the complexities involved – even for land they themselves claim. But what the constructs do, and do quite well in my opinion, is provide Pukapukans with guidelines for action. They offer explanations. They give present-day claims an aura of legitimacy, a sense of fairness (cf. Bilmes 1976). And they provide room for manipulation, for people to adjust social ideologies to the precarious balances that must be maintained between people and resources on a small coral atoll.

Given this context, one can perceive why difficulties exist in defining the degree to which *koputangata* constitute groups versus categories. It depends on the circumstances. In one sense, a *koputangata* is clearly an ancestor-oriented cognatic corporate group. It possesses continuity through time. All people who jointly use certain property trace cognatic descent to the same ancestor. They may well share food with one another, and they may come together for a meeting if one of their members wants to make some change on the jointly held property, such as build a house or plant several coconut trees. In another sense, a *koputangata* may simply be an ancestor-oriented cognatic category. As descendants of Kitewu, for instance, they all trace (or have others trace for them) genealogical links back to a common ancestor. Some in this general category jointly hold property whereas others do not. And they certainly do not all come together for meetings if the property holders can help it. Such meetings would encourage other relatives to lay a claim to the property as well.

The ambiguity between *koputangata* category and group emphasizes the anthropological concern with how one restricts cognatic group membership (see Shore, 1982:307–8, for a summary of the issue). No absolute answer exists for Pukapukans. But they do possess certain guidelines for delimiting *koputangata* in specific cases. The one absolute principle involves possessing a descent link to the apical ancestor. Other criteria are open to negotiation. The more cognatic links one can trace to an apical ancestor, the stronger is one's claim to that *koputangata*'s property. Others might dispute one or two individual links, but a large number of ties to an apical ancestor builds a solid case to support one's right to the property. A tendency exists for people to lay claim to property near their residence. This is partly a matter of convenience. It also involves an emotional tie to a locality. Families residing near (or on) certain property take care of it over time and develop an identification with it. Need is a prime factor. Pukapukans strongly believe that one should help relatives, especially if they are close or are in need. But what constitutes need versus greed can become a subject for heated debate. As a general rule the closer the relationship, the more stringent are the demands for sharing property. Current use of property is important too. Pukapukans find it extremely difficult to evict individuals from a swamp section or piece of land once they have used it for a while. The initial conditions of a temporary tenure tend to be forgotten with the passage of years. One's initially grateful guests may gradually become the property's legitimate occupants. An individual's determination constitutes a final factor. Where some people might become discouraged by the hostility and prevarications of their relatives, others become more insistent. In all but the most obvious cases, individuals need a certain amount of feisty persistence in asserting rights to property.

One should note finally, in discussing ancestor-oriented *koputangata*, that a group's property boundaries are often ambiguously defined. Conflicts frequently arise among neighbors regarding the precise dividing line between adjacent sections of land. In constructing Map 3, for example, I had to take individual owners out separately when surveying property to avoid disputes. The survey indicated that different people clearly had differing opinions regarding the location of property boundaries.

A *koputangata* may constitute an ego-oriented category of consanguineal kin as well as an ancestor-oriented one. In its most basic form, this ego-centered category connotes the sharing of both blood and property. All Pukapukans can, as Hecht notes (1976a:143), presume to be kin in some sense, but generally people do not trace common ties farther back than four or five generations. People rarely, however, marry a relative nearer than three generations removed from a common ancestor (see Beaglehole and Beaglehole 1938:294; Hecht 1976a:103). No clear rule exists for deciding exactly when distant relatives become nonkin rather than kin. Usually it depends on the circumstances. But generally Pukapukans try to maintain a diverse set of ties with a diverse group of kin (see, e.g., Hecht 1981:70). Like Banabans (see Silverman 1971), they prefer to keep a variety of options open.

It is extremely important, in analyzing *koputangata*, to realize that they constitute an alternative to the villages as a means of organizing people and property. *Koputangata*, in being amorphous and fluid, allow people to readjust continually the balance between resources and population either by redefining the group's membership or by redefining the group's property. The villages, as structured corporate groups, allow only for annual changes in membership and for almost no changes in property. Whereas *koputangata* constitute a plethora of overlapping categories and groups connected through a multiplicity of cognatic links, the villages focus on the discrepancies between residence and village membership and the "farming out" of children into other food-sharing units to establish cross-cutting ties. The villages, moreover, have a patrilineal bias in their membership.

Carrying the distinction farther, one can see that *koputangata* possess comparatively less property and certainly less authority than the villages. Though a few select individuals act as stewards (*tiaki*) for *koputangata* property, the village collectively regulates village property. *Koputangata* possess neither *pule* nor representatives on the Island Council, and whereas villages participate in competitive games, *koputangata* do not for a very good reason. They are too ambiguously defined. A person could belong to two teams at the same time. An insulting victory speech against one's opponents might unfortunately refer to many of one's teammates as well.

The 1976–80 Akatawa

At first glance, it might appear that the *Akatawa*'s "revival" in 1976 would necessitate major changes in the atoll's social organization. Under the *Akatawa* people and property are divided between two 'sides' rather than among three villages. The public reserves, food-sharing units, *pule*, and sporting teams all are reorganized under the *Akatawa*. Yet there was no revolution, no renting of the atoll's social fabric in 1976. All that happened, in actual fact, were a few slight alterations. The most radical change probably occurred in my own understanding of the atoll's social organization. It seemed much more fluid, much less structured, than I initially presumed. (This was especially the case after the village system replaced the *Akatawa* in 1980, see Borofsky 1982:225–8.) How did Pukapukans manage these major alterations with so little conflict? It was fairly simple.

The establishment of the *Akatawa*'s bipartite organization in 1976, for example, did not cause significant alterations in the village reserves. All were essentially preserved intact except that Loto's reserve at Motu Uta was split in half. It now became two reserves instead of one. People used the old boundary between the Tawa Lalo and Tawa Ngake sections of the reserve for a dividing line. Yato's reserves at Motu Kotawa and Niua merged with Motu Uta's Tawa Lalo to form one side of the *Akatawa*. Ngake's reserve at Motu Ko merged with Motu Uta's Tawa Ngake to form the other. Aside from that, the concept and the boundaries of the village reserves remained the same. All that it involved was a slightly different configuration of who now owned what. Even the names of the old sections in Motu Uta remained intact. One side of the *Akatawa* called itself Tawa Lalo, the other Tawa Ngake (see Map 4).

Nor were any of the reserves really depleted by the greatly enhanced number of people using them. True, more people laid claim to resources in each reserve, but since Tawa Ngake and Tawa Lalo now both possessed two major reserves instead of one as under the village system, people limited their stays at any particular reserve to a shorter period of time. When Tawa Ngake finished making copra in its section of Motu Uta, it moved on to Motu Ko. When Tawa Lalo finished its section at Motu Uta, it turned to Motu Kotawa, leaving Motu Uta ample time to become restocked with coconuts.

A touchy issue existed regarding the places where newcomers might

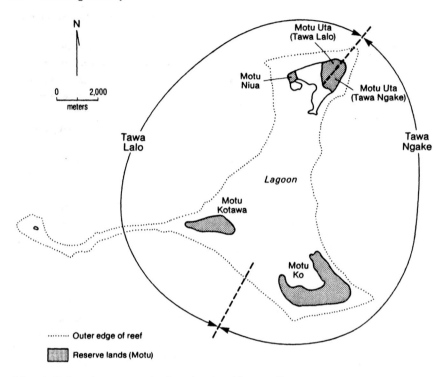

Map 4. Pukapuka as organized under the *Akatawa*.[11]

collect coconuts in Motu Uta and Motu Ko. In both reserves groups of
households had their own special strips (or *kawa*) for collecting coconuts,
but people, at least initially, did not mind including others as guests on
their strips. It was, after all, the gracious thing to do. And since the
Akatawa was initially viewed as temporary (see Chapter 5), the guests
would, presumably, eventually leave.

The reorganization of the villages' taro swamps in 1976 proved of
little difficulty. Every year, each village has to redivide its public swamps
to correspond to new membership roles. Pukapukans simply redivided
the swamps again but in terms of *Akatawa* units rather than villages.
Instead of people cultivating a few large sections in one reserve as before,
they now cultivated several smaller sections in two reserves. Not much
difference existed in the amount of taro each family obtained under the
two systems.

The private taro swamps controlled by various *koputangata* in the
villages' reserves of Motu Uta and Motu Ko initially presented no prob-

lem. People continued to cultivate them as before. The cases in which a person belonged to one side of Motu Uta and worked taro swamp sections on the other did not prove terribly complicated. The individuals concerned simply asked the other *tawa*'s *pule* for permission to visit their swamps. Rarely, if ever, was permission refused. With time, certain difficulties did arise. Since a larger number of people had free access to Motu Uta under the *Akatawa*, more people gradually began laying claim to sections of *Koputangata* controlled swamps there. This also happened at Motu Ko as new people visited that reserve.

On the surface, reorganizing the distributive system, the village's food-sharing units (*tuanga kai*), seemed anything but easy. Certain families had been attached to particular food-sharing units for generations. One set of units could not simply be wiped out and a whole new set put in its place. The change, however, required almost no reorganization. Loto village, as already noted, had preserved the association of food-sharing units with land strips (or *kawa*) in Motu Uta. It already had four food-sharing units associated with Tawa Lalo and four food-sharing units associated with Tawa Ngake. The Tawa Lalo units of Loto, with their names still intact, combined with Yato's six units to form ten food-sharing units in the *Akatawa*'s Tawa Lalo. Likewise, the four units of Tawa Ngake (of Loto) combined with the ten from Ngake village. The changes basically meant that more people collected more produce, which, in turn, was divided more ways, but the means by which they did all of this roughly remained the same.

Since the *pule* guard, like the public taro swamps, were reorganized each year to accord with new membership rolls, no major difficulties arose here either. The *tawa* simply created new *pule*. In regard to the Island Council, one member from Loto by chance already belonged to Tawa Lalo, the other to Tawa Ngake. Consequently, no alterations were required in the council's makeup as a result of the change. All that changed was the constituency that each represented: Rather than two members representing a single village, three members now represented each *tawa*.

Having two teams rather than three in sport competitions did not make a great deal of difference either. Since the new *tawa* teams were larger, most of the same individuals who had played before continued to do so. Only the fact that they now represented two *tawa* rather than three villages changed. Spectators, however, seemed more interested in *Akatawa* competitions. Previously, one village had stood aside while the other two competed. With only two sides playing, everyone was emotionally involved. The two teams, moreover, were relatively evenly matched in cricket. Series of matches sometimes went on for weeks as each team tried to dominate the other.

Thus although the concrete changes required to transform the village system into the *Akatawa* in 1976 appeared major, they were in practice relatively minor. Pukapukans basically superimposed the *tawa* on the established structures of the village with slight alterations here and there to adjust for increased membership.

All this is not to say that problems did not gradually arise. Some did. The issue of whether Tawa Ngake or Ngake village owned Motu Ko came up during discussions regarding the building of an airport on the village reserve. The fact that newcomers depleted some sections of a reserve sooner than others caused resentment among those who now had to search for their coconuts elsewhere. And people from other villages began encroaching on the taro swamps owned by their relatives. In short, some of the same problems that continually arise among *ko-putangata* cropped up with the *Akatawa*.

But, at least initially, no great problems arose. The *Akatawa* provided people with new experiences. They could visit new reserves, compete on new sports teams. The sense I got, especially in the *Akatawa*'s earlier stages, was that it was an exciting change of pace from the island's normal pattern. It embodied, to quote Boon's paraphrasing of Lowie, a certain "playlike component of 'alternicity' " (1982:102), a toying with structures once removed from Pukapukans' own central forms of organization.

Placing the island within a broader perspective

So far Pukapuka has been described as if it were an island unto itself. Before ending our discussion of modern Pukapukan social organization, this impression requires clarification and modification. Communications with the outside world are limited. The only legal way to get to the atoll is a four and a half day boat trip from Rarotonga. Shipping calls averaged 4.7 per year in the period from 1942 to 1965 (Tiro n.d.). During our stay there were slightly fewer. Still, Pukapukans are very much aware and a part of the modern world. Outside orientations and powers certainly exert an influence on the atoll.

The island, for example, imports a large quantity of foodstuffs and has done so for decades. In 1950, a survey showed that Pukapuka imported approximately 10,600 pounds of flour, 1,200 pounds of sugar, 1,300 pounds of rice, 500 pounds of cabin biscuits, and 1,400 pounds of canned meat (Department of Health n.d.:14). Today the amounts are larger. In 1978, it imported roughly 71,700 pounds of flour, 28,300 pounds of sugar, 34,700 pounds of rice, 600 tins of cabin biscuits, and 300 cases of tinned corned beef. (Almost 2,000 tins of canned fish also came onto the island.)[12] The total annual cost of these foodstuffs in 1978 amounted to approximately $63,920 (Turner 1978:19). Nor are food-stuffs the only imported items. The list includes building materials, outboard motors, clothes, and benzine lamps. The total *known* outflow of money from Pukapuka in 1978 to pay for such items was approximately $125,600 (Turner 1978:20).

Unlike Manihiki and Penrhyn, two other atolls in the northern Cooks, Pukapuka possesses no marketable exports aside from copra. (Pearl shell does not grow there because of the lagoon's muddy bottom.) Total income from copra production fluctuates from year to year on the atoll. In 1978, it was approximately $21,000 (S. and T. Kingan, personal communication 1985). Where, then, did the additional money come from to pay for the imported goods? Most of it probably came from government salaries (approximately $61,000) and governmental grants, especially old-age pensions (approximately $31,000) (Turner 1978:18). Without such outside governmental support, the island would have to alter its current life style drastically.

Though the imports are certainly extensive, no Pukapukan family relies solely on them for its diet. Almost all adult men go fishing and almost all adult women work in the taro swamps no matter what their income. The fact that large taro swamps exist on Pukapuka gives the island an advantage over other atolls in the northern Cooks. Pukapukans can, if need be, become basically self-sufficient in food supplies. A nutritional study of the local diet in 1950 – including native foodstuffs such as taro, pulaka, coconuts, and fish but excluding imported products – indicated that the diet met most nutritional requirements except for a mild deficiency in vitamin C and a marked deficiency in vitamin A (Department of Health n.d.:14–20; cf. Davies 1956b:740). The extensive imports are more a luxury than a necessity.

It has already been mentioned that the villages control their own affairs and that the Island Council and the Kau Wowolo (or 'Council of Important People') exert a certain amount of authority over the island as a whole. But today most of the critical decisions affecting Pukapukans are made in Rarotonga by the national government. The government's main representative on the island, the chief administrative officer, possesses considerable political power in island affairs (see Beckett 1964:420–1).

Over the past several years, extensive emigration has occurred (see Hecht 1976a:12–15, 1978). More than half of the people that one might identify as Pukapukan do not now dwell on the atoll. Rather, they live in Rarotonga and New Zealand. There is considerable interchange among these groups. Pukapukans frequently visit their relatives on other islands. Occasionally, others also visit relatives on Pukapuka. Some migrants even return permanently to the island after making money elsewhere. The movement of people is by no means only in an outward direction.

Traditional Pukapukan social organization

The ease with which the three villages transformed themselves into the *Akatawa*'s two 'sides' in 1976 suggests a close connection between the two modern organizational patterns. But how does the *Akatawa* fit with the atoll's *traditional* social organization? That is an important question in trying to understand the *Akatawa*'s past.

Unfortunately, we encounter serious problems in trying to resolve this matter. First, limited and conflicting data exist on the atoll's traditional organization. If we focus on precontact social organization, our information derives mainly from vague second- and thirdhand accounts recorded several decades after the arrival of missionaries in 1857. If we draw a larger net and include the work of anthropologists who from 1934 onward studied the island's traditions, we discover definite differences in their accounts.

Second, and deriving from the first, considerable difficulty exists in specifying a traditional, as opposed to nontraditional, period in Pukapukan history. No quiet, static time exists before the onslaught of recent modernization. The island has undergone considerable change in the past 400 years, especially in population. More than 250 years before contact, a hurricane reputedly devasted the island, leaving only two women, fifteen men, and "remnants of their families" (Beaglehole and Beaglehole 1938:386). In 1862, when Gill visited the island, he estimated the population at 750 (Gill 1862). Following blackbirder visitors in 1863 and an epidemic in 1870, the population reputedly dropped to 300 (Vivian 1871–2). The population was 632 when the Beagleholes conducted their research in 1935. Rather than typifying a new trend, the changes of the past four decades belong to a much longer process.

The picture one gains of the Pukapukan past, in other words, is an ambiguous, changing one. How, then, do we proceed? A central theme of this book is that discrepant and ambiguous accounts provide an opening to understanding. They offer an opportunity to comprehend traditional social organization in insightful, new ways. The rest of this chapter examines the work of the Beagleholes and Hecht, the anthropologists presenting the most comprehensive ethnographic analyses to date of traditional Pukapukan social organization. (In the next two chapters I shall take up Pukapukan accounts of the atoll's past.) By paying close attention to the contexts in which the Beagleholes and Hecht worked and how this affected their results, we gain an appreciation for how they, as anthropologists, interpreted traditional Pukapukan social organization. And we gain insight into how they, as anthropologists, contributed to the differing accounts of the *Akatawa*'s past.

The Beagleholes' perspective on traditional Pukapukan social organization

The Beagleholes conducted their fieldwork on the atoll in 1934–5. They describe three major social groupings relevant to our analysis: matrimoieties, patrilineages, and villages. According to the Beagleholes, traditionally there were two overarching matrimoieties: Wua Kati and Wua Lulu. Each of these was divided into smaller matrilineal units, called *momo*, *keinanga*, or *manga*, which the Beagleholes refer to as lineages or sublineages.

The head of the matrilineage (*wakatauila* or *wakalulu*) was the eldest male or female member of the group.

His functions are light. He acts as gift-giver at the *waele* feasts for first-born children in the families making up the descent group. He represents the lineage at inter-lineage and village meetings, arranges for the carrying out of its activities in games, competitions, and feasts. He has no special status in the community beyond a certain position within his own group based on seniority. (Beaglehole and Beaglehole 1938:227)

Many of the larger swamps outside the village reserves, according to the Beagleholes, belonged to these matrilineal units (1938:44, 228, ms. a under "Names of Ui Keinanga and Ui Po"). Puwatu, for example, was owned by the matrilineal sublineage Kava – or, more precisely, the Kava sublineage (*keinanga*) within the Lulu lineage (*wua*) of the Lulu moiety (*wua*) (1938:225). The Beagleholes note, "Children retain a share in the mother's maternal lineage [taro] beds, but receive no shares in the mother paternal lineage beds. . . . The talo lands [or taro swamps] are controlled by the lineages as corporate entities" (1938:44). And later they add:

Today the maternal sub-lineages, not the lineages or moiety groupings of lineages, have effective economic functions in the control of land, principally the control of talo beds [talo is the Pukapukan word for taro]. The talo beds owned by a sub-lineage are divided among both male and female members of the sub-lineage. There is no permanent subdivision of these talo beds; but they are divided at regular intervals as composition of the sub-lineage corporation is altered by birth and death. (1938:228)

On the basis of information collected in a household census of Ngake and Yato villages, the Beagleholes suggest that "there is no tendency to either moiety or lineage localization" for the matrilineal units (1938:226). The general impression one gets is that the matrilineal units provided a set of cross-cutting nonlocalized ties among the more localized patrilineal units.

The Beagleholes note, "The maternal lineage functions as a unit in fishing and sporting contests, and in certain types of food divisions" (1938:228). "Team membership for fishing and sporting contests was formerly always based on maternal lineage membership. One moiety contested against another moiety" (Beaglehole and Beaglehole 1938:231). Food divisions that took place after various competitions were previously always "in terms of either maternal or paternal organization . . . [and] food divisions at marriage and birth feasts were formerly . . . in terms of maternal units" (1938:232; see also ms. a under "Activities Organized on Wua Lines").

The matrilineal units, in other words, constituted corporate groups with their own organizational structure and their own jointly held property. Aside from owning property, their functions were relatively light, as illustrated by the limited responsibilities of the lineage's head. Still, they served an important social purpose on the island, providing cross-cutting ties between localized patrilineal groupings.

At least seven major patrilineages previously existed: Muliwutu, Maatanga, Yangalipule (or Tilotilowia), i Tua, Yamaunga, Yayi, and Yaalongo (Beaglehole and Beaglehole 1938:229). Members of each patrilineage owned certain strips of land (*kawa*) (Beaglehole and Beaglehole 1938:41–4, ms. a, "Land Boundaries and Divisions"). These strips existed not only in the nonreserve sections of the island where people built their houses but also within the village reserves – Motu Uta, Motu Ko, Motu Kotawa, and Motu Niua. Members of a patrilineage were buried in cemeteries located on the nonreserve sections of these strips. Each patrilineage, moreover, was affiliated with a particular village – the village within which its land strips (or *kawa*) were located. Ngake village included Muliwutu and Maatanga, Loto village Yangalipule (or Tilotilowia) and i Tua, and Yato village Yamaunga, Yayi, and Yaalongo.

Regarding the ownership of property, the Beagleholes state:

The coconut trees, talo beds, and bush timbers on all sections [or *kawa*] are of two kinds: first, those owned by the people of the lineage in common and shared among all members; second, those individually owned by male and female members of the lineage who alone are allowed to plant or to own trees on the section. Coconut trees of the first type descend in the lineage corporation and are not alienable. Trees of the second type are inheritable among individual members of the lineage, but are not alienable outside of it.

Each section (*kawa*) is further subdivided into homestead lots named *yikuanga*. . . . Only people belonging directly to the lineage that owns the sections on which the lot is located may plant or privately own trees or talo beds or be said to own house sites on the lots. (1938:42, see also ms. a, "Kawa Land Strips")

The Beagleholes go on to note that "at the death of the household head, his house site and the nut [i.e., coconut] trees descend in the paternal line. The children of the deceased act as joint owners of the property through the trusteeship of the eldest male of the family" (1938:43). Patrilineages, like the matrilineal sublineages, owned taro swamps. The swamps, at least outside the reserves, tended to be smaller than those owned by matrilineal units (see ms. a, "Names of Ui Kein-anga and Ui Po, 2"). The patrilineages owned swamps as corporate entities and redivided allotments within them from time to time. Rights to specific sections of a swamp were alienable solely within the patrilineage.

The Beagleholes record that the patrilineages had two distinct aspects: the *po* (or common burial site) and the *yoolonga* (or localized grouping):

When a man talks of his *po*, he means his paternal lineage and the piece of ground where he will be buried. The importance of the burial ground as giving a symbolic locus of reference for the varied functions of the lineage is shown by the fact that when asking the paternal lineage membership of a person one does not say: "What is his *po*?" but, "Where will he be buried?" (*Ka tanu i wea*?) The answer always provides the name of the burial ground. On the other hand, in narrative the name of the *po* is always used as an adjective to indicate paternal descent affiliation, as "*Ko Pakula, e tane Ma[a]tanga*" (Pakula was a man of Ma[a]tanga *po*). (Beaglehole and Beaglehole 1938:229).

In contrast, the *yoolonga* division

is in terms of patrilocal residence. That is, all members of the same household or family organization living patrilocally are considered to belong to the same Yolongo [*sic*] organization. In food shares, the head of the family, usually the oldest male, receives a food share for and on behalf of the patrilocal group living with him.
The Yolongo group will thus exclude blood members of the family who are adopted elsewhere and are not in residence with the patrilocal group, but will include nonblood members who reside with the patrilocal group through marriage, or through adoption. (Beaglehole and Beaglehole ms. a, "Organizations for Food Division and Games, etc., Yolongo")

The patrilocal rule of residence emphasized the persistence of localized patrilineal groupings through time. The Beagleholes indicate that "the amount ... of po [i.e., patrilineage] localization ... is comparatively large" (ms. a, "Po Localization"). "Of 39 male heads of households in Ngake whose residence is patrilocal, 37 or 95 percent are members of the two Ngake [patrilineages] ... Ma[a]tanga and Muliwutu" (ms. a, "Po Localization"; see also 1938:230, 250). For Yato, the figure was 82 percent.

The patrilineage's leaders consisted of a subchief (*langatila*) or chief (*aliki*) (depending on the lineage) and, in former times, a priest who directed the worship of the lineage's gods (Beaglehole and Beaglehole 1938:235–7, 321–5). The priest consulted the gods on intralineage matters. The chiefs handled matters affecting the island as a whole and dedicated themselves to the welfare of the people within their respective patrilineages as well as to various village projects. The chief of the Loto patrilineage i Tua was the high chief of the island (*aliki wolo*).

Political authority on the island was split among three groups:

Village meetings (*wakapono lulu*), attended by the chiefs, subchiefs, and all adult males of the village discussed matters affecting the village and the reserves, and settled intravillage disputes. Meetings of the old men's group (*wakapononga no te tupele*) discussed island affairs. Meetings of the chiefs (*wakapononga a te wui aliki*) discussed island and inter-lineage matters. . . . Informants believed that the supreme chief called the minor chiefs together at unspecified times to discuss matters referred to him by the council of old men (*tupele*). All decisions of the old men were presented to the high chief or the council of chiefs for final approval. Whether or not this approval was nominal depended on the prestige and power of the high chief. (Beaglehole and Beaglehole 1938:245)

The present-day Kau Wowolo is a continuation of the chiefly meetings.

The localized patrilineal groupings (*yoolonga*) formed the basis for certain food divisions and sporting contests. The Beagleholes state:

Food divisions following fishing contests and other games are always in terms of either maternal or paternal organization. . . . Before the division of food for a fishing contest (*malama*), the food dividers asked me how I wished the food to be divided. As I left the responsibility to them, they decided to make the division on the paternal (*yolongo*) [*sic*] principle. (1938:232)

Long ago, the Beagleholes record, "team membership for fishing and sporting contests was . . . always based on maternal lineage membership. . . . [But] at a later period [of Pukapukan history,] organization was in terms of either *wua* or *yolongo* [*sic*] units. [Today] village membership is the rule" (1938:231–2). The Beagleholes' unpublished field notes make essentially the same point (see ms. a, "Activities Organized on Yolongo Lines").

The patrilineages, like the matrilineages, thus constituted corporate groups, with their own property and organizational structure. In comparison with the matrilineages, however, they possessed more property and a greater degree of political organization.

The Beagleholes' description of the villages suggest that they were organized much as they are today, especially regarding property and the allocation of resources. The villages owned the same reserve lands, and they allocated village resources in roughly the same way. Minor differences existed in the length of time each *pule* guard held office. Previously it was for one month rather than two weeks. Though the Beagleholes do not specifically mention the *tuanga kai* food-sharing units, material such as the above quotes on food distribution makes clear that the *yoolonga* constituted the food-sharing units in 1934–5. (This fits with the general impression of people today regarding a relationship between village food-sharing units and patrilineally controlled strips of land [*kawa*].)

Residence and village membership was far more overlapping in earlier times than in 1978–81. To avoid conflicting loyalties and the transfer of "village secrets," when a person changed village membership he or she generally changed residence as well (Beaglehole and Beaglehole 1938:221). Thus the pattern of cross-cutting village membership and residence ties did not exist in the past to the same degree that it does today, but given the importance of matrilineal groupings in 1934–5 presumably they, rather than village/residence links, served as the basis for cross-cutting ties.

Various data suggest that the modern villages at least partially evolved out of the atoll's patrilineal organization.[13]Strips of land in both the reserve and nonreserve lands of Loto, for example, are related to distinct patrilineages. Even today particular families focus on certain strips when collecting coconuts. And the Beagleholes indicate that missionary effort hastened the predominance of village organization in competitive games (1938:232). (This fits with a missionary preference for village organization noted in other areas of Polynesia; see, e.g., Crocombe 1964:64–7, 1967:98.) Collectively, the data suggest that the relationship among matrimoiety, patrilineal, and village units clearly changed over time. When one adds the known fluctuations in the island's population, it seems all the more likely that what the Beagleholes saw (and recorded) was not a static, timeless form of social organization, but an evolving, fluid one.

The anthropological contexts of the Beagleholes' research

Examining the anthropological contexts surrounding the Beagleholes' research raises a number of important issues. Significantly, portions of the Beagleholes' analysis appear to unravel on closer examination. One may doubt, for example, whether matrilineages and patrilineages corporately owned taro swamps and whether residence was as patrilocal as the Beagleholes depict. Such comments are not meant to be a direct criticism of the Beagleholes' ethnography. Pearl and Ernest Beaglehole were excellent fieldworkers. The problem was that they conducted their research within a particular intellectual context that affected the formulation and presentation of their results.

Colson (1985) indicates that up into the early 1930s American ethnology generally concerned itself with salvage ethnography, with historical reconstruction. Two interactive themes were at work in various ethnographic accounts of the period. On the one hand, salvage ethnography often minimized meaningful contextual relations. Anthropologists had to collect and describe remnants of patterns no longer existing during the period of their fieldwork. As Gruber states:

> The needs of salvage . . . so readily recognized through an awareness of a savage vanishing on the disappearing frontier of an advancing civilization, set the tone and the method for much that was anthropology in the earlier years of its prosecution as a self-conscious discipline. . . . Such an approach could lead only to a collection of data rather than a body of data. The very operation of the collection itself infused the data with a sense of separateness, a notion of item discontinuity that encouraged the use of an acontextual comparative method and led only to the most limited (because they alone were observed) ideas of functional correlation. Moreover, the sense of salvage with its concern with loss and extinction, stressed the disorganization in a social system at the expense of the sense of community; it stressed the pathology of cultural loss in the absence of any real experience with the normally operating small community. (1970:1297; cf. Wagner 1981:27–8).

On the other hand, anthropologists often created ethnographic abstractions – timeless, homogeneous tribes uncontaminated by contact. They used memories and momentos to construct holistic pictures of vital, functioning societies. Since such societies were frequently defined in precontact terms, to distance them from the disruptions of the present, the accounts by definition were often unverifiable (see Leaf 1979:146–9). They were not based on direct observation. They existed as abstractions or ideals of what might (or even should) have been.

The fact that many anthropologists possessed the same biases in formulating their accounts as folklorists a century earlier suggests certain underlying themes in recent Western efforts to reconstruct past cultures. Whether they are an adaptive response to the social transformations of the past two centuries, as Hobsbawm suggests (in Hobsbawm and Ranger 1983:4–8), is a question requiring further investigation. But readers should realize that anthropological reconstructions are themselves part of a Western tradition with a considerable past. (Burke's 1978 account makes this point particularly well.)

A second broad trend of the 1930s, aside from historical reconstruction, concerned the development of anthropology as a scientific study with its own literary genre. As Clifford states, "In the 1920s, the new fieldworker-theorist brought to completion a powerful new scientific and literary genre, the ethnography, a synthetic cultural description based on participant-observation" (1983a:124). Emphasizing a scientific orientation with observer neutrality, anthropologists gradually began supplanting travelers, missionaries, and administrators as authorities on native life.[14]

American anthropologists emphasized two broad data-gathering techniques within this scientific genre. They combined direct observation of present-day conditions with intensive interviews of select informants regarding the past. How did they choose such informants? "You would get the expert," recalls J. Whiting, who received his training at Yale during the same time the Beagleholes did (personal communication 1985). One would choose a person who had the requisite knowledge, who was articulate enough to answer one's questions. The ethnographer's job, Cohen suggests, was to discover authoritative spokespersons and to record cases that supported or invalidated their accounts (in Ellen 1984:223).

Such data collecting often left room for different interpretations. Eggan, who worked among the Hopi of the American Southwest at the same time the Beagleholes did and who praised their fieldwork, suggests that his account of a particular Hopi village might well differ from the Beagleholes' as a result of their differing theoretical orientations. He notes that although he and Titiev worked together on the Hopi, they at times drew somewhat different conclusions. "We had to work on the whole system of initiation from a few hints here and there so there was room for that" (F. Eggan, personal communication 1985).

A final theme of the early 1930s concerns anthropologists' ties to colonial regimes (see, e.g., Asad 1973; Ellen 1984). "White rule or colonial domination was a given context for their work," Clifford suggests, "and they adopted a range of liberal positions within it. Seldom 'colonists' in any direct, instrumental sense, ethnographers accepted certain constraints while, in varying degrees, questioning them" (1983b:142). White rule and colonial domination clearly formed the context for much fieldwork in the 1930s (see, e.g., E. Beaglehole 1944:11–12, 127–8), but it would be an overgeneralization to state that, as a result, anthropologists always distanced themselves from informants or that such conditions created insurmountable distortions (as some have implied; see Asad 1973). Certainly the Beagleholes do not easily fit into such a pattern. Forty years after her fieldwork, for example, Pearl Beaglehole kept in touch with informants, and the Beagleholes' applied research in Hawaii and New Zealand indicates a sensitivity to the social plight of Polynesians.

The preceding account is too brief a summary to give the flavor of the subtleties and diversity of the period. (Interested readers can consult the notes for further references.)[15] But it does provide a background for looking at the specific influences on the Beagleholes' research.

It is easy to move from the general trends of the 1930s to more specific concerns in the Beagleholes' monograph on Pukapuka. Both strive to present salvage ethnography within a scientific framework. But one should not simply assume that the Beagleholes' work constituted a knee-jerk response to these trends. The Beagleholes clearly knew many of the limitations of these approaches and sought to overcome them. How they came to write a traditional ethnography, in spite of this knowledge, is an interesting story.

Since more data exist for Ernest Beaglehole than for Pearl, the following account will focus on him. This is reasonable given that Ernest Beaglehole collected most of the material on Pukapukan social and economic organization and wrote the bulk of the *Ethnology of Pukapuka* (Beaglehole and Beaglehole 1938:3). Still readers should realize that Pearl Beaglehole was a quite skillful linguist and, according to Sapir, showed outstanding originality in her work (Inactive Personnel Files, Bishop Museum Archives, letter from M. May, May 13, 1935). Unpublished translations of chants and myths indicate that she possessed an impressive comprehension of Pukapukan given her limited stay on the atoll.

Ernest Beaglehole, after undergraduate training in psychology at the University of New Zealand, went on to receive a doctorate from the London School of Economics for his work on the social psychology of property (E. Beaglehole 1932; Ritchie 1966; Rudmin n.d.).[16] His main anthropological training occurred during his postdoctoral work at Yale. The department at Yale during this time was an eclectic one (see Ebihara 1985:105–8). According to Whiting, "There were a number of strong and diverse interests" (personal communication 1985). Material in Beaglehole's personnel file at the Bishop Museum suggests that he spent most of his time working with Sapir and Buck (though he did take courses with other anthropologists such as Wissler). In the forward to his *Notes on Hopi Economic Life*, Ernest Beaglehole credits Sapir with "introducing [him] to American anthropology and for the stimulus of his teaching and friendship" (1937c:1). Whiting, who participated in the same seminar with Sapir as Beaglehole, recalls that the "seminar was on psychology, on personality theory. It was not based on fieldwork so much as reading of psychologists, psychoanalysts and personality psychologists. That was the text. Then Sapir talked about how this [material] applied to ethnography and to anthropological data" (personal communication 1985; see also Ebihara 1985:108).

Buck, far more than Sapir, influenced the central issues of the Beagleholes' Pukapukan research. Precisely speaking, Buck was not a professionally trained anthropologist. He received his training as a medical doctor. He was, to quote Condliffe (1971), his biographer, a "home-made" anthropologist. Buck's interest in anthropology derived from a broader concern with Maori health and the revitalization of Maori culture (see Condliffe 1971; R. Rose, personal communication 1985). Half

Maori himself, Buck formed an early alliance with Ngata of the Young Maori Party to improve conditions among the Maori, culturally as well as physically. For Buck, salvage anthropology was as much an emotional and political issue as an academic one. (He used his Maori name, Te Rangi Hiroa, in many of his writings.) Though his doctorate was entitled "Medicine amongst the Maoris in Ancient and Modern Times," his first major published work in anthropology examined the evolution of Maori clothing. It concerned the technological processes used in the manufacture of Maori garments and their evolution over time. From weaving, Buck extended his interests to other aspects of material culture. His goal, Condliffe notes, became to record "what was left of the material culture of the Polynesians before it vanished for ever" (1971:33).

Buck became an expert in his specialty of describing and classifying Polynesian material culture, but illustrative of Gruber's statement above regarding salvage anthropology of the 1930s, Buck had little interest in the broader cultural contexts of the artifacts he examined. He focused on limited functional correlations, on the way an artifact's use dictated its mode of manufacture or shape.

While at Yale, Beaglehole took several courses from Buck and developed a close friendship with him (Inactive Personnel Files, Bishop Museum Archives; Condliffe 1971; Ritchie 1966). A mutual interest in Polynesia combined with their common New Zealand background presumably encouraged such a relationship. Clear evidence exists that it was Buck, both as a teacher and through his affiliation with the Bishop Museum, that guided the formation of Beaglehole's research plans for Pukapuka. In a letter to Judd in 1933 regarding possible projects he might undertake if appointed a Bishop Museum Fellow, Beaglehole writes, "I have in mind a study of tradition, social organization, custom and material culture of [Pukapuka] along the lines of Dr. Buck's work on Manihiki and Rakahanga" (Inactive Personnel Files, Bishop Museum Archives). His actual fellowship application for funds to conduct the Pukapukan research justifies the importance of the study by noting that

it seems desirable from the viewpoint of a comparative study of Polynesian culture to supplement Dr. Buck's work on the eastern atolls, Manihiki, Rakahanga, and Tongareva [i.e. Penrhyn] . . . by a study of the intermediate island of Pukapuka. . . . Field work in Pukapuka is important . . . not only to complete our knowledge of the northern Polynesian atoll culture but also to collect further material for the student of such comparative Polynesian problems as relate to social organization, material culture, language, and religion. (Inactive Personnel Files, Bishop Museum Archives)

Beaglehole's research statement fits well with the Bishop Museum's commitment to completing a regional survey of Polynesia, a concern Buck shared (see Condliffe 1971:188, 193). Given the radical disruption of traditional Polynesian social organization following Western contact, the museum's survey focused on salvage anthropology (cf. Wagner's comment in this respect, 1981:27–8). Developing out of the first Pacific Science Conference (meeting in Honolulu in 1920), it also had a definite scientific orientation (see Te Rangi Hiroa 1945). The survey's results, for instance, were presented in a scientific genre (in the museum's bulletin series), and trained anthropologists, from Gifford and Handy to Linton and Emory, participated in it.

Ernest Beaglehole did not fully share Buck's interest in material culture. As Pearl Beaglehole recalls, Ernest "had less interest in material culture [than Buck did]. But because Peter [Buck] had been our teacher and was into material culture, Ernest went to a great deal of trouble to get the material" (personal communication 1977). The *Ethnology of Pukapuka* contains numerous pages on material culture. There is an important reason for this. By the time the Beagleholes were preparing their monograph for the museum's bulletin series, Buck had become director of the museum. Both Ritchie (1966:111) and Condliffe (1971:193) indicate that Buck helped the Beagleholes organize their data for publication.

A final factor influenced the Beagleholes' Pukapukan research: their earlier fieldwork among the Hopi. Anthropological techniques they experimented with among the Hopi, such as collecting census data (P. Beaglehole 1935), became important data-gathering tools during their Pukapukan research. Fieldwork among the Hopi also brought them into firsthand contact with a matrilineal, matrilocal society. By the time they went to Pukapuka, not only were the Beagleholes conversant with the patrilineal biases of early Polynesian anthropologists (from their reading courses at Yale); they also had a concrete understanding of a matrilineal system. The combination proved valuable in constructing their account of Pukapukan double descent.

The Beagleholes' construction of a Pukapukan ethnography

The above contexts, especially that of conducting salvage anthropology within a scientific framework, directly influenced the Beagleholes ethnography. It led them to emphasize cultural uniformity and structure at the expense of diversity and ambiguity. The Beagleholes realized that they did not always take into account individual variations in their published reports. Their field notes state that "there are all sorts of individual variations of behavior attached by the individual Pukapukan to these patterns . . . the idea and actions [*sic*] patterns that we have grouped together under the title of Pukapukan Society would have endlessly different meanings for our various informants" (ms. a, "Theory of Anthropology, Introduction, 1–2"). "It is literally true that vast reaches of

Pukapukan culture as we present it here, are the peculiar property of but few individuals . . . [who] have certainly given to the information . . . the imprint of their own personalities in ways that can hardly be identified" (ms. a, "Theory of Anthropology, 3").

At least four factors account for the Beagleholes' focus on cultural uniformity in their work. First, in order to facilitate cross-cultural comparisons, their results had to fit within the existing framework of the Bishop Museum's surveys. Ernest Beaglehole committed himself to such comparisons, especially in relation to other Polynesian atolls, when applying for a museum fellowship. Stressing individual subtleties and complexities would only confuse these comparisons.

Second, the Beagleholes' fieldwork lasted only seven and a half months, from November 3, 1934, to June 13, 1935. The limited duration left certain avenues of research uninvestigated. They did not map sections of land or collect long genealogies. Instead, they relied on the statements of select informants for constructing a picture of who owned what property. With few informants, with limited case histories, Pukapukan culture understandably seemed more uniform than it actually was.

Third, simply by publishing their data in a limited number of pages they were forced to reduce the complexities of their account. Although they recorded different versions of several tales in their field notes, only one set of divergent accounts, the matrimoieties' origin myth, is really discussed in their book. The fact that contradictory assertions exist regarding the ownership of various taro swamps is never dealt with. And various theoretical issues raised by their census of Ngake and Yato village are downplayed. Compromises, in other words, had to be made in publishing the *Ethnology of Pukapuka*. The inclusion of miscellaneous tales, diverse details, and assorted intellectual digressions apparently did not appeal to the museum (or its director). In fact, two of the Beagleholes' manuscripts – one on myths and chants, the other on string figures – still await publication.

Finally, the Beagleholes' appreciation of the monograph's intended audience likewise influenced their emphasis on the uniformity of Pukapukan culture. The material had to have a coherent organization, a lucid pattern, that others could readily grasp. (Their field notes are too disorganized in this respect for publication.)

In a more subtle, indirect sense, the book's scientific style emphasizes the same general point. It lends the Beagleholes' analysis an impersonal aura. Ernest Beaglehole, like Laura Bohannan (1954) after him, sought to separate his personal experiences, frustrations, and embarrassments from the image of himself as a objective scientist. Though he acknowledges authoring a novelistic account of his fieldwork (1944), he warns readers not to construe it as a fragment of personal history. In the *Ethnology of Pukapuka*, the context and the concerns that influenced the Beagleholes' collection of data are not discussed. What we primarily have are the data – often organized in the form of tables, figures, and statistics – and the conclusions the Beagleholes drew from them. Ambiguous and contradictory material, which might cloud the certainty of various conclusions, is not emphasized.

These factors working together clearly influenced the Beagleholes' depiction of Pukapukan culture. We can see this, for example, by examining their description of the atoll's residence patterns. Informants, according to the Beagleholes, reported Pukapukan postmarital residence as patrilocal. Census data collected from fifty-four households, mostly in Ngake and Yato village, they state, confirmed this assertion. In respect to kin affiliation (the reason a person affiliated with one household rather than another at the time of their census), the Beagleholes indicate that 82.5 percent (of the 348 people examined) lived patrilocally. The patrilocal orientation, one should note, fits well with the focus on patrilineality common among Polynesian scholars in the 1930s.

But as occurred with my analysis of modern Pukapukan residence patterns, a closer look suggests that the relationship between locality and patrilineality is less precise than it initially appears to be. A problem, first of all, exists in fitting somewhat fluid, ambiguous data into neat ethnographic categories. The anthropological image implied in postmarital residence patterns – of stable groupings in which the only significant residence change occurs at marriage – oversimplifies a rather complex situation in Pukapuka. Today individual Pukapukans may reside in a variety of locations, even in a variety of villages, before marriage. Once married, moreover, the couple may not stay in a single location. They may make two or three moves. The terms *patrilocal* and *matrilocal* also obscure residence options that have rather different implications regarding the formation of social groupings. Moving into one's husband's father's household (viripatrilocality) implies a different form of kin affiliation than moving into one's husband's mother's household (virimatrilocality).

Given these ambiguities the Beagleholes made two choices that, although facilitating the presentation of their data in statistical form, raise doubts regarding their final conclusions. First, they generally used a person's place of birth as his or her premarital residence. Second, when both spouses were born in the same village – which meant that postmarital residence could not be determined from their census data – they listed the couple's residence as patrilocal. When I reclassified their census data to allow the latter category to stand simply as unclear (rather than subsuming it under patrilocality), postmarital residence was 49 percent patrilocal (i.e., virilocal), 17 percent matrilocal (i.e., uxorilocal), and 33 percent unclear.

Personally, I have a hard time following the basis for the Beagleholes' classification of kin affiliation within households. Partly this stems from an inability to follow their method of classification in a few complex cases, but also a critical difference exists between their field notes and their published monograph regarding the classification of individuals who possess a tie to a husband living matrilocally but who possess no tie to that husband's wife. The field notes indicate that the situation constitutes a case of patrilocality, the published text matrilocality. If one again separates out the unclear cases regarding spouses born in the same village (rather than subsuming them under patrilocality) and sticks to the precise published definitions, I obtain the following tentative results for kin affiliation within households: 46 percent patrilocal, 21 percent matrilocal, and 33 percent unclear.

The overwhelming bias toward patrilocality, in other words, appears less definite on closer analysis. The pattern of residence seems more ambiguous, more fluid than the uniform, structured account the Beagleholes present. It does not mean that ultimately they were wrong, but it does mean that in analyzing their data for publication, for presentation to an audience of Western scholars, they tended to fit the data into somewhat arbitrary, somewhat inaccurate categories that overstated the degree of cultural uniformity, the degree to which Pukapukan households were patrilocal.

The Beagleholes' account possesses another bias. It emphasizes stasis and the merging of distinct temporal orders. As sophisticated field-workers, the Beagleholes clearly knew the problems surrounding historical reconstruction. Their field notes state, "We are under no illusions as to the vitality of many of the patterns we present. Many of them are dead, and we have resurrected them from the memories of our informants in order to present comparative data for other Polynesian communities" (ms. a, "Theory of Anthropology, Introduction, 1"). They carefully distinguish patterns of social organization persisting at the time of their fieldwork from those then defunct, and they note that some of their data, based on historical reconstruction, are "reasonably reliable" whereas others are "definitely weak" (1938:7–8).

Still, as we shall see, their account of Pukapukan social organization emphasizes a static rather than dynamic perspective. At least two factors probably contributed to this. First, both the Bishop Museum's and Buck's concern with salvage anthropology encouraged merging information from diverse time frames into one, somewhat timeless premodern period – a practice common (as noted) with historical reconstructions of the 1930s. Although the population changes preceding and following contact are listed, their implications for social change are never drawn out. Nor is the fact that modern village organization probably evolved out of the traditional patrilineages particularly developed. Patrilineages and villages are described as two distinct forms of social organization, not a single evolving one.

Second, the presentation of the Beagleholes' material within the confines of a book encouraged a more static image than they probably wished to convey. Ongoing changes stopped where they had been recorded. Fluid, changing ideas become static, published ones – frozen in print and time.

A third factor does not fit with the above two, nor does it simply concern the merging of different temporal frames. Still, it is a critical factor that seriously influenced the Beagleholes' account. The Beagleholes failed to grasp the temporal biases in their informants' descriptions. Informants' perceptions of the present in terms of the past led the Beagleholes into confusing the two in their account of Pukapukan land tenure.

A concrete example regarding the Puwatu taro swamp illustrates what I mean. According to three of the Beagleholes' most reliable informants – Pau, Veeti, and Mitimoa – Puwatu belonged to the "Kava keinanga [or submatrilineage], specifically to members of this keinanga living in Yato" (ms. a, "Names of Ui Keinanga and Ui Po, 2"). If we set aside what these informants indicated and reconstruct from modern patterns and the Beagleholes' census the matrilineal affiliations of people actually cultivating sections of the swamp in 1934–5, we obtain a rather different picture (Map 5). Only five of the swamp's thirteen probable cultivators actually belonged to the Kava submatrilineage. Seven did not. (One individual's matrilineal affiliation could not be determined.) Of the seven not belonging to the Kava submatrilineage, six belonged to matrilineages in the opposite matrimoiety, Wua Kati. One belonged to the same Wua Lulu matrimoiety but a different submatrilineage. A major discrepancy, in other words, exists between what the Beagleholes' informants state and what one can reasonably reconstruct about the situation in 1934–5.[17]

Why did reputable informants such as Pau, Veeti, and Mitimoa state something so seemingly inaccurate? To begin with, what they stated was not actually incorrect. If one goes back to the apical ancestor (or *pu mua*) of the swamp, Kitewu, she did indeed belong to the Kava submatrilineage (see Figure 1). Also, an examination of Map 5 indicates that perhaps half the swamp's plots were being cultivated by members of the Kava submatrilineage (or their daughters). The problem was that a few generations after Kitewu, male descendants began inheriting swamp sections, thereby injecting non-Kava cultivators into the swamp.

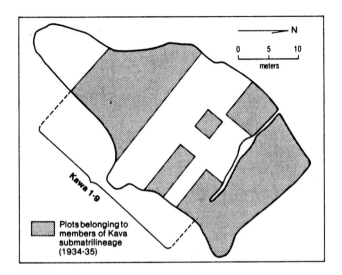

Map 5. Reconstruction of matrilineal ownership for Puwatu taro swamp, 1934–5. For additional information, see note 17.

In discussing the organization of the swamp in 1934–5, the Beagleholes' informants presumably were emphasizing principles of the past rather than actualities of the present. It is quite conceivable that the matrilineages did not actually own (or even nominally control) taro swamps in 1934–5. A cognatic pattern may well have prevailed during the Beagleholes' fieldwork.

What about patrilineal swamps? Pau, Veeti, and Mitimoa claimed that the Awale taro swamp belonged to the Awale branch of Yaalongo patrilineage (ms. a, "Names of Ui Keinanga and Ui Po, 2"). Reconstructing the swamp's organization from present-day patterns and the Beagleholes' census indicates that only two of the twelve individuals cultivating the swamp in 1934–5 actually belonged either to Yaalongo or to the Awale subbranch of that patrilineage. Five other cultivators belonged to different patrilineages localized in Yato (Tokelau, Malamalama, and Maatanga Yato) and five to patrilineages localized in Loto (Tilotilowia, Mulii, and Po Aliki).[18]

Did the Beagleholes' key informants thus mislead them regarding the ownership of Awale? Again, it depends. The apical ancestor for the whole swamp, Tetawa, did indeed belong to Yaalongo patrilineage. His daughter, Lakini, belonged to the Awale branch of this patrilineage; his son, Waiva, to the general Yaalongo patrilineage – like his father (see Figure 2). Also, the two members of Yaalongo patrilineage possessed

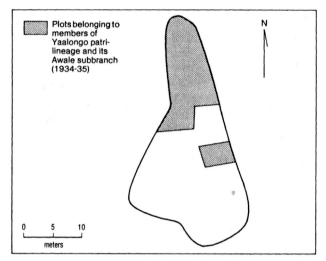

Map 6. Reconstruction of patrilineal ownership for Awale taro swamp, 1934–5. For additional information, see note 18.

a relatively large section of the taro swamp (given their number) in relation to non-Yaalongo cultivators in 1934–5 (see Map 6). Presumably again, Pau, Veeti, and Mitimoa were perceiving the present in terms of the past when explaining 1934–5 inheritance patterns.

A similar picture occurs when we examine the five sections of non-swamp land discussed in Figure 3 within the Yaalongo *kawa* (or 'strip of land'). Only one of these sections' owners actually belonged to the Yaalongo patrilineage in 1934–5. The others belonged to patrilineages localized in Loto village.

The uneasy feeling one gets from all this is that Pukapuka probably did not constitute a case of double-descent land tenure in 1934–5. Informants had cultural constructs involving double descent. That is clear. But this is not the same as stating that Pukapukans actually possessed a system of land tenure involving double descent. Biases in the Beagleholes' analysis derive, in other words, from their listening too closely to key informants. Because these informants merged different time frames in discussing land tenure, so did the Beagleholes.

This point raises an important question. How did the Beagleholes collect their data for the *Ethnology of Pukapuka*? In his application for a Bishop Museum Research Fellowship, Ernest Beaglehole described his "plan of attack" with the statement "The usual anthropological field methods will be followed" (Inactive Personnel Files, Bishop Museum Archives). This meant, as the published and unpublished field materials make clear, that he would gather information through interviews with selected informants, group discussions, observation, and the collection of census data, texts, and artifacts. Combining key informant interviews regarding past conditions with direct observations of present practices was a common methodology of the period. The collection of texts was a familiar Boasian practice (Stocking 1983b:10). It certainly fit with Sapir's linguistic orientations. And the collection of material culture fit with Buck's interests. (The Beagleholes brought back almost a complete collection of Pukapukan artifacts.)

The Beagleholes frequently checked the validity of various data with groups of informants. They collected a limited number of genealogies and accounts of traditional history from a group of "as many as 50 men" during the early part of their fieldwork. "More select were later sessions . . . usually attended by about five of the best informants. The systematic consideration of each phase of Pukapukan culture was taken up in these . . . intimate sessions" (1938:4; see also E. Beaglehole 1944:125). Material in their field notes indicates that the Beagleholes often checked, or rechecked, uncertain information with a few select informants.

How did the Beagleholes choose their key informants? As an affirmation of what their field notes term "character references of informants," the Beagleholes cite the following information in the *Ethnology of Pukapuka*:

Principal informants were: Ve[e]ti and Mitimoa, both over 65 years old; Eliu and Pau, both about 50 years old; and Talainga, about 40 years old. Pau was undoubtedly the scholar of this group. Though comparatively young, he was a keen student of things Pukapukan, equally well informed on all aspects of the culture. Ve[e]ti and Mitimoa were well informed in their own right but functioned more as consulting authorities than as original informants. The youngest of the group, Talainga, made up for disadvantages of age by keenness and conscientiousness. At our suggestion he wrote several notebooks full of old chants and stories which are models of Pukapukan prose and verse. Eliu was a reliable and willing informant. His wife, Molingi, about 33 years old, was a most capable and enthusiastic informant on the women's aspects of Pukapukan life. (1938:4; see also ms. a, "Introduction")

The Beagleholes emphasized several criteria in assessing who were or were not knowledgeable informants: seniority, group consensus, knowledge of textual materials, and ability to explicate difficult matters. One can perceive their concern with seniority in the above statements regarding age. While acknowledging that what their informants knew of "heathen days" was hearsay, the Beagleholes observed that older informants had closer contact with these earlier times. Pau's knowledge, they wrote, "derived from [his] father and others who were probably young men . . . at the time of [the early] missionaries" (ms. a, "Introduction"). Obviously, however, age was not the only factor since both

Talainga and Molingi were included, and the high chief of the island, though quite old, was overlooked because of his senility.

Consensus among informants was probably a more critical factor. In sorting out the confusing list of paternal lineages and sublineages various Pukapukans presented (1938:229), for example, the Beagleholes checked their conclusions with a variety of informants (ms. a, "Revised List of Po and Their Akavae"). They did not rely on a single individual. Likewise, information regarding the matrilineal and patrilineal owner-ship of certain taro swamps was not given by one informant but by three (ms. a, "Names of Ui Keinanga and Ui Po, 2"). In regard to informants they rejected, Ernest Beaglehole notes:

Our experience with Alaikonga as a reporter of times past was short-lived. I found very soon on checking his information with that provided by obviously more capable students of old Pukapukan customs that Alaikonga knew little about the past save what he could evolve from his own fertile imagination. He was never at loss for an answer, never in doubt, never bewildered. (1944:191)

An individual's knowledge of texts was also an important criterion for judging his or her competence in traditional matters. Most of the textual materials the Beagleholes obtained were either dictated by Veeti and Pau or written down by Talainga (ms. b:972). Talainga's knowledge and dedication in recording long texts of material, in fact, probably account for his inclusion in the select group of informants the Beagle-holes worked with (see E. Beaglehole 1944:146–7). Talainga, to my knowledge, is not mentioned as an authoritative informant in any other contexts in the Beagleholes' field notes.

Finally, the Beagleholes selected informants who could explicate dif-ficult materials to them. Regarding the chants Ernest Beaglehole found difficult to understand, he comments in his novelistic account of field-work, "I would say that I would no more attempt to translate a Puka-pukan chant without a really intelligent Pukapukan constantly at my elbow than I would try to fly an aeroplane without an instructor" (1944:150–1). He makes clear that his best guides, in this respect, were Pau and Veeti. They "could discuss the chants with freedom and fluency and feeling" (1944:127).

Caution is in order here regarding the Beagleholes' preference for informants who could coherently explain things to anthropologists. An early informant, quite likely Alaikonga, listed the owners of Puwatu as Yato women (ms. a, "Taro Patches"). The description is vague, im-precise, and certainly less anthropologically intriguing than what Pau, Veeti, and Mitimoa provided. However, it probably more accurately reflects the situation encountered in 1934–5 than that described by the

Beagleholes' "more capable students of . . . Pukapukan customs" (E. Beaglehole 1944:191).

Overall, the Beagleholes stress two main criteria in evaluating the validity of their data:

We believe [that one or all of our informants] would recognize that the majority of the statements contained herein hold true in one sense or another for some aspect of his experience, and it is this belief and the fact that the formal patterns of Pukapukan society configurate fairly well with the patterns of other Polynesian communities that are the sole guarantee of the measure of truth in the generalizations presented. (1938:8)

By such standards, the ethnography was clearly successful. Certainly Pukapukans in 1977–81 felt that the Beagleholes provided a generally accurate picture of their culture. Several comments made to me regarding the Beagleholes' informants' reactions suggested that they, too, believed the account to be valid. And Polynesian scholars, both in the past and today, look on the Beagleholes' work with respect.

But as we have just seen, the above criteria have certain flaws. Indigenous constructs contain their own biases, their own cultural concerns, that influence their "objectivity" (in a correspondence sense of truth). The examples of Puwatu and Awale taro swamps make that clear. And we saw that earlier anthropological descriptions of Polynesian groupings as primarily patrilineal in nature turned out, on closer analysis, to have misinterpreted a rather complex situation.

My intention in this section is not to raise criticisms of the Beagleholes' work. I have already stated that, in my opinion, their fieldwork was very good. The point I wanted to emphasize is one made by Foucault (1965, 1972), Gadamer (1975a, 1975b), Mannheim (1952, 1953), and others. Research occurs within an intellectual context and, certainly in the case of anthropology, this context affects the production of its scholarly literature. To what degree we can overcome such biases and write valid ethnographies is a basic concern of this book. But before exploring the issue further, I want to discuss Hecht's analysis of Pukapukan social organization. As one might expect, at a somewhat different time, with somewhat different interests and a somewhat different group of informants, she constructed a somewhat different account of traditional Pukapukan social organization.

The anthropological contexts of Hecht's research

Hecht conducted her fieldwork on Pukapuka for thirteen months in 1972–4, "concentrating [her] efforts on the cultural symbolism of kinship and land tenure" (1977:183). Her interest in cultural symbolism derived, at least in part, from her work with Schneider at Chicago. Hecht took several courses from him. More important, Schneider was Hecht's graduate adviser, the principal investigator for the National Science Foundation grant under which she conducted her fieldwork, and a member of her dissertation committee. Hecht states in the preface to her dissertation that Schneider's concern with cultural analysis was a "continuing inspiration" for her own research (1976a:ii).

At least three elements in Schneider's cultural perspective are related to Hecht's work. First, Schneider views culture as an independent "system of symbols and meanings" (1976:198). Or as he states, "Culture needs to be studied on its own, in its own terms, as a system apart from and not reducible to other systems" (1976:213). For Hecht, "Culture may be defined as a meaningful system of symbols, hypothesizing that meaning has its locus in the interrelations between units, not in the units themselves as analytically isolable entities" (1976a:6).

Second, to learn a cultural symbol's meaning, Schneider suggests, one should explore the range of contexts in which people use the symbol, in which they communicate with and through it (1976:212–13). Hecht states in her National Science Foundation proposal (1972:2) that an "effort will be made to elicit . . . Pukapukan ways of speaking about kinship, affiliation, and residence." And it was through "listening to what . . . informants were saying about their criteria for decisions about names, parentage, siblingship" (1976a:9), Hecht indicates, that her cultural analysis of Pukapuka began to take shape.

Third, Schneider emphasizes that cultural analysis provides insights that a standard account of social organization might well miss. "Consideration of cultural principles, based upon eliciting and analyzing symbolism," states Hecht, "leads to a fuller analysis of several issues that the Beagleholes either did not investigate fully or found contradictory or obscure" (1977:185).

The focus of Hecht's fieldwork "became the elicitation of Pukapukan culture as a meaningful system of symbols, in order to examine the implications of categorizing this cultural system as a case of 'double descent' " (1976a:6). How did she go about it? In her own words, "The procedure involved in eliciting the data was fairly standard, i.e. language learning, observation of and participation in on-going activity, eliciting texts about contemporary and traditional patterns and practices for analysis, and focusing on particular details in question" (1976a:7; see also 1985:156).

Rather than pick informants herself, Hecht let Pukapukans recommend knowledgeable elders to her. As she recalled, she initially had no way of evaluating who was or was not knowledgeable about traditional social organization. So she asked Pukapukans she was friendly with (personal communication 1982). She worked intensively with the informants they suggested, often as a group (see Hecht 1985:156). It became clear to her in time that Molingi and Petelo were superior to other informants in these group discussions, especially in their knowledge of genealogies. They not only provided more information but presented their knowledge in a more sophisticated manner. Hecht presumed that such competence derived from their backgrounds. Molingi's former husband knew a great deal about genealogies; Petelo had worked with Catholic birth records for many years (personal communication 1982).

The genealogies Hecht collected in these group discussions involved the tracing out of various kinship lines in the abstract. She did not tie them to specific rights of ownership or specific pieces of property. In this way she avoided tense arguments. Still, there were some disagreements, she recalled, such as in the compression or expansion of generations. Sometimes her informants seemed to reach a consensus; sometimes they did not.

Hecht visited various informants outside these group discussions to follow up on specific points as well as to elaborate on issues better discussed in private. She also mapped out certain land sections. She had to be particularly careful when discussing ownership of specific trees or specific sections with groups of people. Such discussions, focused as they were on particular issues and contexts, often became fractious when several individuals were involved.

Hecht's most significant problem concerned historical reconstruction. She had to merge present-day retrospective accounts with material collected by the Beagleholes:

Since Pukapukan "patrilineal and matrilineal sub-lineages are now virtually defunct" (Beckett 1964:417), and have practically been so since the Beagleholes' time, a certain number of gaps in the data must be expected. The actual social relations of actual people in the past, the patterns of behavior, are of course lost in the past, and I can only postulate the range of patterns of behavior from the statements of my informants about the past, from patterns of modern behavior and my informants' statements about them, and from limited documentation in the form of local records and London Missionary Society reports. This procedure required careful evaluation of the distribution of knowledge and informant reliability, by cross-checking between informants, documentary evidence, and content analyses of oral traditions, for consistency, and the repetition and patterning of symbolic themes. (Hecht 1976a:8)

Hecht believes that her cultural analysis exists at an implicit level in what people told her and in the overall patterns of their lives, both in the past and during her fieldwork. It builds on informants' concepts. But she admits that she went beyond what was immediately observable, beyond informants' statements, to develop her own synthesis. What she sought was a "congruence," "a unitary symbolic structuring," in Pukapukan symbols and behaviors (1976a:9, 52). Sometimes, such as with the genealogies, she did not have a complete picture. She got bits of the story, as she said, regarding who lived where, cultivated what areas, or married whom, but gradually she built up a coherent picture. In her own words, "Through analyzing normative statements about how people should behave, eliciting the cultural attributions that informed the normative statements and abstracting cultural attributes, [she was] able to describe some of the meaningful structure of traditional Pukapukan social organization" (1976a:162).

Comparing Hecht's and the Beagleholes' ethnographic constructions

Before elaborating on some of the differences between Hecht's and the Beagleholes' descriptions of traditional Pukapukan social organization, it is important to stress that their accounts very much overlap in certain areas. Relatively few differences exist between the Beagleholes' and Hecht's accounts of village organization, for example. They concur on the village patterns of ownership, allocation of resources, and structuring of authority. Small differences exist regarding the organization of food-sharing units, length of service for *pule* guards, and election of island councilors, but these reflect changes in the intervening years between their fieldwork.

They differ mainly in their descriptions of the more ambiguous, less structured aspects of Pukapukan social organization. Three topics concern us here: Hecht's concern with cultural analysis, her emphasis on cognatic ties, and her reservations regarding the corporate nature of the matri- and patrilineal units.

In her cultural analysis, Hecht shows that certain parallels exist in the ways Pukapukans symbolically structure gender, space, and the life cycle. She notes, for instance, that "the cultural associations of maleness/femaleness are . . . dry/wet, up/down/, periphery/centre" (1977:188):

Wetness is . . . associated with the lower swamp land in the center of the islets, and the center or interior in other contexts. Dryness is . . . associated with high coconut land, and with the contextual periphery. In life the male province is at the periphery, the female province is central or interior. The child grows within the female; the male provides from outside. While men gather outside in the public arena; women remain inside. Men tend the dry coconut land on the higher periphery; women tend the lower, central swamp. Men voyaged on the sea; women remained on the land. Where blood identity was pertinent, for example, in the demonstration of skill in wrestling competitions, the matrilineages had control; the burial lineage claimed the 'soul' for the afterlife, transcending the island, and linking the generations through men. (1976b:3)

The child's blood, the "strength and skill of the living body" (1977:193), belonged to the mother and the matrilineal category. From her the child inherited predetermined characteristics, such as ability in competitive sports. "Matrilineal concerns were with the lifetime" (1977:195). Consistent with an

ideology of involuntary . . . performance styles, the matrilineages or sublineages were the basis for exogamic groupings and for the organization of sports competitions. The matrilineal sublineages were also the blood vengeance groups, again consistent with the ideology of shared blood, and a specific concern of the lineage with its members' lives and lifetimes. (1981:59)

The patrilineal unit, or what Hecht terms burial category, focused on death. The cemetery constituted a central patrilineal concern. Through interment, one affirmed a common link with one's ancestors, a common link across generations:

In the Pukapukan cultural model, it appears that burial creates rather than expresses descent. One can not say for sure if a person belongs to a particular burial lineage until he is actually dead and buried. . . . Patrifilial identity is ultimately common location of burial, and continuity of the line is created by and depends on successive links of burial. (1976a:79)

In contrast to matrilineal identification, which followed the mother and was set by birth, patrilineal affiliation was relatively fluid and tentative during one's lifetime. "Matrilineal affiliation is normatively unchangeable; burial lineage affiliation is expressly subject to change" (Hecht 1977:195). Through adoption, for instance, one might come to be buried in a different cemetery from that of one's biological father. Also, though it involved risking ancestral wrath, a person might change cemeteries "according to his own wishes" (1976a:78). Hecht believes that the terms *burial category* and *burial lineage* express this fluid, tentative character of affiliation – which becomes definite only at interment – far better than *paternal lineage* (the term used by the Beagleholes).

Although Hecht's cultural analysis is too subtle and complex to be given full justice in this short space, the following passage expresses her main theme:

The cultural premises about maleness and femaleness relate to a broader worldview in which the sexual associations of fertile wetness and lifeblood with the female, of death, burial and inter-generational continuity with the male are acted out in the disposition of the child to his parents as female fertile lifegiving is complemented by male death and burial. Formally, the burial lineages maintained contact across the perimeters of Pukapukan physical and spiritual existence; the matrilines were concerned with activities interior to these boundaries, in mundane and secular contexts. (1977:195)

One obvious reason Hecht's analysis differs from the Beagleholes' concerning social organization is that they focused on different research themes. The Beagleholes shared Hecht's interest in symbolic analysis, but because of their limited time on the atoll, the fact that their fieldwork preceded others', and the role Buck and the Bishop Museum played in their research, the Beagleholes never followed up this interest in any depth. Hecht could. She resided longer on the island, had the Beagleholes' fieldwork to build on and the financial support of the National Science Foundation for investigating this subject. Even if the Beagleholes had focused more on symbolic analysis, their accounts presumably would have differed somewhat from Hecht's, however. The Beagleholes were interested in the psychological aspects of symbols, Hecht more in the cultural ordering of symbols.

In addition, Hecht was conducting research for her doctoral dissertation. Such research, by nature, has to deal with new issues. Simply to repeat the Beagleholes' fieldwork might have pleased some researchers, but it might not have resulted in Hecht obtaining a Ph.D. Her doctoral research had to develop new perspectives based on new data.

In the process of building upon the Beagleholes' ethnography, Hecht's analysis affirms Schneider's claim regarding the value of cultural analysis. Her work opens up new perspectives, offers new insights not readily perceived in the more standard account of social organization presented by the Beagleholes. Her symbolic ordering of wet/dry and of land/sea, for example, ties in with Barrau's analysis of contrasting Indo-Pacific environments (1965). It also resonates with analyses of land/sea, peripheral/interior elsewhere in the Pacific (see, e.g., Alkire 1968; Sahlins 1976; Shore 1982). And it provides intriguing insights into how the symbols of blood, land, locality, and nurturance convey far broader meanings than the Beagleholes realized, especially in relation to general Polynesian concerns with male and female, brother and sister (see, e.g., Shore n.d.).

In addition to its concern with cultural analysis, Hecht's account of traditional social organization differs in another way from the Beagleholes' work. Hecht emphasizes the cognatic nature of land tenure. She asserts that "cognatic descent categories of shallow depth were the source of the personnel of most proprietary aggregates" (1976a:163). What Hecht realized far more than the Beagleholes was the degree to which control over taro swamps and dry land was invested in ancestor-oriented cognatic descent groups. "The aggregate of persons actually involved in the exploitation of a section of dry land or swamp at any one time," she states, "probably traced their connections as members of cognatic descent groups rather than as lineage mates" (1976a:118).

Hecht goes on to suggest that "it is not so much the cultural recognition of descent constructs which requires our attention as the symbols and symbolic configurations validating that recognition" (1976b:9). A recurrent theme, Hecht asserts, is "the significance of sex-role differentiation. Ideological and normative data on land tenure, adoption and marriage suggest the idea of descendants of brother and sister as they are separated and reunited through time and space" (1976b:9).

One of the reasons Hecht's account differs in this respect from the Beagleholes' derives from the different character of their data and their use of different informants. Hecht, building on the Beagleholes' research and spending a longer time on the atoll, focused far more on collecting genealogies. The Beagleholes collected relatively few genealogies. They relied mainly on the accounts of key informants for analyzing property holding. Through her map work, Hecht could relate particular genealogies to specific pieces of land. Moreover, Hecht utilized different informants (with presumably different perspectives). When I investigated traditional land tenure practices five years after Hecht, interviewing several of the same key informants she worked with, people overwhelmingly used cognatic constructs for explaining traditional land tenure practices – unlike the Beagleholes' informants.

Hecht's concern with nonunilineal groupings also reflects changes in anthropological theory since the Beagleholes' time. Following from the work of Firth (1957, 1963), Goodenough (1955, 1961), and many others in the past three decades, cognatic descent theory has become a topic of considerable interest among anthropologists. This was not so in 1934–5.

A final difference between Hecht's and the Beagleholes' accounts centers on the corporate nature of the matrilineal and patrilineal (or burial) social units. The Beagleholes viewed both types of units as corporate, with their own leaders, their own food divisions, and their own property. Hecht perceives them as possessing much less property, much less authority, a much weaker corporate character. For her, "matrilineage and burial lineage organization focused on the activities of occasional groups, for sports competitions, warfare, life-crisis events – activities that are in a sense rituals of unilineal identities" (1976b:5). Beyond these ritual and ceremonial activities, "there is little evidence for any functions of the matrilineal and burial categories" (1981:60). Matrilineal elders did possess nominal control over certain central taro swamps, as did burial lineage elders over strips (or *kawa*) of dry land. But she notes that "neither exploitation of swamp nor that of coconut trees requires concerted and on-going group activity" (1976b:7).

This difference in perspectives directly derives from the previously mentioned difference. The Beagleholes perceive unilineal groupings as the property-owning units. Hecht views land tenure in more cognatic terms.

One must realize that this area of Pukapukan social organization has probably been relatively fluid through time to allow for population/

resource adjustments. It is understandable, therefore, that differences would arise in the Beagleholes' and Hecht's accounts. Both are trying to describe an ambiguous set of categories and groups from differing perspectives using different informants. Such differences should not be viewed in negative terms. They have clearly contributed to our understanding of Pukapukan social organization. As a result of these differing perspectives, we now possess a first-class cultural analysis. We better grasp the ambiguities surrounding the degree to which various unilineal groupings did or did not own property, were or were not corporate. And we can appreciate a point I made earlier in relation to the *koputangata*: Some parts of Pukapukan social organization are easier to describe than others.

In turning to how Hecht conducted her fieldwork, we find certain striking similarities with the Beagleholes' research. Does this mean that they must both be right since they concur? Not really. I would suggest that Hecht shares some of the same biases as the Beagleholes. She emphasizes uniformity at the expense of diversity, stasis at the expense of change.

Hecht realizes that her account implies a greater sense of coherence and uniformity than might actually have existed in earlier times (personal communication 1982). Still her approach tends to encourage this orientation. One must remember that, for Schneider, culture is distinct from patterns of action. Patterns of action may be diverse or conflict ridden, but this does not hold for the symbols and meanings out of which these patterns are constituted. Schneider defines culture as "a total system; it does not have loose ends and unintegrated pieces and parts that do not articulate with other parts. It holds together as a meaningful system" (1976:219). By following in Schneider's footsteps, Hecht was naturally drawn toward emphasizing coherence.

The act of translation also encouraged such tendencies. Hecht presents her data to a Western audience generally unfamiliar with the details of Pukapukan social organization. Page limitations and the complexities of the material understandably lead to simplification. She cannot present the rich, detailed subtleties of her genealogies, for example. No one would publish them. And if by chance someone did, few non-Pukapukans presumably would find them interesting enough, let alone comprehensible enough, to read. As a result, Hecht does what most anthropologists do. She summarizes the data in her analyses. Marcus and Cushman note, "The general anthropological readership tends to be most concerned with the overall arrangement of a work and with the way theory is brought to bear upon the facts under consideration. . . . Accuracy or clarity of detail is less important than the shape and coherence of the 'story the text tells' " (1982:51).

Hecht's simplifications and concern with homogeneity create certain problems with her analysis, however. Take, for example, her assertion regarding the somewhat fluid, tentative nature of burial lineage membership (before interment). Working with a broader sample of informants only six years later, I found the matter to be more subtle and complex than she depicts. Let me set aside what the Beagleholes' data suggest for the moment – since it appears that Hecht does not derive her analysis from them – and simply focus on people's perceptions in 1977–81. The sample involves the same thirty informants discussed in Chapter 1. Four of Hecht's most prominent informants are among those included.

When I asked informants if Pukapukans changed burial lineage (*po*) membership in prior times, 60 percent said no, 30 percent said yes, and 10 percent expressed uncertainty. But these figures cover up a general consensus regarding the limited conditions under which Pukapukans could change membership. Of the nine who said yes, for example, most emphasized one of three conditions under which it was possible: if the father gave his consent, if the child was adopted, or if the cemetery became full or closed (see Beaglehole and Beaglehole 1938:231). Most informants, I suspect, would concur with these conditions. Only a single informant expressed a rather marginal belief – that one could change burial lineage membership if upset with one's father or father's relatives. Before dismissing this belief completely, however, we should note that the woman who expressed it, Molingi, was the informant Pukapukans, Hecht, and I all viewed as one of the two most knowledgeable people on the island regarding traditional matters. (We can see that Pukapukans do not always agree with what she says.)

Only in a very limited sense did Pukapukans perceive burial lineage membership as tentative despite the above possibilities for change. I interviewed all the adults on the island regarding their expected site of burial (another phrasing of the burial lineage one belongs to). Only two expressed uncertainty on the matter. When I mentioned these cases to other Pukapukans, they appeared amused that even two adults would not know their expected burial site. It seemed the epitome of ignorance.

Two cultural constructs embodied adult Pukapukans' views regarding burial lineage membership in 1977–81. First, a clear majority, more than 80 percent of my sample, held that people in olden times could change burial lineage membership only with their father's consent.[19] People did not follow this rule simply as a matter of propriety. A large number of the sample believed that the individual, the individual's relatives, and/ or the descendants would be punished by ancestral ghosts if the individual willfully went against the father's wishes. Of those who elaborated on the subject under further questioning, the great majority described various troubles that inevitably resulted from such willfullness. Only two individuals, Molingi and a semisenile elderly woman, definitely asserted that nothing happened to people who went against their father's wishes.

A second cultural construct concerned a set of interrelated factors Pukapukans used in determining an individual's future burial site. Readers should note that an individual's future cemetery may not be immediately obvious to modern Pukapukans. Few occasions now exist for publicly displaying burial lineage membership before death. And in contrast to earlier times, Pukapukans today trace cemetery affiliation cognatically. One factor Pukapukans consider is the burial location of the individual's parents and their close relatives. Unless adopted, an individual is almost always buried in the same cemetery as one or more of these people. Another factor, understandably then, focuses on whether a person is adopted (*tama kokoti*). A final factor concerns information collected informally over time – from gossip as well as from statements by the child's parents. Collectively, the three factors usually provide enough data for Pukapukans to make a reasonable guess as to an individual's future burial site. Accuracy in this matter is facilitated by the fact that people phrase their assessments in fairly general terms, referring to villages rather than specific cemeteries within each village.

Nonetheless, detailed private interviews with six knowledgeable informants indicated that people did not always agree on who was to be buried where. All six informants explained their assessments regarding where specific informants would be buried in terms of the above three factors. But different people used different information in their formulations. Hence they got different answers. One disagreement among the six, for example, involved whether a particular person had or had not been adopted (*tama kokoti*). Those who said that he had emphasized one burial site; those who said that he had not emphasized another. The Beagleholes in 1934–5 indicated that the individual had been adopted. The individual in 1978 claimed not to have been. The situation is an ambiguous one at best, especially since the person preferred not to discuss the issue.

The point I wish to make is this. Hecht is correct in stating that burial lineage membership is tentative if she means that other Pukapukans may not precisely know which specific cemetery an individual plans to be buried in. But almost all Pukapukans in 1978 claimed to know where they themselves would be buried. The idea that even two adults lacked such information several Pukapukans found amusing and absurd. Hecht's generalization regarding burial lineage membership, in other words, sidesteps subtle complications that weaken the conclusions she wishes to draw.

Aside from overemphasizing coherence, a second major bias in

Hecht's analysis involves the merging of different temporal orders. Hecht, in a sense, is forced into historical reconstruction by the nature of her problem, the organization of Pukapukan double descent. Patrilineal and matrilineal sublineages, she noted in 1976, had practically been defunct since the Beagleholes' time. Consequently, she had to combine the recollections of her informants with the Beagleholes' material. Clearly, Hecht is aware of the problem, as the earlier quote regarding her methodology indicates (see also 1977:184). Yet she cannot really escape the difficulty. In her need to deemphasize change, especially between the Beagleholes' research and her own, she tends to overemphasize the static qualities of culture at the expense of dynamic ones. Clearly, her informants' recollections exist within a different temporal framework than the recollections of the Beagleholes' informants. She cannot simply presume that certain cultural patterns persist over time. This is something she must prove instead of assume.

Even in the few years between Hecht's and my research, informants' conceptions of the matrimoiety system changed – a result presumably of the various cultural revivals that occurred during the period (see Chapter 5). In 1977–81, people often described the matrimoiety system as paralleling the *Akatawa*. Most emphasized that the matrimoieties, as social groupings, were formerly called into being by the Kau Wowolo (or 'Council of Important People') to participate in certain sport competitions initiated by the council. Hecht's top two informants described the matrimoiety system to me in the following terms. Many other informants made similar comments:

The Kau Wowolo confirms when the matrimoieties will occur [or begin, *tupu*], when the work of the matrimoieties will be performed. . . . One matrimoiety did not just get it into its head to do it. (Molingi)

If the Kau Wowolo of the island wants to do this, in regard to some games, they will say, "Is it all right if we, this year, live by matrimoieties?" They will discuss it . . . then the Wua Lulu will work together . . . so will the [Wua] Kati. . . . This is how it operated, by notification of the Alonga Mana [the Rarotongan word for the Kau Wowolo]. It was something just to show people. "Is it bad," the Kau Wowolo will say, "if we do it this way by matrimoieties for this year, for one or two years?" (Petelo)

Discussions with Hecht indicate that informants were not describing the matrimoieties in this manner in 1972–4. Their descriptions emphasized the points Hecht enunciated above.

Leaving biases in Hecht's analysis aside, I want to deal finally with the criteria she uses in validating her account. These too affected her construction of traditional Pukapukan organization. Hecht emphasizes two criteria. The first focuses on coherence. If various data fitted together in "complementary configurations," if they possessed a "unitary symbolic structuring" and consistency, if they constituted "a recurrent theme," then they represented a valid cultural pattern (1976a:52, 1976b:9). The second criterion concerns the native viewpoint. If certain elements of the analysis expressed the indigenous view or built on indigenous conceptions, then these too were probably true (1981:75). Numerous anthropologists, I suspect, would concur with Hecht regarding both criteria. She is certainly not alone in espousing them.

But it turns out, in examining the Pukapukan data, that not all that fits together in a coherent manner or that expresses a general native perspective can be viewed as valid. Hecht's analysis, as noted above, indicates that a complementary patterning existed between matrilineal and patrilineal concerns. Matrilineal concerns focused on the living, patrilineal concerns on the dead. In a conversation in 1985, Hecht referred to this as one of the most thoroughly formulated aspects of Pukapukan traditional social organization. Her description of the relationship very closely resembles Pukapukan statements I collected on this matter. One knowledgeable informant in his forties, Yingonge, illustrates the commonly held view during my research:

At the time of living (*olaanga*), all the children of the marriage follow or go to the matrimoiety of the woman [or mother]. If the mother is a [Wua] Kati or a Wua Lulu, they will follow behind her. At the time of death, it is different . . . the bones from the living person will be taken to the place of the father.

Petelo, one of Hecht's key informants, made a similar comment in a group discussion I held at my house one evening regarding traditional forms of social organization:

During the life of the person, he belongs to his mother [or really mother's side]. He belongs to her matrimoiety. . . . Here is the meaning (or reason) . . . a woman gives birth, provides a child. . . . At death, the right (*mana*) goes to the man [or father]. Because the man perpetuates [or preserves, *akakatili*] the woman's seed (*wua*) by his descendants.

Again and again informants would affirm the same general complementary patterning when we discussed traditional Pukapukan social organization together. The matrilineal groupings concerned the individual's life; the patrilineal groupings, his death. Pukapukans phrased the situation this way so frequently, in fact, that I would concur with Hecht that it constitutes one of the best-formulated constructs relating to traditional social organization.

Yet the construction contradicts an important Pukapukan conception regarding the past. Adult Pukapukans almost unanimously agree that people previously came together in both matrilineal or patrilineal groupings during the members' lifetimes for sporting events. In other words, both matrilineages and patrilineages, not just the matrilineages, focused on activities during their members' lifetimes.

When I pointed this contradiction out to a group of informants the same evening Petelo made the above statement, they initially disagreed with me. Two informants politely, but repeatedly, tried to convince me that no contradiction existed. They restated, in various ways, the above formulation. When I persisted in my point, they took it as ignorance on my part mixed with a bit of stubbornness and tried harder than ever to convince me of my error. After our conversation had gone on for several minutes, Molingi interrupted. She stated that perhaps there was a point to what I said. The construct did not fully make sense as Pukapukans usually phrased it. They all knew that patrilineages as well as matrilineages involved themselves in various competitions during members' lifetimes. A long pause followed as people thought about Molingi's comment. No one else publicly agreed with me that evening. In fact, nothing much more was said about the topic in our discussion that night. But during the next evening's discussion, when I raised a closely related matter with them, several people laughed. Yes, they agreed, there had been something to what I had said.

This change in perspective was not simply a matter of Pukapukans being polite. (They had found no difficulty in disagreeing with me the night before.) There was a clear realization among some of them that an ambiguity existed in the previous formulaic phrasing of the relation between the matrilineal and patrilineal groupings. What several informants found amusing was that an outsider should perceive something about their past that they themselves had not.

One knowledgeable informant, who had not been at the above meeting, also apparently took note of what we had discussed. When the topic came up in a private interview, he explained that Pukapukans have a certain phrasing for explaining matrilineal and patrilineal concerns, the one quoted above. He added that the cultural construct, though clear and systematic, was not actually correct. People sometimes explained the idea poorly or were confused about what it really meant. His opinion was that, in actual fact, patrilineages as well as matrilineages involved themselves in the ongoing lives of their members. Illustrating his thesis, he pointed to patrilineally organized games. Such a perspective stood in marked contrast to one he had enunciated several months before.

We can see that anthropologists must be careful in relying on coherence as the basis for validating ethnographic accounts. Coherence may be an important element in the formation of cultural constructs, but it may ignore certain ambiguities and contradictions that anthropologists must take note of in their cultural accounts.

Concluding comments

We have come, in this chapter, to a better understanding of some of the contexts and concerns that shape ethnographies. Although the Beagleholes' and Hecht's accounts were sensitive and sophisticated in outlook, we have seen that they contain implicit biases resulting from the contexts in which they operated, the problems they sought to solve, and the audiences for which they wrote. By placing their work in a broader cultural and historical context, we understand more clearly both their ethnographic accounts and the social organization they sought to portray.

Having discussed matters of social organization, we can return to a question raised earlier. Does the *Akatawa* fit within the general scope of the atoll's organization? I would say so. Like the villages and *koputangata* of today, as well as the patrilineal and matrilineal groupings of the past, the *Akatawa* emphasizes that there are alternative means of organizing people and property on the atoll. True, the *Akatawa* adds a new dimension. Instead of alternative groupings coexisting *in* time, the *Akatawa* coexists with the villages *through* time. Still, the result is the same. It deemphasizes the parochial nature of groups, strengthens cross-cutting ties, and reduces intergroup conflict (by changing the constitution of the groups competing). We perceive the cross-cutting ties Sahlins (1958) emphasized for atolls. We might add an important corollary here, however. A tendency exists on Pukapuka for one of the two groupings to control more resources on a more permanent basis than the other.[20]

The overall pattern fits well within Shore's (1982, n.d.) model of Polynesian social relations. Competitions occur between (what Shore terms) symmetrical, or structurally equivalent, social units. Villages compete against villages, *tawa* against *tawa*, patrilineages against patrilineages, and so on. But sport competitions do not occur between complementary groupings that affirm alternative means of allocating people and property. Villages never compete against *koputangata*. Patrilineages never competed against matrilineages.

The case of the *Akatawa* emphasizes the fluid, flexible nature of Pukapukan social alignments. Clearly, the fluidity serves a positive function. It prevents opposition between competing units from becoming too intense, from spilling beyond the controlled arenas in which it is normally acted out. J. Huntsman (personal communication 1985) notes a similar pattern in the Tokelaus, a group of Polynesian atolls to the northwest of Pukapuka. An interesting parallel occurs as well among the Ramkokamekra (Ge) of Central Brazil. Shifting moiety divisions within Ramkokamekra communities change social alignments from season to season as well as from year to year (see Lave 1975). Such examples suggest that the issue of shifting social alignments deserves further attention, especially regarding the way it maintains social integration within small-scale communities.

What for Pukapukans constitutes a cultural solution to atoll life has proved to be something of a problem for anthropologists. It has taken them time to grasp the fluid, flexible nature of Polynesian social alignments (see Howard and Kirkpatrick 1989). Early anthropologists, we noted, often erred in overemphasizing stability. That is perhaps why at first glance the changes surrounding the *Akatawa* seemed so dramatic to me – and why, on second glance, they seemed quite natural and appropriate.

One might add here that the Beagleholes, Hecht, and I do not disagree about the relatively structured, corporate village groupings that have played a central role in Pukapukan social organization for the past few decades. Our disagreements center on the more flexible, "alternative" aspects of Pukapukan social organization. These, we noted, defy easy description.

Rather than acting as a hindrance to our understanding of Pukapukan social organization, however, our various disagreements opened us up to new insights and understandings. Differences between the Beagleholes' and Hecht's accounts, for example, raised important questions regarding the implicit assumptions shaping the analysis of each. It was in the areas of consensus that their biases were less obvious.

Perceiving that Pukapukans possess "ways of knowing" that are different from those of anthropologists, the point taken up in the next two chapters, helps clarify some of our own hidden assumptions, some of our implicit understandings regarding the construction of ethnographic knowledge.[21] A mutually beneficial dialogue is at work here. In realizing that Pukapukans order their traditions differently from anthropologists, anthropologists learn about the biases of their ethnographic accounts. And informants, pondering an outsider's view of the atoll's patrilineal organization, see ambiguities in their own cultural formulations. By understanding our differences (and the reasons behind them), we both gain insight into our divergent constructions of the atoll's past.

3

Acquiring traditional knowledge
Pukapukan ways of knowing, Part I

Since the techniques Pukapukans use to acquire traditional knowledge may be unfamiliar to many readers, it is appropriate to begin with a concrete example.

The day before Tengele started repairing a large old Pukapukan canoe, we had a talk. He told me that Lima and Unu (two close relatives in their twenties) would assist him so that he could teach them how to fix old-fashioned canoes. (He had wanted helpers and had chosen these two.) From my conversations with Lima and Unu and from the way they worked, it was clear that they, too, had the same idea. They were assisting so they could learn more. But very little direct teaching occurred. Rarely did Tengele give explicit instructions on how to perform a particular task. Lima and Unu learned far more (in my opinion) from observing and experimenting than from direct advice Tengele gave them.

It seemed apparent from watching Lima and Unu that, although both had had some experience in hewing, neither had actually hewn such a large outrigger before. They frequently hesitated in their work and often paused to see how it was progressing. (Later conversations with each of them confirmed this. Lima had previously hewn one short outrigger by himself; Unu had only assisted in the hewing of one.) Since Tengele felt it appropriate to teach them, he also must have known their limitations.

Yet Tengele did not give them any overt instructions. He just started to shape the outrigger himself. Lima and Unu hung around, casually watching him and talking with me. Tengele seemed almost uninterested in whether they watched him. Similarly, they seemed only partially interested in what he was doing. When Tengele got tired, he handed the adze to Lima and told him to take over. Tengele then sat down and ate a coconut. Only occasionally, and in the most casual manner, did he take a look at how Lima was progressing.

At first, Lima was hesitant; he seemed unsure of how to proceed. But he never asked Tengele for help. He simply started in and, as he built up a little confidence, began taking bigger cuts. Only when the cuts became deeper did Tengele give a few specific directions mixed with minor criticisms. "You are

74

starting to make your cuts in that direction too deep, make them smaller. Sometimes cut from the other direction as well. Cut a little more off the front." Lima kept working without saying a word.

When he got tired, Unu, who had been carefully watching Lima, eagerly took over. Unu, too, initially seemed hesitant about how to proceed. But Tengele seemed to ignore Unu. Tengele appeared far more engrossed in telling me about Vakayala and Uyo, two legendary Pukapukan figures. (In contrast to his teaching of Unu and Lima, he directly questioned me several times to make sure I followed the conversation.) As Unu became more confident and started making deeper cuts, Tengele also gave him a few directions. They involved details regarding where and where not to cut. But no overall formal directions were given.

Throughout the whole period, Tengele never once uttered a word of praise to either Lima or Unu. I had the impression that they were most relaxed when Tengele was not watching. Just the absence of attention seemed praise enough. When he watched carefully for any period of time, it seemed to imply (at least to me) that something was wrong.

When the fine hewing had to be performed, Tengele again took over. He made no effort to show either Lima or Unu the subtleties of what he was doing. He just did it. Nor did Lima and Unu seem really absorbed in watching him. They casually looked on as they talked to me and ate coconuts.

Finally, with only a few small details left, Tengele handed over the work to both of them. Some bark still had to be skinned off the log and a few rough spots had to be smoothed out. Lima and Unu took turns alternately using the adze for hewing and the knife for skinning. Tengele seemed to ignore the person with the knife; he watched only the one using the adze. But again he said very little unless a mistake was being made.

When it came to lashing the outrigger two days later, the same pattern occurred. Tengele simply started lashing a joint. He seemed mainly interested in finishing the task. Overtly at least, he displayed little interest in teaching Lima or Unu what to do. They appeared to watch him in a casual, low-keyed manner. (I seemed far more interested in learning the exact details of what he was doing than they did.) Only when Tengele needed some specific help – to hit the sennit after each turn so that it would be tight – did he call Lima over and give him specific instructions.

After Tengele had finished two lashings, Unu and Lima both tried to do one on their own. Though it was clear from the way they worked that they had had some previous lashing experience, it was also clear (to me) that they were not perfectly sure how to proceed with the lashing Tengele made (see Beaglehole and Beaglehole 1938:179). Every once in a while, one or the other would look over at Tengele's lashing. Lima and Unu tried to be careful in their work, and when they were finished, both of their lashings looked identical to Tengele's from the top. But only Unu's matched Tengele's on the underside. Lima's was different.

Apparently, both Unu and Lima had made educated guesses as to how Tengele had done the lashing on the underside on the basis of what they could see from the top. But they had guessed differently. The difference was not major, just a matter of making or not making a diagonal before going under the bottom piece. But it was still apparent upon close examination. Lima noticed it when he finished his lashing and went back to look at

Tengele's. Since no one said anything, he just left it. During the whole time, Tengele only occasionally looked up from his work to see how Unu and Lima were progressing. As long as they seemed absorbed in what they were doing, he said nothing.

On another day, Tengele and Unu lashed the three *tutuki* (or 'support') sticks to the outrigger poles. (Lima was also supposed to help but did not show up.) Tengele cut some sennit for Unu and some for himself. Tengele told Unu to lash the front joint. Then Tengele started lashing the back joint. When Unu did not immediately move toward the front, Tengele looked at him with a little surprise and asked him if he knew how to do the lashing. Unu said nothing. He just stood watching Tengele start his own.

As Unu passed by me on the way to the front of the canoe, he whispered softly to me, "I don't know how to do it." But he said nothing to Tengele. He just went to the front joint and, after watching Tengele for another minute or so, started on his own lashing. When Tengele undid his lashing so I could draw the details of the way it was done, Unu kept on with his. After finishing four turns on each side – the general limit one can go in this type of lashing before proceeding with a different pattern – he just paused casually as if to rest. He waited for Tengele to catch up and go ahead of him. Unu would frequently look over at Tengele's lashing and experiment with different styles, before finally deciding on a particular procedure.

Tengele, by and large, seemed to ignore Unu. Only occasionally did he look over to see if Unu was working. Once, however, he did give Unu direct instructions. Seeing the way Unu had incorrectly wrapped a piece of sennit around a stick, he told him that the wrapping should start from the top of the stick rather than the bottom. Unu unwrapped the section and started over again.

When Unu was finished, his lashing, though looser, resembled Tengele's fairly closely. The main difference between them lay in the time it took to finish: Unu took considerably longer than Tengele. Still, Unu was clearly pleased with his work.

As this illustration suggests, traditional education in Pukapuka is often less explicit and formal than in Western schools. Over the past decade, social scientists have tended to label such education "informal" because, as Scribner and Cole state, "it occurs in the course of mundane adult activities in which the young take part according to their abilities" (1973:554–5). Or as Howard observes for the Polynesian island of Rotuma, "One absorbs the information informally, usually without anything being made explicit" (1970:65). More recently, the adequacy of this terminology has come under criticism as social scientists have sought to delineate precisely the processes and consequences involved in learning in non-Western settings (see, e.g., Lave 1982; Strauss 1984). Certainly one must be careful not to stereotype all Pukapukan learning as informal. Both formal and informal patterns occur on the atoll (see Borofsky 1982:144–8). And within the informal category, one might well distinguish various subcategories, such as the "ill-defined" and "attention-directing" strategies discussed by Strauss (1984). But however one labels the above techniques, they clearly differ from those favored in many Western schools. How and why they operate as they do is the topic of this chapter.[1]

Status rivalry

Before proceeding farther, however, we must clarify the terms *status* and *status rivalry*. In accord with Goldman:

By status . . . I mean the principles that define worth and more specifically honor, that establish the scales of personal and group value, that relate position or role to privileges and obligations, that allocate respects, and that codify respect behavior. (1970:7)

Status rivalry refers to competition over issues of status. As various social scientists indicate, rivalries over status constitute a pervasive theme throughout Polynesia (see Goldman 1970; Howard 1972:818). The Ritchies comment, "It seems to us, and to most people who have looked at Polynesian cultures, that . . . the central preoccupation of Polynesia [is] one of status and rivalry between people of similar . . . statuses" (1979:80). Marcus (1978) and Shore (1982) provide excellent descriptions of status rivalry for Tonga and Samoa, respectively.

As in the rest of Polynesia, Pukapukan concerns with status and status rivalry involve two interacting principles. One focuses on hierarchy, dependency, and deference toward superiors. The other emphasizes autonomy and equality with one's peers. Pukapukans often defer to those in positions of power not necessarily because they know more about a subject but simply because they possess a superior status. But social deference to such authority is often downplayed on the atoll, given its egalitarian orientation. Almost as a way of affirming their own individual statuses, Pukapukans challenge, qualify, or elaborate on what others claim to be true. Rather than hierarchy, equality – which is qualified mainly by sex and age – pervades public discussions. In certain contexts, adult Pukapukans continually challenge each other's assertions, or improve on them, so as *not* to be viewed as deferential.[2] In questioning or qualifying the validity of each other's statements, people affirm their own status and worth. A constant one-upmanship exists, as a result, regarding who knows more about this or who can better perform that.

Concerns over status and status rivalry exist within the confines of the cultural principles discussed in Chapter 2 and are muted by them. Pukapukans seek not to disrupt the elaborate system of cross-cutting ties that envelops them. They tend to avoid direct interpersonal conflicts that lead to lasting disruption of close personal relationships. Status rivalries tend to be most overt in the ritualized competitions among villages. They tend to be downplayed among close relatives and friends.

A humorous undercurrent also frequently pervades Pukapukan status rivalries. There is less of the intensity and physical conflict that various writers depict for high islands such as Samoa (see Freeman 1983; Shore 1982). Pukapukan status rivalries often have a joking, bantering quality.[3] As the following example illustrates, they may add a certain zest to an activity.

While Molingi was making a particular string figure (*waiwai*), Nimeti, her husband, jokingly criticized her efforts. When she failed to do it right the first time and had to try over again, he turned to me and stated that she did not know how to make such things. Here was the proof; she could not do this string figure. Molingi appeared to ignore his comments. She seemed absorbed in trying to work out where she went wrong in making the figure. Again Nimeti criticized her efforts. Finally Molingi turned to him and stated that he was getting senile. (Both of them are in their seventies.) Didn't Nimeti recognize, she rhetorically asked, that she was an expert on traditional matters?

As a result of Molingi's comment, Nimeti picked up a string and started making a figure himself. Molingi scoffed at his efforts. My daughter Amelia came by and asked Nimeti what he was doing. He proudly showed her his figure. Molingi criticized Nimeti's string figure as something any child could do. Finally Molingi finished her figure and showed it to me. She pointedly noted that Nimeti did not know how to make one like her's. Nimeti laughed at the implied challenge and began work on a different string figure. Here was another one, he commented, that Molingi did not know.

In understanding the dynamics of life on the atoll it is important to remember a concern with status and competition permeates many, if not most, social activities, but one should also remember that a subtle humor frequently graces such rivalries as well.

The learning process

Learning within situationally relevant contexts

The manner in which Tengele instructed Lima and Unu regarding the canoe illustrates an important point. Knowledge in Pukapuka is often acquired in the context of some activity. It is embedded in some purpose; it is situationally relevant. As Firth notes, one of the "cardinal points of education in a native society such as Tikopia [another Polynesian island, is] . . . its practicality – not in the sense of being directed to economic ends, but as arising from actual situations in daily life" (1936:134; see also Ritchie and Ritchie 1979:107). In the above case, Lima and Unu learned because Tengele had a task to do and needed help.

We can grasp the importance of context by listening to people's descriptions of how they acquired certain knowledge. In the following, Kililua recalls how he learned place names along a particular reef:

Many times my father and I would go in the lagoon, my real 'father' and his 'younger brother,' to catch some fish. . . . If we went on my uncle's canoe to fish in the lagoon I would at times ask questions (*uwiuwi maalie*): "What is the name of the place, of this place; what is the name of this islet (*motu*)?" I would then be told, "This is the islet of Te Tali." "What is the name of . . . ?" "That is the islet of Tau Yili." "What is the name of that place?" "That is the islet of Te Mako." . . . When I came back to this place, I might ask someone else, to Tiele or someone else . . .

As I grew older, we young men would go along the reef and say we are coming to such and such a place, we would say we are approaching the islet of Tau Yili; then we would go on to the place called the Aua Loa and stay there fishing. Consequently, I learned all the places, all the islets.

Yala describes how he gradually mastered the names and descriptions of various fish:

If a 'parent' (*matua*) said, "Go get some *eve* for us," I would go fish for some *eve*. I understood what an *eve* looked like so when I caught one I would say, "Yes, this is an *eve*." When I brought it back, my 'parent' he would say that it was correct. I had caught an *eve*.

It would be inaccurate, however, to view all education in Pukapuka as tied to a particular activity or a purposive context. Some knowledge is learned for its own enjoyment. Here Molingi describes learning legends in her youth:

At nighttime, at the time we were getting ready to sleep, the children would ask (*uwiuwi*), "Tell us some stories." Then our old 'grandfather' would tell the legend of Wutu and other similar tales. It was a common thing for all the 'fathers' to do; we might also hear the stories at some other homes. . . . The children would ask their 'parents,' "Please tell the legend of so and so, the legend of Lata, the legend of Yii." The legends of all the old people . . .

We would ask (*pati*), the children would ask, "Some other home tells a certain legend to their children. We heard about it. Please tell us the legend of so and so because so and so told it to their children. Please tell us so we can listen." Then our 'father' would tell it to us.

Variation exists, in other words, in the degree to which education is placed in a context or tied to specific tasks. Fish or place names generally are more easily explained and learned in concrete settings. Also, they are part of everyday life. Other education may not be so closely tied to specific needs or projects. Telling legends, for example, is really a form of entertainment and a means of acquainting the younger generation with Pukapukan traditions. But overall, most knowledge is acquired within situationally relevant contexts. As the above quotations regarding fishing indicate, what is learned often arises from carrying out concrete tasks in everyday life.

One must keep this contextual aspect of education in mind in reading the following sections. Context helps to limit the diversity that might naturally develop in a particular situation. What people observe and what they hear may be open to a variety of interpretations, but the context helps indicate the appropriate one. The word *paapaa*, for instance, may mean either 'father' or 'grandfather' depending on the age of the person speaking. For young children today, *teeti* usually refers to 'father' and *paapaa* to 'grandfather.' Among older people, *paapaa* indicates 'father.' Likewise, the word *wua* has more than ten meanings, some quite distinct from one another. It can refer to a pill, a group of fishermen, or a section of taro swamp. From either word alone, one cannot possibly understand which interpretation is meant. One must have details regarding the speaker and/or sentence. Context clarifies a word's meaning.

Observation and imitation

A generalization the Munroes suggest for many traditionally oriented cultures holds true for Pukapuka: "Explicit verbal instruction is rarely given . . . [the child] learns by observation and subsequent imitation" (1975:88). "In every Polynesian society," the Ritchies assert, "children, so long as they do not interfere, may be participant observers in most aspects of family, village, informal, or ceremonial life" (1979:85; cf. Ochs 1982). Rarely, if ever, are children excluded from events open to the general adult population. Each of the four times I watched the annual adult wrestling competitions, for instance, children sat or played along the sidelines. When the children grew tired of observing, they wrestled among themselves. Likewise, when they grew tired of wrestling, they again watched the adults. Unless the children proved disruptive, grown-ups generally ignored them. I might add that Pukapukan children do not usually request permission to observe adult events. They just do it.

Pukapukans often regulate their participation in the learning process. If something does not interest them, they simply avoid involvement in it (if they can). Lima, for example, did something else the day Unu and Tengele lashed the *tutuki* sticks. Here we see a subtle aspect of the Pukapukan concern with status. Though Pukapukans defer to those teaching, learners try to maintain their own position or status, vis-à-vis teachers by deciding when and where they will learn.

Children are not alone in acquiring knowledge through observation and imitation. Adults do so as well. As the following example illustrates, learning wrestling chants by adults is often a casual affair. What they pick up in one practice session – by listening, observing, and imitating – is what most adults rely on when reciting chants at the annual wrestling matches. (I observed this practice session four years in a row and each time it followed the same pattern.)

Several older men, including Petelo, were sitting on the beach with some younger men, mostly in their forties and fifties. Petelo started a chant and others proceeded to join in. Kililua, who had been elsewhere, came up and immediately began chanting too. After each chant was finished, one of the older men started a new one. It seemed to me that a few of the younger men (in their forties) did not know several chants and were trying to bluff their way through them. Since the chants are performed in a group and certain words tend to merge, the younger men could do this – as long as they had the right sounds and actions.

During the pauses between chants, one person or another would make a comment regarding who did and did not know the chants. One elderly man jokingly challenged Apela's knowledge of a verse. Apela laughingly replied that the other man's comment was absurd. Another elderly man commented about the lack of knowledge among the young men in their twenties.

On a more subtle level, a competition existed between Petelo and Kililua regarding who could think of new chants more rapidly or who stumbled through fewer verses. Neither wasted his time commenting about the other's skill. But it was clear (to me) that Kililua was trying to assert himself as the master of these chants and Petelo was subtly challenging his claim.

Adults' retrospective statements indicate that observation played an important part in their acquisition of skills:

I mainly watched the people making things and then I would try myself to do it. I would try doing it and it would be correct. That is the way I learned making hats; we (*taua*) would watch the people who knew how to make hats; then we would know how to make them. (Taavini)

I learned by observing while next to . . . the old people as they made these things. I would watch and then I would know how to make them. I did not ask people questions. (A woman in her sixties)

Another way to grasp the importance of observation is to realize that the word *kite* has two basic meanings (cf. Levin 1978a:6). *Kite* is commonly used in the sense of 'to see,' 'to observe,' 'to witness.' *Na kite koe i te payii?* 'Did you see the ship?' *Kooku te kite i to laua pekapeka*, 'I am the person who witnessed (or I was witness to) their quarrel.' *Kite* also means 'to know,' 'to possess knowledge.' In her statement above, Taavini says, *Onoono wua taua ki te kau e iloa e te waii, kite ai taua i te wai i te mea ia*, 'We would watch the people who knew how to make such a thing; then we would know how to make this thing.' In the statement by the woman in her sixties, it is not exactly clear which sense of *kite* she is in fact using. *Na kite au koi tawa au . . . ke maani naa mea a te kau maatutua*. The phrase could be translated either as 'I gained knowledge (or learned) while next to the old people as they made these things' or 'I observed while next to the old people as they made these things.' My translation combines both of these senses because the context suggests to me that is what she means, but the phrase is somewhat ambiguous. The point to emphasize is that knowledge is something

Carrying the day's catch home

grasped visually. As Koskinen (1968) points out, most Polynesian cultures have a visual orientation toward knowledge.[4]

To summarize, children and adults learn by observing before and/or as they participate in an activity. As Levin (1978a:4) states for the

Polynesian island of Tubuai, "Learning is based on close observation" of others. Formal instruction and questions are kept to a minimum. Such an approach raises a number of questions. Why, for example, do Pukapukans prefer observation to formal instruction as a learning technique? How do people acquire the same sorts of knowledge when instruction is not standardized? And why do Pukapukans ask few direct questions? We shall begin with the last problem since it overlaps with the above discussion.

Listening in relation to asking questions

Listening, though secondary to observation, plays an important role in the acquisition of knowledge. Pukapukans often assert that they learned about their cultural traditions simply by listening to other people's conversations:

[Did anyone specifically tell you about these legends?] No, for instance at the gatherings of Ngake village, ... all the knowledgeable people would tell these sorts of tales. ... I am a person who likes to sit at all the meetings so that I can listen to all that is said. If a group gathers somewhere, I will sit down beside them so that I can listen to and learn what is said. (Paani)

[How did you learn about such things as the old patrilineages (*po*) and matrimoieties (*wua*)?] From the old people, the elderly (*ai metua*); they taught me, they told these things to me. ... [Did you ask someone who was especially knowledgeable?] I just listened to what some people said in their meetings. (A man in his seventies)

As several people emphasized to me, extensive questioning by children is generally discouraged. Yala, in his normally colorful and lucid way, gave the best explanation of this:

Sometimes a little child, if he says, " 'Grandpa,' what is this, huh 'grandpa'?" I tell him, "It is a such and such." "What is that thing up there, that thing that is hanging?" "That is a such and such, that is what it is." "There is another thing, 'grandpa'; look, what is that?" "Why do you like to ask so many questions?"

This type of child, the 'parent' will get tired explaining all these things. This type of child is always asking questions (*kano uwiuwi wua*) to us. But if he just looked, he would see what it is. "A lizard." "What is that thing that is crawling?" We (*taua*) would explain "a beetle." "What is that?" "An ant."

Then the child asks about some other animal, then asks again about some different animal. This is the time that we get angry. We don't get angry if there is one question, two questions, or three questions. But if he starts asking a lot of questions, that is the reason the person gets angry.

[Why?] Because the child just likes to ask questions; he is just a child, for what reason does he ask these things? You explain that this thing is a beetle; what is he going to do with this beetle? He is not going to do anything with this beetle. He does not then follow that beetle. It is just that he likes to ask questions.

"Hey, what is that hanging?" You explain "clothes." He does not go and get the clothes, so why does he ask about them? That is the reason that I will get angry. "You come here just to ask questions." Nothing of value is going to result from this. Consequently, the 'parent' gets angry. "You just like to keep asking questions? Here, take [or eat, *kai*] this" [the idea is that the child is being beaten]. That is why all parents get angry.

I know from personal experience that people grew tired of being asked questions. Most people seemed pleased when I initially interviewed them. They took it as an honor; it implied that they were knowledgeable. But no matter how intelligent my questions might make people feel, several became tired of them over time. After a lengthy interview lasting two to three hours, some preferred not to be interviewed again for three to four weeks (even though I offered recompense, such as cigarettes and gifts, for their help). Their refusal was not meant as a personal slight. It was simply that, from their perspective, they had better things to do than sit down and answer (what they viewed as) scores of questions. Some Pukapukans found it unusual and a bit amusing that an adult could even formulate the number of questions I did. Where, two or three of them joked, did all my questions come from? Is that what I learned at the university, a man half-seriously asked.

Yala's statement above illustrates another important point. It would be inaccurate to say that questions per se are discouraged. Under certain circumstances questions are encouraged. If parents see that something of value will result for their children or themselves, they will often encourage children to ask questions so they better grasp the principles involved. Likewise, if children ask a question about Pukapukan traditions that the parents can answer, the parents are generally glad to answer – if they are not busy and the children ask properly. That is why Kililua, in describing how he asked questions regarding certain place names, used the phrase *uwiuwi maalie*. It literally means 'asking questions slowly' but in this context is better translated as 'occasionally asking questions.' The idea is that he did not ask too many questions at one time.

People are doing you a favor by answering your questions. Molingi, in describing how she asked to be told legends, used not only the word *uwi* (to ask in the sense of seeking information) but also the word *pati* (to ask in the sense of requesting a favor). In another section of Kililua's interview on the way he learned various place names, he emphasized just this aspect – that his asking for information was really requesting a favor. Certain place names "I would really want to know; it was a request (*pati*) by me. I asked, 'Please tell me so that I will know the name of this place. I do not know.' Then they would tell me." (Other informants made similar statements.) But if one asked too many questions, especially about something not perceived as having much value, the other person might get angry. This goes back to the importance of context. Questions about concrete situations that have concrete applications are not discouraged, but questions of no perceived import are frowned upon.

Related to this is the fact that people do not like to answer the same question twice. If a person raises some question a second time, it implies a failure to have listened carefully to the first explanation. What psychologists term reliability – informants repeatedly yielding the same results on certain tasks – is consequently extremely difficult to measure on the island (cf. Weller 1984a). Changes in people's accounts over time may thus not always be discernible, either to Pukapukans or to anthropologists.

Even though Pukapukans do question one another under certain circumstances, my data suggest that adults rarely ask direct questions of other adults. Why? The answer goes back to the issue of status discussed earlier. One informant explained the issue in this way:

[You have said several times over the past year that you were interested in learning more about Pukapukan legends and you mentioned asking Paani some day about a few. Yet you have not done so. I wonder why.] Well, there is no time for me to ask him. But maybe, if there is any time for Paani to come to my home for some other purpose, I think that would be a good time to ask.

[But you would not go to Paani's house?] No, no. [Why?] Well, I do not want to go to someone's home to ask questions like that. Maybe they will say that "that person is a fool to come to our house and ask those questions." I wait for the appropriate time. Sometimes, in a meeting or when there are three or four persons that might meet outside the post office, something like that; that is a good time to ask.

[Would you be ashamed (*akamaa*) to go to Paani's house?] No, I would not be ashamed. I would not be ashamed. But I do not have any time to go to his home . . . I can go to his house on some other purpose, but not on that purpose. [I am not sure that I fully understand.] Well . . . [he heaves a long sigh as if tired]. I do not know. That is our custom.

[Do you mean that they would criticize you?] Maybe, maybe. Well, because I am a Pukapukan and they are Pukapukan too. If I go to Paani's house for this purpose, they might say, "Hey, he is a fool." They believe that all the Pukapukans should know that. And yet I go to him and ask him those questions. It is simple for them to say that "it is a waste of time for him to come and ask these questions because his 'parents' know about these things." Because all people on the island believe that everyone on the island knows their culture. It's like that.

Maybe this person does not say anything critical and he agrees with you in a friendly way. He welcomes you and says good things to you. He explains what you want to know. But for the people of the home, and for other people in other homes . . . they may say "there is a fool." Maybe your question is very simple for them. Maybe they know the answer to that.

Children have little status to lose vis-à-vis adults. Hence, they frequently ask direct questions. But as people get older, especially when one adult deals with another, they tend to avoid asking direct questions, especially if they imply one's ignorance. They would rather, as the informant suggests, wait for an appropriate moment to raise the matter indirectly, in a casual manner.

For askers to be effective in posing a question, they must be sensitive to the replier's status concerns as well as their own. Most Pukapukans will respond to sincere questions asked in a deferential manner, but adults tend to ignore questions with a provocative, testing quality. Two informants explained the matter to me:

If an ignorant (*valetiko*) person asks me a question, I will answer him. But if it's an adult who knows these things, I will not answer because if I answer he will criticize me. (Vave)

If Petelo comes to me, if Petelo asks to me about some genealogy, "What is the name of some particular person"... such as who is the 'parent' (*matua*) of Pepeu, his 'mother' (*matua wawine*)? I will say, "I do not know. I do not know the name of his 'mother.' Perhaps if I reply you will criticize me." (Yolo)

These informants are absolutely correct. Questioners do frequently scoff at the answers they receive if they differ from what they expect. It is a common form of teasing in Pukapuka.

Readers should not form a mistaken impression. Pukapukans are at times willing to admit they do not know something. People, for instance, admitted they did not know some of the answers to questions I asked. But overall I have the impression that in areas viewed as common knowledge (especially in respect to certain important Pukapukan traditions) many, if not most, adults try to avoid showing their ignorance or avoid opening themselves to ridicule. It is a matter of degree, admittedly, a matter of context. But with certain qualifications – in regard to the topic, the individuals involved, the number of times one has to admit one's ignorance, and who else is listening – Pukapukans clearly try to avoid displaying their ignorance in public. Now one can perhaps understand why Lima and Unu never asked Tengele a question while working on the canoe.

How, then, do adult Pukapukans ask questions regarding matters they would like to learn more about? It involves a certain delicacy, a certain awareness of the replier's sensibilities. Some questions are vaguely worded or open-ended. Some are asked with such tact that it is not always clear they even constitute questions. They may seem more like abstract musings – as something that puzzles a person, as something various people have presented conflicting accounts about.

Here is a common pattern I perceived many times:

Toa and I were discussing certain genealogical matters related to Tokelau cemetery (see Map 3) as we stood one day in the shade by the cemetery. A man who was on his way back from feeding his pig saw us. He came over to chat. As an introduction, he made a mildly sarcastic remark about how we were just fooling around. We did not know what we were doing. Toa said no, in fact, he was teaching me something about Tokelau cemetery and its reputed founder Koulangi. When Toa did not offer more information, the man made a further comment. He said that he did not really believe what people nowadays asserted about the affiliations of various cemeteries in Yato. People just said contradictory things, which confused him. He did not know really who to believe. The man never asked Toa directly what he knew. He just waited to see· if Toa would respond.

After a moment's hesitation, Toa took the up the cue. He noted that his 'father' had told him that previously Tokelau had been affiliated with Walepia cemetery – not all of Walepia, just the part under the frangipani tree. Toa suggested that Koulangi, in fact, derived from the Walepia patrilineage (*po*). This appeared to intrigue the man. (I knew from an earlier interview with him that he knew little about Koulangi's parents or their genealogical ties.) But at the same time, he seemed hesitant to believe Toa. After all, he and most other people felt that Tokelau cemetery belonged within Yayi *kawa* (or 'strip of land') not the *kawa* that included Walepia.

The man never directly challenged Toa. He just smiled and said that he had believed all these years what other people had said – that Tokelau belonged to Yayi *kawa*. Toa commented that he had heard that too, but it was not true. Some strips of land, he asserted, did not simply go in an unbroken line from the lagoon (*tai*) to the ocean side (*tua*) of the island. As part of his proof, he noted that Yamaunga *kawa* went up only to Ipui cemetery – it did not go all the way to the ocean side of the island. All the land between Loto village and Yaalongo *kawa* belonged to Yayi *kawa*.

In interviewing informants during various surveys, I generally kept my opinions to myself. I would ask people certain questions and record what they said. I tried not to lead them in a particular direction or give them any clues as to what I thought. I often wondered, however, how Pukapukans might interview informants. Hence I was intrigued one day to see Lama, a man in his fifties, asking Molingi several questions.[5] I went nearby to observe.

In some ways our styles were the same. He was quite respectful to her and asked his questions politely. He was clearly showing that he appreciated her time and effort. But beyond this, a significant difference existed. He asserted far more of his own opinions than I would have. Though respectful, he seemed to be continually trying to show her that he knew quite a bit too. Molingi would at times simply let him go on. At times she would throw in something of her own. At other times she would correct him.

When she pointed out some error to him, Lama often would sound surprised. He might say something like, "You don't say, really. And here all these people in Loto village had told me something different." Molingi would laugh at the remark and then go on to justify her position. Lama would take careful notes on what she said. Or sometimes he would pause to think a second and say, "Yes, now I remember. That is correct. You know I had gotten this confused with so and so" and he would name some other person. Then he would take down Molingi's explanation.

I demurred from displaying what I knew because of my scientific orientation, my desire not to interject personal biases. Lama had other concerns. By continually adding his own comments, he was making it clear that he, too, possessed a degree of competence in these matters. He, too, had status.

In asking questions, Pukapukans focus mostly on contexts and concerns they are familiar with. As the apical ancestor construct (discussed in Chapter 2) implies, Pukapukans often use genealogies as a way of locating an individual within an understandable framework of rights and statuses. When my wife Nancy and I showed pictures of our families in America, for example, Pukapukans focused their questions on people's relationships to one another and on where they lived. People rarely asked about what our relatives were like as individuals or what occupations they had. Pictures of scenery seemed to bore them. They passed over beautiful Hawaiian vistas with just a glance.

Some Pukapukans are aware that they tend to ask certain types of questions. The following example, one of three I recorded, made that clear to me. Tukia, a school teacher, and I were one day discussing anthropology and what anthropologists did. He emphasized that anthropologists had an important role to play in preserving Pukapukan traditions. I replied that Pukapukans were quite capable of preserving their own traditions. They did not need to rely on outside help. He disagreed. Yes, he admitted, Pukapukans could ask their elders questions. That was not what he was referring to. He had discussed various matters with older people. Yet all he had gotten back (in his opinion) was vague, worthless information. He thought that I, as an anthropologist, learned at the university what types of questions to ask. Sometimes, he noted, he overheard an adult telling legends to younger people. The audience would ask, he commented shaking his head, the most trivial sorts of questions – just about some detail of location, the relation of various participants, or the behavior that precipitated a particular response. They asked nothing of broader significance, such as the legend's general meaning or its relation to other known traditions. He believed that, as a trained anthropologist, I knew the broader questions to ask. He felt that I knew how to fit various data together.

The importance of repetition

The styles of observing and listening, though important, are not the crucial factors that facilitate Pukapukan learning. The critical factor is repetition. What is missed in one observation or in one listening is picked up in another. What is only partially learned at one stage is improved on through repeated experiences. Learning in Pukapuka is a gradual process. Practice helps bring mastery.

A sense of how much repetition is involved in the learning process

Petelo
(J. Hecht)

Molingi

Kililua

Yala

Tukia   Paleula

Two of the Beagleholes' informants

Pau   Veeti
(Bishop Museum)   (Bishop Museum)

can be gained from examining an early practice session held by the Yato Village Youth Club in preparation for a chant (*mako*) competition. During this session, in which the club attempted to learn four verses, they repeated the first verse approximately thirty times. Since they must have had fifteen or more additional sessions after this one, I estimate that the verse was eventually repeated at least 200 times. An examination of various statements cited above also indicates the importance of repetition. Kililua specifically mentioned it regarding place names. Molingi conveyed the same impression – that as a child she repeatedly heard some of the same tales.

The importance of repetition in learning was pointedly driven home to me by the way my wife Nancy and I learned certain dances:

About three months after we arrived on the island, Tawa Ngake (one of the *Akatawa*'s two units) had its one and only practice session for the next day's victory dance. Because people were busy with various things, the practice did not begin until around 8:00 P.M. It lasted for approximately four hours.

The leader initially discussed various steps with some adults around him. He would try out a step or two, and others would suggest modifications. Because of the general context, the existence of these modifications, and the way many performers laughed when first trying out the steps, I assumed people were learning a new dance.

Nancy and I participated in the practice, though we found it rather difficult. Nancy asked me later, "How could people learn the dance steps so quickly?" People could barely see what was going on half the time because of the poor lighting. By the end of the practice, we certainly had not learned the steps.

Almost two years later, it was quite a different story. By most standards, the time set aside to create and practice dance steps for the Christmas Day dance competition is short. Ideally, there are about two hours. Men from one *Akatawa* unit come together with the women from the other unit to learn dances for the competition. (This is the only time during the year that these men and women practice together.)

For the Tawa Lalo men and Tawa Ngake women on Christmas Day 1979, there was less time than usual. When one of the leaders announced that we had only forty-five minutes left in which to learn new steps, a wave of tension went through the dancers. We had wasted more than thirty minutes getting the band sorted out and still had no clear idea what movements we would perform. Several people remarked that we could not possibly win the competition.

Yingonge then took over. He immediately told the band to play the Banana Court number he had composed for a special celebration five months earlier. As the men swung into a familiar step, people's spirits started to pick up. Though it had originally taken the Tawa Lalo men several lessons to learn these steps, we needed only five or six repetitions to remember the pattern. The Tawa Ngake women had little difficulty fitting in because they used, as Nancy said, a general movement that went with various men's steps.

Yingonge next explained a few new movements he had thought up based on the original dance. In about fifteen minutes we had mastered these. With twenty minutes left we slowly began making our way toward the judges' stand. All did not seem lost as before, but it certainly was going to be close. Yingonge showed the women a slight variation. A woman in her thirties immediately caught on and demonstrated it to the other women. As the women practiced this step, the men went over their own.

Then Yingonge, working with Viliamu, created a simple but humorous new step. It was similar to one we had done at the special celebration and was not difficult to learn. It had a certain sexual bawdiness that made us more enthusiastic. With about five to eight minutes left, we moved closer to the judges' stand. It looked as though we finally had something competitive.

As we went through our final practices, we seemed to be gaining more and more confidence. We were not good, especially toward the rear of the line, but we had the idea. Those in the very front looked quite professional.

We delayed our final movement toward the judges' stand because the leaders were intent on making sure everything was set. The band had the rhythm; the dancers seemed to be performing credibly. Everything seemed to have fallen into place. Finally, we moved up to the judges' stand and performed.

For part of the dance, I watched from the sidelines so I could see how we looked. I thought we were as good as if not better than the other side. But did we win? We lost. The judges stated that both teams had performed well and they could not decide between us, but since we had arrived at the judges' stand a few minutes late, they would award the prize to the other side.

Pukapukans build up a core of constructs and skills from repeated experiences. Each situation is not exactly the same as the next. Some may, in fact, seem quite different. But the underlying elements are often similar. Gradually, over time, Pukapukans develop a sense of how certain patterns fit together (cf. Lord 1960). As a result, they can often, with little effort, learn new dance steps. Learning the Banana Court dance the first time involved considerable practice (see Borofsky 1982:146–8), but once we had learned the steps, developing new steps (based on the old) was relatively easy.

Repetition seems especially important in the earlier stages of learning, but as time goes on and people acquire certain basic skills, repetition becomes less significant. Criticism and ridicule take its place.

Ridicule and the absence of praise

Ridicule is a pervasive element in Pukapukan education. As a means of asserting one's own competence and status, people frequently criticize the foibles of others. Rarely is praise given. Levy's statement about Tahitian upbringing is just as applicable to Pukapukan childhood. The child "is not coached 'positively' – 'Do it this way.' But his errors are corrected – 'You are doing it wrong.' He begins to learn that both learning and proper performance consist of scanning for and avoiding errors" (1973:460; cf. Levin 1978a). This is what happened when Tengele taught Lima and Unu about hewing the outrigger. He corrected their mistakes. Tengele never offered an overt word of encouragement.

The following description of the Yato Youth Club at a later stage in their practicing for the chanting competition mentioned above conveys the flavor of the way such criticism operates:

After a few minutes, a twenty-year-old girl started the *uyunga* (the high-pitched introduction to a chant). An older man (in his early fifties), who was assisting the club, immediately stopped her and said she was doing it wrong. She tried twice more and each time the older man made a critical remark. One of the boys (in his early twenties) yelled at another girl (also twenty) to try. The girl just sat where she was and said nothing. Again the boy yelled at her to try. Again she said nothing. So a woman in her early thirties tried. Halfway through the *uyunga* she began laughing in embarrassment. This made several people "snarl" at her in disgust. Then the girl who had unsuccessfully attempted to do it in the first place tried again. This time she succeeded, and everyone picked it up from her.

For the second verse, this woman and the thirty-year-old woman (who had laughed in the middle of her previous effort) did the *uyunga* together. Another boy in his early twenties turned to a teenager and told him to pay attention. In general throughout the chant, people made such little sniping remarks to each other. The remarks usually took the form of jokes that made others laugh. It was more one-upmanship than anything else. When the second verse was finished, the older man said that the pace of the chant should be slower.

Then there was a small break. Three people spoke to the group and each commented on something that had been wrong with the practice. The older man focused on the way the group was pronouncing the chant incorrectly. Two boys stressed that people were fooling around too much.

And so it went for most of the session. Some of the critical remarks added spice to the practice; they relieved the repetitive routine. But many of them had the effect of pressuring people into following a certain pattern.

In a way it is not fully correct to call this ridicule. Many Pukapukans view their comments as helpful. One time, for example, when I was assisting Viliamu with some work, he told me I was hitting nails like an old lady. I suggested to him that it would be wiser not to criticize his helpers. They might not want to help as much. He looked at me with mild surprise. He said he was not trying to ridicule (*avili*) me. He was just trying to help me hit the nails better. I should hit them with a firm, hard stroke.

It would also be inaccurate to say that no praise is ever given in the learning process. My notes indicate, for example, a few positive comments made here and there during the early practice sessions of the Yato Youth Club, particularly when the group's performance markedly surpassed what others had been led to expect. It would be more appropriate to say that praise is simply uncommon, especially among people who are familiar (*maatau*) with each other. Praise to newcomers can be lavish, but not to one's friends or children. For them one reserves sarcastic praise (*waiakanau*) – such as complimenting people on their cricket batting after they have just been bowled out twice. As the example of Tengele and the canoe implies, the absence of criticism may itself be a form of praise.

A comparison between two teachers helps to clarify the differences between this Pukapukan perspective and one common in the West. During my stay on the island, our family became close friends with an Australian Volunteers Abroad teacher who taught at the government school. The teacher was quite dedicated and well liked. He frequently used positive reinforcement with the children at school, encouraging them with compliments and treating them, within reason, as equals. This, he felt, was the most effective way to stimulate self-expression among the children, both in their discussions and in their writing. Without some sort of encouragement, he thought, they would not be eager to learn.

Another teacher, a Pukapukan, was also quite dedicated and competent, but he thought the Australian teacher was too soft on the children. Students, he asserted, must learn how to persevere in the face of adversity. One must challenge students and not let them feel content with what they have done. By giving too much positive reinforcement, students develop a "swelled head" about their capabilities. They become self-aggrandizing in their relations with others (cf. Ritchie and Ritchie 1979:156).

The lack of positive reinforcement was brought home to me directly in two ways. Paleula, who speaks some English, was helping me go over a few questions in Pukapukan that I wanted to use in a questionnaire. I had had trouble translating *praise* into Pukapukan and I had asked him how he would do it. At first he thought I meant praise in the sarcastic sense noted above (*waiakanau*). I explained that I meant it in a positive sense. It took us about twenty minutes of discussion to get the idea of the sentence correct: *E ni toe tangata na tautuluina koe i au wakamaunga ma te talapaya*? 'Did some people encourage you in the learning process through the use of praise?' When I asked certain Pukapukans that question, particularly people in their twenties, they did not understand what I meant. I had to spend several minutes explaining what the question referred to. They were not even sure of *talapaya*'s meaning in this context.

The Australian teacher was widely admired on the island. When he was getting ready to leave, I asked him if anyone had complimented him on the excellent job he had done. No, he said, no one really had.

A few Pukapukans, who were visiting the island from New Zealand and Rarotonga, had been very complimentary – but not the Pukapukans that he knew well. True, several people had given him mats. A few people had also mentioned at various feasts (*imukai*) held for departing passengers that he had done a fine job. But, he noted with a smile, they did that for everyone. Yet none of this should be taken to mean that he was not very much admired and appreciated. He clearly was. People simply did not express their respect directly to him (cf. Kirkpatrick 1983:153).

Challenging as an educational tool

Because of status rivalries, Pukapukans frequently challenge one another's opinions on a subject. Children, as well as adults, learn information by picking apart (or listening to others pick apart) someone's remarks. The following example, observed by the Australian teacher and dealing with a Pukapukan legend, illustrates the process well:

A dispute developed among the students in the form 5 class regarding the punishment accorded to Vakayala (a legendary figure) for his crimes. After most of Vakayala's flesh had been beaten off, were his testicles exploded by the placement of hot stones on them, or was he thrown into the water to drift with his testicles still intact? The argument went on for about twenty minutes.

One teenage boy, Taputu, asserted that Vakayala's testicles had been exploded. Since two other boys frequently viewed Taputu as being haughty, they criticized his account on general principle (as the teacher phrased it). They indicated that Taputu did not know what he was talking about. He was just making up his account. As it turned out on further discussion, the two boys were not that sure of the legend themselves.

Another teenage boy, Waletini, asserted that Vakayala's testicles had not been exploded. As proof, he mentioned that his father had told him this story and had not mentioned anything about exploding testicles. This brought still another boy, Atuvilo, onto Taputu's side. Atuvilo liked to tease Waletini, especially regarding how Waletini felt he knew so much because of what his father told him. Several others, both girls and boys, also participated in the discussion. But that day, the discussion was left unresolved.

Some children then went home and apparently asked others about the legend. Waletini asked his father again. One of the teenage girls asked Molingi. Atuvilo asked his 'mother.' When they discussed the matter the next day, the general consensus was that the testicles had not been exploded. Most of the children accepted Molingi's opinion because they viewed her as the most knowledgeable person queried. She had not mentioned anything about exploded testicles to the teenage girl. But there was not complete agreement. Taputu and Atuvilo still had doubts that Molingi knew everything there was to know about the legend of Vakayala. They still felt that they were at least partially right.

(Interestingly, the Beagleholes recorded both versions of the Vakayala legend in their field notes.)

In adult discussions the process may be more subtle. Adults do not usually criticize others directly. They may listen, wait, and then suggest an alternative view, as the man in his late fifties did with Toa. Or they may turn the criticisms into jokes, as the elderly man did with Apela in the wrestling chanting practice. Pukapukans may imply (as a manifestation of their status rivalries) that their challenges and counterchallenges are quite direct, but to me as an outside observer, they appeared to be diluted through jokes, tact, and innuendos. This principle is illustrated by the way informants described their discussions with Hecht. People told me that numerous conflicts arose during the genealogical sessions, but Hecht did not describe the sessions in such terms. She thought that the arguments were fairly subdued. Concern with status rivalry was tempered by the desire to avoid disrupting close social relations.

The important point is that, whatever the actual degree of direct challenging, Pukapukans feel the pressure; they feel the competition. Often it acts as a stimulant to learning. People compete to see who knows more. During the wrestling chant practice described above, Petelo challenged Kililua's efforts at dominance. Others got swept up in the competition and tried to show off. The elderly man's remark to Apela implied that he himself was no novice.

To stand up to a challenge is an affirmation of one's competence. The word *wakalalilali* is a derogatory one in Pukapukan. While I was working on a Pukapukan dictionary with several teachers (Mataola et al. 1981), some of them suggested that the term meant a good-for-nothing person as well as one who was "a waste of time." I found the combination of meanings somewhat confusing, but when people explained it further, the term's meaning became clear. It referred to a person who was not much of a challenge to compete against. *Ia koe i te wakalalilali ke poopoko mai kia aku*, 'It is a waste of time for me to wrestle with you [since you are not much of a challenge].'

Like context and repetition, these critical remarks or challenges play an important role in the development of a common fund of knowledge, at least in terms of what people say publicly. With some exceptions, assertions that seem too out of the ordinary bring ridicule on a person. Though people may have a great variety of opinions on a subject, not all of them are publicly expressed. People tend to focus on the safe ones, the ones that other people will basically agree with.

In this context Toa's conversation with the man in his late fifties is seen in a new light. While I had heard various opinions about how strips of land (*kawa*) had traditionally been organized in Yato village, I had never heard anyone else suggest what Toa stated – that the strip named Yamaunga went only up to Ipui cemetery. Though his assertion had an intriguing reasoning to it, which both the other man and I could appreciate, it differed from what everyone else I had interviewed asserted – that these strips ran in a general line from the lagoon side of the island (*tai*) to the back or ocean side (*tua*). This fact probably explains why the man in his late fifties was apparently hearing Toa's idea for the first time, even though they were on fairly good terms and had known each other for years. Presumably, Toa had been hesitant to assert such an idea before in public.

One can thus see that challenging and criticism, like context and repetition, play important roles in limiting diversity of knowledge, at least in what is expressed publicly. They also emphasize that learning occurs within a context. In Pukapuka, a person does not just learn a skill. The person also interacts with others in the process (see Finnegan 1977:241).

Yet all this leaves some questions unanswered. Why do so many Pukapukans shy away from direct individual instruction? And why do they gravitate toward observation and listening?

Subordinating the learner as a teaching style

Most older people profess an interest in teaching the young. A man in his sixties expressed a common theme when he stated, "If the person is craving (*umiti*) to learn and comes to me, I will tell him what I know. I will not be stingy if he comes to my house." But few of the younger generation seem to come; few of them appear interested in being taught.

For children, being "taught" can be a rather humiliating experience. To punish a child for certain wrongs, Pukapukans not only beat the child with an object (such as a coconut spathe or a bunch of coconut leaves tied together), but may do so until the child stops crying. What Ernest Beaglehole noted in 1934–5 holds true today. The "Pukapukan technique requires that the child be whipped until he stop [*sic*] crying. I have never seen a child cease crying immediately in an effort to avoid further punishment. . . . He cries as long as he is whipped" (1944:162). Admittedly, the children are rarely hurt seriously, but the punishment does generate a feeling of helplessness and frustration. Not only does it teach the children to avoid repeating an offense; it also teaches them that they possess a distinctly subordinate role in the learning process. The beating constitutes a lesson in social relations. Though the following illustration is a bit more vivid than most I observed, it contains elements of a common pattern:

As I was sitting by the road, I saw a man (in his fifties) come up to the water tank with his 'son' (of about three and a half). The man was holding a coconut spathe in his hand. In a firm voice he told his 'son' to turn on the faucet and fill up the bottle he was holding. The boy, with a little trepidation, obeyed.

I asked the man what was going on. He explained that he was training the boy. Apparently, his 'son' had initially refused to go get water for the household. The man decided that his 'son' should be taught to be more obedient. (The boy, being the youngest child in the family, was admittedly a bit spoiled.)

The boy finished filling the bottle and held it up to look at. The man pointed the spathe toward home and nonverbally indicated that his 'son' should move in that direction. The boy seemed rather pleased with himself for having gotten the water. He started walking toward home with a smile on his face, a little oblivious of his 'father' behind him. Seeing his 'son's' nonchalance, the man poked the boy gently with the spathe. The boy appeared to ignore the poke. The boy's continued nonchalance seemed to perturb the man. He hit his 'son' firmly with the spathe.

This caused the boy to go into a tantrum. He started crying loudly. This in turn motivated the man to hit the boy harder to stop the crying. The boy went into a worse tantrum. The man continued to hit his 'son' until the boy, in rage and frustration, dropped the bottle and ran for home. This irritated the man even more. After a moment's pause to decide whether or not to pick up the bottle, he headed for home himself, leaving the bottle where it was dropped. About ten minutes later, one of the man's older children came from the house and fetched the bottle.

One can understand what one of Levy's Tahitian informants meant when he stated, "In childhood . . . one is too much under the control of others" (1973:42), or that the joy of becoming a young adult is that one is no longer hit: "In my childhood, one was hit. You went to school and were mischievous and you were hit. You returned to the house and you were ordered to do things. If you didn't go [and do them] you were hit. Now, no" (Levy 1973:468). One can also get a sense of why so many students liked the Australian teacher. He showed them respect.

This does not mean that the Pukapukan childhood is necessarily an unhappy one. The Australian teacher, Nancy, and I all viewed Pukapukan childhood as being fairly enjoyable. After all, the whole island constituted a playground and parents tended to leave their children alone to play among themselves (a point Ritchie and Ritchie, 1979, suggest is common throughout Polynesia). But this one aspect of subordination, perhaps because of its prominence, seemed to rankle children immensely.

Teachers stand in a position of superiority over their students. Learners must show proper respect and appreciation for what they are getting. Kililua indicated this in discussing the conditions under which he would teach others (a point I heard many others make as well):

I will teach some other people. But first I want to see what type of people they are. If I perceive that he is just boasting and will soon lose interest, I will start to lose interest too. . . . If it is someone who has criticized me before, what I have said before, I won't help him.

One can now better understand why Kililua described his learning experiences the way he did in earlier sections of this chapter. He was implying that he had showed the proper respect to his teachers.

Given that people do not like to abase themselves in front of their equals, given the issue of status rivalry, one can sense why so many people are not eager to be taught formally. It goes back to why people do not ask too many questions. It is just not worth all the trouble; it is just not worth all the humiliation. It is better to wait, to observe, to ask indirectly.

These comments are closely related to an aspect of Pukapukan vocabulary. There is no specific word for *student* in Pukapukan. The closest one that comes to it is 'child' (*tamaiti*). Students at the government school are called 'schoolchildren' (*tamaliki apii*). There is one word that can indicate *student* in a very special sense, *apiianga*. It refers to theology students (who must leave the island for formal schooling). But for the general term *student*, people either use the word *child* or some circumlocution.

The subordination implicit in formal instruction helps to explain the reactions of several women when Tukia offered them suggestions before an important volleyball game:

Tukia did not try to be excessively aggrandizing in instructing them. He tried to be helpful (though his tone was patronizing). Some of the younger girls, in the late teens and early twenties, who had worked with Tukia at the school, listened quite carefully to his advice. But not the women Tukia's age. A woman in her late twenties made several joking remarks about the instruction to other members of the team. The situation obviously embarrassed her. Another woman, in her early thirties, totally ignored Tukia. Every time he spoke, she stared up at a coconut tree until he was finished.

One can perhaps better understand now why Lima and Unu seemed so casual in watching Tengele hew the outrigger and lash the canoe. They did not want to appear subordinate.

The following example summarizes many of the complications and subtleties involved in this process. It also reinforces another point: that people stress the practical applications of knowledge. (The woman found my collection of genealogies a bit amusing because, from her perspective, they would have limited applicability in America, where few Pukapukans live.)

As I was collecting genealogies from Molingi, a woman (in her midforties) came up behind me to watch what I was doing. She made a joking remark about how I was collecting Pukapukan genealogies to show to people in America.

I consequently suggested that she might like to learn some of the genealogies I was recording. She gave a huff and replied that, of course, she knew most of these genealogies. Was I trying to imply that she did not know about her own forebears? No, I said, I just thought she might be interested.

Perhaps, if she listened, she might learn something new. Again she huffed. How could she know all that Molingi knew? she asked me. Was she as old as Molingi? She was still relatively young. (The implication here was that she had not had enough experience to learn certain genealogies.)

I suggested that she nonetheless might want to listen. She looked at me a little perturbed. Why, she asked, should she learn more if Molingi already knew these things? (Molingi smiled at the offhanded compliment.) There was no real reason for her to learn. She could always go ask Molingi if she needed to know a genealogy related to some land dispute.

I then went back to working with Molingi. The woman stood watching for about ten minutes. Then she sat down near me because, as she said, her legs hurt. As time went on, she tried to answer a few of my questions about specific genealogical relationships. Sometimes, when the question concerned fairly recent relationships, she would give me the answer before Molingi did. Rather than becoming a student, she had decided to teach me too!

After another ten minutes or so, the woman became intrigued by one of my questions and asked Molingi to develop it further, to explain how it fit with something else she knew. During the rest of the interview, she mostly listened to Molingi. Occasionally she would try to answer one of my questions before Molingi did. If I expressed doubt about her answer, she would turn to Molingi for confirmation.

When the interview was over, the woman smiled at me. Now, she asserted, I had proof that she was quite knowledgeable. If I wanted, I could interview her too. That way I would have more genealogies to take back with me to America.

Because of concern over status, people frequently emphasize that they learned things on their own. (Levy notes a similar pattern for Tahiti, 1973:220, 452.) This point was made clear to me during my early months on the island when I conducted a survey of the way people learn fish names. The vast majority of the ten-year-old boys I interviewed asserted that no one had taught them the names they knew. They had learned them on their own. Only with considerable probing did they mention adults who had also perhaps instructed them.

The ambiguity between teaching and learning can be seen in the Pukapukan word *apii*. Confusion exists as to whether the term means 'to teach' and 'to learn' or simply 'to teach.' Though I was never able to determine which was the case – since several people gave me different answers – I find the confusion about the term's meaning relevant. One can see exactly the same confusion in the way that teaching seems to merge with learning. Was it teaching or learning when Paani listened to the talk of the older men? Was it teaching or learning when a ten-year-old boy heard older men describe the names of various fish? It is difficult to say.

Learning from public displays of knowledge

Given the above concerns with status and subordination, one can see why public occasions provide an ideal opportunity for Pukapukans to acquire knowledge. While elders display what they know, others can listen quietly, taking it all in. But this having been said, a problem exists that complicates the situation immensely. Public events occur within the normal Pukapukan framework of challenges and counterchallenges. A great deal of information is presented, but it is not exactly clear which information is correct.

The inspection tour by the 'Council of Important People' to Motu Ko, the reserve of Ngake village, was the occasion for two huge feasts. After the first one, various people got up and made speeches. The first person who spoke was from Ngake. He praised the feast his village had prepared. The next two speakers belonged to other villages. Though voicing their appreciation for the meal, both expressed doubt that it matched up to the feasts their own villages had put on for the council. Yet out of compassion (*wakaaloa*) for the effort of the Ngake people, they both added, they would donate a small gift of money.

The fourth person to get up was Petelo. He waited for everyone to quiet down before beginning. (Normally people try to speak over the noise.) By his manner, he was able to draw people's attention to what he was about to say. After praising the feast of his village, he decided to ask the assemblage several questions. Many people, particularly from other villages, might claim to be knowledgeable, he said. But when tested publicly, did they really know that much about the traditions of the island?

After a pause, to make sure he had people's attention, Petelo continued. He asked the assemblage what was the true meaning of the word *kula* – not the obvious meaning, 'red,' but the ancient meaning of the term. His next question concerned the meanings of the terms *kula pupuni* and *kula moemoe*. He took in breath, as if to ask a third question, but then paused. He stated that that would be enough for now, but the clear implication was that there were many more questions that he could ask if people wanted him to.

Poyila, a man in his late fifties and Ngake's official 'speaker,' was the first to reply. I knew, from private discussions with Poyila, that he was unsure about many matters of tradition, but apparently he felt he knew one of the answers to Petelo's questions and was eager to display that fact. In his opening remarks, Poyila noted that it was appropriate that he, as the official 'speaker' of Ngake, should answer Petelo's first question. The question referred to the greatness of the village to which they both belonged. He also expressed his appreciation to Petelo for presenting his questions so as to educate the youth of Pukapuka.

Poyila was not completely sure of the whole story and asked for Petelo's help if he forgot any part of it. As he understood it, someone from Pukapuka had gone to a foreign island, where he found a bright red object. He then brought this back to Pukapuka. Because the person was from Ngake, the object eventually became associated with that village. In fact, it became another name for the village itself.

Petelo listened to Poyila carefully and courteously, but when he was finished, Petelo just stood there quietly, waiting for others to speak. Lavalua, the chairman of the 'Council of Important People' got up. He admitted that he was not sure what the term *kula* meant. Nonetheless, he doubted Poyila's explanation. As everyone knew, one of the old names for Ngake was Te Langai Kula, not Kula. Obviously, there was something wrong with the explanation. He thought he would turn his attention to the second of Petelo's questions, which seemed more interesting. *Kula pupuni* he felt referred to the child in the womb. He could not see; his eyes were closed (*pupuni*). *Kula moemoe* referred to the child just after he was born. Since the child slept a lot (*moemoe*), he was given this name.

Papu next stood up and spoke. Essentially, he agreed with Lavalua's answer, he said, though he had a few minor reservations about its completeness. Since the first question was obviously more difficult, he would focus on that one instead. He felt that *kula* dealt with a trip (*tele*) of some sort. At various times in his speech he expressed both definiteness and uncertainty concerning this assertion. For example, to paraphrase him, he stated, "For sure the word has something to do with a trip, that is certain. But I am not sure in what way. Perhaps it is a trip, perhaps it is something else. I am not sure. At least that is my opinion."

Petelo then rose to speak again. He urged people to think deeply about these questions. They dealt with the past that was being ignored by today's generation. Then he proceeded to debunk the definitions espoused by the chairman of the 'Council of Important People.' Lavalua, though making reasonable guesses Petelo said, was wrong. As a hint, he suggested that people think about the old chants to figure out what the terms meant.

He turned to me and asked me if I knew. He added that I should not worry about the terms *kula pupuni* and *kula moemoe* since they were not difficult. But did I know what *kula* meant? (His question must be seen in light of the fact that I had been interviewing him extensively for the past two weeks.) Having no idea, I said nothing.

Vave, a Yato 'chief,' then got up and spoke. He began by jokingly stating that the term *kula* referred to the color of cooked coconut crabs and meant the food at Ngake's feast. Various people smiled at the joke. The answer obviously was not that simple. Vave went on to express his general agreement with Papu that *kula* referred to a trip, but in a slightly different sense than what Papu suggested. It referred to the people who were involved in the trip.

As proof of his assertion, Vave offered the following phrase: *Kavea te kula ki olaanga*, which he translated into modern Pukapukan as *Kave te kula [or tele] ki Motu Kotawa, Ko, ma Uta*, 'Take the party of people to each of the publicly owned village reserves – Kotawa, Ko, and Uta.' *Olaanga*, in the sense of being life, he said, referred to the public reserves (*motu*), which gave people sustenance. These were the reserves that the 'Council of Important People' was now visiting. Hence Petelo's question was quite timely. (In my later private questioning of Vave, he admitted that the phrase did not come from an ancient chant but from a religious song he knew.)

Tengele, one of Loto's Island Council representatives, next stood up and said the questions were not really as difficult as people seemed to imply. In fact, they were quite simple. *Pula pupuni*, he said, was obvious. Papu looked up at Tengele and asked with a wry grin if Tengele meant *kula pupuni* or *pula pupuni*. Tengele, with an innocent smile, replied *pula pupuni*. *Pula pupuni* referred to a patch (*pula*) sewn on a piece of clothing to cover (*pupuni*) a hole. This brought several laughs. Tengele had obviously changed things around so that he could give a clever answer. Clearly, he was talking about something quite different from what Petelo meant.

Pula moemoe, Tengele continued, referred to someone who slept on a rough surface, such as gravel. Because the top of the head rubbed against the ground, the person gradually lost his hair. He became bald (*pula*). With an outstretched hand, he vaguely pointed in the direction of Poyila, who was partially bald. This brought even more laughs.

During these speeches, Petelo just listened. He took everything in but said nothing. Likewise, Kililua listened carefully to each speaker. Kililua seemed hesitant to speak himself, however. Molingi occasionally listened to the speeches, but she did not seem particularly interested in them. Though she laughed at Tengele's jokes, she was mainly absorbed in eating coconut crabs.

Akima, the chairman of the Island Council, next stood up. He made a brief statement thanking Ngake for its feast and presented the village with some money in an envelope. He completely sidestepped Petelo's questions. The next speaker did the same.

Then Petelo stood up again and explained what the terms meant. People had gotten confused, he said, because they had not examined the two questions properly. The *kula* of the first question was somewhat different from the *kula* of the second. In the first question, *kula* referred to something that the parents, the patrilineage (*po*), the localized patrilineal group (*yoolonga*), held very precious or dear (*wakaemaema*). The proof of this statement, he noted, lay in a phrase from the chant of Malo: *ngalo ai to tatou kula*. It meant in respect to the *po* that it was becoming extinct, that there were no more descendants to carry it on. *Kula pupuni* referred to when the child was born, when he came out of the mother's womb. The eyes were covered with blood and hence the baby could not see. *Kula moemoe* referred to a child when he was about five or six months old, when he began to recognize people. At this time, the child mainly ate and slept. He was not very much involved with people. Having thus answered his own questions, Petelo sat down.

Subsequently, several people stood up and gave speeches similar to Akima's. Some emphasized the puniness of Ngake's feast in comparison with the magnificent feasts their own villages had put on. Others briefly expressed their gratitude. But all gave a little money.

That night I asked Papu what he thought about Petelo's speech. He said that Petelo had been correct. As he elaborated on his answer, he stressed that Lavalua had been wrong. When I pointed out to him that he had basically agreed with Lavalua in public, he smiled. That, he said, had just been to be polite. Was Petelo right about the term *kula*? Papu suspected so because it fitted with some things his mother had told him when he was younger.

The next morning, at the second of the feasts, Kililua got up to speak. He said that he now wanted to reply to Petelo's questions. With a smile, he looked at Tengele and said that the term was *kula pupuni* not *pula pupuni*. It was meant to be a joke, but it did not come off because people were still too busy eating. (Kililua had gotten up too soon to speak. People did not seem intent on listening to him.)

Kula pupuni, Kililua said, referred to the child up to three or five days after birth. About this time the umbilical cord (*pito*) dropped off. Before this time, the umbilical cord must be covered – so that it would not become detached and cause bleeding. *Pupuni* referred to covering the umbilical cord. The term *kula*, in the sense of red, referred to blood. *Kula moemoe* concerned the period in the child's life when he slept most of the time – from just after birth to about six months, when the belly button (*pito*) and digestion were all right. The child got the name *kula moemoe* partly because he slept much of the time and partly because the child's skin was a bit reddish. Satisfied with his explanation, Kililua sat down. No one else got up and spoke – partly because everyone was engrossed in eating, partly because Petelo had already answered his own questions. People seemed to ignore Kililua's remarks.

A few days later, I asked Lavalua about Petelo's speech. He thought it was a fine idea to teach young people about the old traditions. But the sad thing about Petelo, Lavalua commented, was that he was now really too old. He was getting a bit senile. Take, for example, what Petelo had said regarding *kula pupuni* and *kula moemoe*. Lavalua felt that his own answers had been closer to the truth.

When I asked Tengele about Petelo's speech, he laughed at me. Go ask the people in Ngake, he told me. They knew. Kililua was a bit embittered by the fact that people had not listened more closely to what he had said, yet what could you do if they criticized you and did not want to listen? he asked. But he knew he was right. Petelo was wrong. Vave had a slightly different perspective. He was surprised by my question. Weren't everyone's answers exactly the same, he asked?

It is difficult to know what *kula*, *kula pupuni*, and *kula moemoe* mean in any definitive sense. There was a great deal of overlap, of course, in what various people said. *Kula pupuni* and *kula moemoe* concern the child around the time of birth and a few months thereafter, but as to details, people clearly differed. (The Beagleholes discuss the terms as well, 1938:233, if readers are interested in still another perspective.)

Public occasions such as these offer opportunities for people to learn. Supporting the atoll's egalitarian orientation, different people offer diverse views on a given subject. Listeners take it all in, avoiding the subordination that often occurs in other contexts. But the fact that divergent accounts exist means that the audience may well leave the meeting somewhat uncertain about who is correct. There are still ambiguities for people to resolve on their own afterwards.

The appearance of being knowledgeable

Pukapukans generally have a pragmatic orientation toward knowledge. They are interested in the application of knowledge to specific ends – to resolving problems faced in particular contexts, with particular audiences. To go beyond this pragmatic orientation, to a more correspondent sense of truth, clearly poses difficulties. Even if we assume that there is a single, correct answer to a problem, which well might not be the case, it is not immediately obvious how an individual might discover it. A Pukapukan would patiently have to seek out opportunities for indirectly asking knowledgeable elders about the matter. If the people queried did not all agree – which is quite likely – the individual would then be forced to choose among them on the basis of his or her own reasoning. And if the individual did discover what appeared to be the correct answer, it would not necessarily follow that others would accept it. They might criticize it as a matter of principle – just as the two high school students criticized Taputu's version of the Vakayala story.

Under such circumstances, it is often easier and more feasible to sidestep direct investigation and simply presume to know certain things – to assume, in spite of one's own limitations, the appearance of being knowledgeable. We already saw that Unu did not know how to lash the *tutuki* sticks, but he did not bother telling Tengele that. He bluffed his way through, just as several men did with the wrestling chants. They may not have known certain facts, but they knew how to disguise their ignorance.

What becomes important in Pukapuka is knowing how to appear knowledgable and how to display knowledge to others. What was significant about Petelo's speech was not just what Petelo said, but the manner in which he said it – how he used his knowledge. Petelo is a master at this. He defined the issues and used his manner to dominate the scene. Papu, Vave, and Lavalua were all drawn into competing on Petelo's terms. Only Tengele decided it would be more advantageous to compete on other terms. Kililua is certainly knowledgeable, but he did not have the presence, the charisma, to make his interpretations stick.

When Kililua privately complained to me one day that Petelo did not know everything there was to know about Pukapukan traditions, he was correct. Petelo does have gaps in his knowledge. (I know from all the questions I privately asked him.) But Petelo knows how to manipulate a situation to his advantage, choosing his terms, using his charisma. We may be in doubt as to what *kula*, *kula pupuni*, and *kula moemoe* mean and whether Petelo was correct, but we can certainly be impressed by a skill Petelo does possess. He is a master at the art of appearing to know in front of others.

4

Validating traditional knowledge
Pukapukan ways of knowing, Part II

For Pukapukans, uncertainty regarding aspects of the cultural past extends beyond the meaning of words such as *kula pupuni*. It includes a variety of traditional matters. At the end of most interviews, I asked informants to assess the validity of what they had told me concerning the past – the degree to which they felt their accounts were accurate. A surprising number voiced uncertainty in respect to one point or another. Here is a sample of what people said:

I am not really clear about this. . . . I just told you what I believed. Is there a person who can ascertain what I said to you is true? [He chuckles to himself.] (A man in his seventies)

Here is my way of ascertaining the truth of these ancient (*tawito*) things we have discussed. I listened to all the old people discuss these things . . . but was what they said true (*tika*) or not, we do not really know. (A woman in her late sixties)

A number of individuals expressed uncertainty regarding important aspects of traditional Pukapukan social organization. Most adults believe, for instance, that a group of patrilineally owned strips of land (*kawa*) running from the lagoon to the ocean side of the island traditionally existed within each village (cf. Beaglehole and Beaglehole 1938:41–2; Hecht 1976:76). Today, there is considerable confusion regarding the exact location of these strips.

The traditional boundaries between various strips of land (*kawa*) in Yato village puzzled me, and one day I went to see Yala about them. After some discussion on the subject, he referred me to two other people he thought knew more about the matter. The issue was a bit hazy in his mind, he said, and it would be better to ask people who really knew. (He incidentally expressed an interest in hearing what they told me.)
The first person Yala referred me to was an old man in his nineties. The man admitted that he himself was not completely sure of where the

boundaries were in Yato. What he recalled being told as a child was that the boundary between Walepia and Yaalongo *kawa* began along the entrance path to the minister's house. The other person Yala referred me to was a woman in her seventies. She, too, was unsure as to the exact boundaries, but she recalled being told the boundary between Walepia and Yaalongo *kawa* began elsewhere.

The two informants concurred about some of the boundaries we discussed, but they clearly disagreed about others.

When I told Yala about the matter, he smiled. Yes, it was puzzling, he admitted. He had heard the same types of assertions before. He clearly viewed them as discrepant and was not sure who to believe. He tended to side with the old man, however, more than the old woman. The old man's versions, he said, made a bit more sense.

Other people with whom I discussed the issue had an even vaguer idea of where the traditional boundaries were. Readers should note that this uncertainty does not derive from land disputes. At the general level at which my questions were phrased such disputes were not involved. Rather, people puzzled over how to apply an abstract construct regarding *kawa* to the specific context of Yato.

Traditionally, a relationship existed among patrilineally owned strips of land, cemeteries (*po*) on that land, and particular food-sharing units (*tuanga kai*) (as indicated in Chapter 2). Today, people in Yato recognize four main strips of land (Walepia, Yaalongo, Yayi, and Yamaunga) and six main cemeteries (Walepia, Yaalongo, Yamaunga or Malamalama, Ipui, Tokelau, and Maatanga).[1] So how many food-sharing units were there formerly in Yato? I asked this question of two men in their seventies. On the basis of what they claimed to have observed in their youth, these two men suggested two different answers. One said four (based on the four *kawa*), the other six (based on the six cemeteries). Both held the same cultural construct regarding the relation among the strips of land, cemeteries, and food-sharing units, but they differed in the way they applied the construct to the Yato context. Other people with whom I discussed the issue felt uncertain about the matter. A few suggested I see the two elderly men just mentioned. When I explained what they had said, people sometimes smiled. It made one wonder, several reflected, exactly how many food-sharing units traditionally existed in Yato.

It might be suggested that ambiguities such as these – the above being just a small sample of those recorded – were brought into focus by my asking people questions. That is true to a certain degree, particularly in the above example, but in several other cases this was not so. Take the following example as a case in point. It again involves the relation between patrilineally owned strips of land and cemeteries.

One afternoon, I was sitting with three men (who were in their thirties and forties) discussing the various cemeteries (*po*) in Pukapuka. The conversation became focused on Ovete cemetery because it seemed anomalous. Though located in Ngake village, some people suggested that it belonged to a patrilineage (*po*) in Yato. Others doubted this since traditionally cemeteries were generally affiliated with the patrilineally owned strips of land on which they were located.

Having respect for one of the men's fathers, I asked the man what his father thought about Ovete's affiliations. The man avoided answering my question, and the conversation continued on to some other aspect of the problem. As we talked about various people's opinions, the man then gave an indirect answer to my question. He said, "When you mention something to the old people, such as my father, they seem so vague. They just say, 'Maybe, it could be like that.' " He laughed a little and then added, "It just as well might not be. Who knows?"

Evaluating an account's validity

How, then, do Pukapukans go about determining the validity of assertions about the past?[2] Two of their general techniques involve examining the contexts and sources of various people's statements.

Evaluating the contexts and sources of one's information

One day the Australian teacher asked his form 5 high school class how they determined whether a person was telling the truth about an issue. Among the points the class stressed were the following: (1) the way the person looked at you, (2) the person's manner of talking, and (3) whether the person started joking with you. Adult Pukapukans, in informal conversations with me, often stressed similar points. Something about the style in which a statement was made, or something about the topic, tipped off the listener regarding the truth of an assertion. Tai expressed it as follows:

Sometimes it will be hard for me to decide, but at other times, I will just look at his attitude (*tu*) while he is talking – the way he speaks, the tone of his voice, how he said it. Because I know when a person jokes (or lies), he might turn around sort of [i.e., not look you straight in the face]. Or he might laugh slightly.

Pukapukans found it difficult to go beyond such generalizations in explaining the matter to me. It was something they just knew, they stated, something they learned through experience.

Another aspect of this topic – which no Pukapukans directly mentioned but which I observed several times – involved challenging other people's comments to see how they defended themselves. Maina, a field assistant in his forties, would occasionally do this while helping me with interviews. When informants answered certain questions, he would

Preparing for a feast

sometimes jokingly imply that they possessed a rather limited knowledge of the topic. When I questioned him about this, he replied that this was his way of checking to see if people were lying. He reasoned that if they did not defend themselves or did not elaborate on their answers, they probably felt uncertain. In fact, research supports Maina's position. It suggests that "the answer that shows more resistance to badgering is more likely to be accurate" (Bernard, Killworth, Kronenfeld, and Sailer 1984:510).

The emphasis on context in the preceding paragraphs fits well with a point stressed in Chapter 3. As with such words as *wua* and *teeti*, it is not just what a person states, but the context or milieu in which the statement is made that is important.

Pukapukans may also rely on a person's past record to evaluate the accuracy of his or her statements. Akima made this point one evening in a conversation we had:

> You will think about the nature of the person who told you something you question. . . . Initially we do not know what is really inside the mind (*manako*) of the person. Perhaps it is something true; perhaps it is something false (*pikikaa*). Consequently, for the initial time, we do not agree (*akatika*) to what he says [or actually we hold in doubt the validity of his assertions].
>
> The second of the times he may say . . . , "Rob has said to me to tell you to go to his place." But I do not go, because I do not trust (*ilinaki*) this person. Then I see you and you ask me, "Hey, why did you not come? I told so and so to go tell you to come." I reply, "I thought that that was just some sort of joke (*pikikaanga wua*) what he said." This is the second time the person has said something like this to me.
>
> Therefore, I realize that he is an honest person. If he says to me a different time, "So and so told me to tell you to go to him, for you to talk to him," I will believe what that person has said, because I am sure that he is an honest person (*e tangata talatala tika*). He is not a liar. But some other people . . . they just lie to you, they tell you lies.

Again and again I heard Pukapukans in conversations among themselves and with me invalidate someone's assertion, not on the merit of that person's views, but because of what he or she had said in the past.

Referring to recognized authorities

Pukapukans frequently assert that they accept the opinions of recognized authorities. One can see this in the way the form 5 schoolchildren resolved their argument regarding the destruction of Vakayala's testicles. They obtained the opinion of Molingi, someone viewed as an expert on legends. Yala suggested the same approach to me for delineating the *kawa* boundaries in Yato village: I should see people especially knowledgeable about the subject. I used this approach at times:

One day, after gathering some poles in Loto's public reserve for building the roof to my cook house, I stopped at a *pule* guardhouse to rest and talk with two of the guards. They were both women, one in her late thirties and the other in her late twenties. One thing led to another, and we started discussing whether it was the legendary figure Waletiale or Malangaatiale who possessed an enlarged penis. Both of them asserted that it was Malangaatiale. They admitted uncertainty as to exactly who Waletiale was but basically felt that he was another character entirely. I, however, asserted that Waletiale possessed the enlarged penis and that the legend of Malangaatiale concerned a man struck by lightning.

We discussed our differences of opinion for a while without coming to any agreement. Then the younger of the two women asked me how I knew my version of the two legends was correct. I replied that this was what several old people, especially Petelo and Molingi, had told me.

As I listened, they again discussed the issue between themselves. What I had said did not seem right to them, but then they themselves, they admitted, were not sure of either legend. Finally, they decided that I might indeed be right. Unlike them, I had discussed the issue with Petelo and Molingi, both recognized experts on Pukapukan legends.

Properly speaking, the category of recognized authorities is not limited to people. It also includes chants and published material on the island's past. As the discussion of *kula* and *kula pupuni* indicates, people use chants (*mako*) to buttress their arguments. In a group discussion with several informants, Molingi cited a chant to justify her definition of the word *matoyinga* (or 'village'; Beaglehole and Beaglehole 1938:231). "All the traditional words of Pukapuka are in these chants," she noted. "They are all inserted in the various chants; there are none that are not." Occasionally people also cite texts. The Beagleholes' (1938) ethnography was referred to several times, for example, in interviews as a valuable source of information on the atoll's traditions.

But the majority of Pukapukans clearly emphasize people in referring to recognized authorities. This is related, of course, to the oral nature of their culture. They possess few written records. They have limited access to materials in libraries or archives. Many chants are not immediately comprehensible to the majority of adults. To make sense of them, adults often need a knowledgeable elder's exegesis.

How, then, do Pukapukans decide which individuals to listen to, which individuals are recognized authorities? Fitting with the atoll's egalitarian orientation, each person decides that for himself. But Pukapukans have a general set of criteria. They involve an individual's background, the individual's public display of knowledge, and how others respond to the individual's ideas in group discussions.

Regarding matters of background, the form 5 high school students indicated that they trusted older informants more than younger ones in traditional matters. Elderly informants, they felt, had had an opportunity as children to listen to still older people. Also, the students suspected that those "contaminated" by Western ways, those having lived abroad, were less reliable in traditional matters than those who had resided on Pukapuka their entire lives.

Adults made similar remarks to me. In assessing an individual's competence, people often emphasized seniority in age:

They are the old people; they know all about such traditional things. (A woman in her midsixties)

They are the ones who listened to the old people who lived a really long time ago. (A woman in her late sixties)

An individual's genealogical background was also an important factor. Some informants were less knowledgeable about traditional matters, people told me, because their parents or grandparents came from other islands.

I had a group of Pukapukans collectively narrate the origin myth of their island (see Beaglehole and Beaglehole 1938:375–7). Afterward, I recorded one individual's rendition of it in the presence of the others. When the transcript was typed, I showed it to another informant. Upon reading it, he asserted that I had listened to a fool. The beginning of the story was Manihikian not Pukapukan.

Who, he asked, had told it to me? I explained that a particular individual had spoken the final version into the tape recorder, but in the presence of Molingi, Petelo, and Kililua (i.e., people well recognized as knowledgeable authorities on such matters). After a moment's reflection, he indicated that the narrator's ancestors had come from another island. He was not, he cautioned me, that well versed in Pukapukan traditions.

It is relevant to add here, in discussing matters of background, that Pukapukans say very little about ascribed social position. No one in Pukapuka, for example, is knowledgeable primarily because he is a chief. In accord with broader Polynesian patterns, seniority and general genealogical status are important (cf., Firth 1970:62–3; Oliver 1974:784), but so are an individual's own experiences.

Exploring further, one can perceive elements of Pukapukan status rivalry in the way Pukapukans assess the matter of seniority. Two informants in their seventies, Petelo and Molingi, were viewed as the most knowledgeable people on the island during my stay. In survey after survey, they always came out on top. But in these surveys they were also the people most criticized for being too old or senile! In a survey dealing with traditional forms of social organization, for example, seventeen people (out of a sample of thirty informants) cited Petelo as being extremely knowledgeable on the subject. Ten cited Molingi. (The next closest individual was cited five times.) But five individuals in the survey criticized Petelo for being inaccurate, forgetful, and too old to remember things correctly. Four did the same for Molingi. (The next closest person was cited twice.) Most of those who voiced these criticisms were slightly younger people in their fifties and sixties who felt they knew just as much as Petelo and Molingi.

We can perceive the atoll's egalitarian orientation at work here. The position of a knowledgeable authority is not inherited. It is open to a variety of Pukapukans. And achieving recognition as an authority does not necessarily increase one's status in the eyes of the general community. One's immediate juniors may often become more critical, in fact, may often accuse one of senility, in an effort to affirm their own competence.

Turning from matters of background, how individuals display knowledge to others is extremely important in assessing their competence. Knowledgeable people, according to Pukapukans, display what they know openly and coherently. They are not evasive or ambiguous in answering questions. In an informal conversation Vave stated a point that several other people made as well:

Some people, they just talk about nothing (*talatala wua*). They do not put things in the right order (*ko ye akapapa wakalelei*) inside their mind. If the individual talks about the subject in question, the other person will get angry. The individual just talks away. . . . But the intelligent people, they do not talk like fools. He would look (or think) carefully about what to tell the person, he will seek out the appropriate words, so that the other person will be happy, so that the other person will listen carefully.

A large number of people suggested that knowledgeable informants presented information in public that others did not know. For example:

The reason I say Paani is really good in regard to chants is because he possesses knowledge of all the things that are gone today, some things that I do not know. (A man in his sixties)

They can tell all the old stories. Some other people just sit around like coral heads when the time comes to tell tales. (A man in his seventies)

An interesting variation of this theme is related to asking questions (comments reinforce a point already made):

These knowledgeable people have held onto [or not forgotten] what they learned. . . . But other people, who are ignorant, they have to ask questions. (Petelo)

People come to me and ask about something they have forgotten. That is how I know they are not knowledgeable. (Yolo)

The form 5 high school class stressed two criteria regarding knowledgeability that one might include under this general heading. First, the students indicated that people were knowledgeable if they were good at the work they performed. By way of illustration, several of them mentioned two men skilled at building canoes. Second, the students focused on how people responded to questions. Knowledgeable people not only answered a particular question in depth but also included other relevant points. When they talked about a legend, for example, they described how the legend was related to other tales not specifically asked about.

A third factor Pukapukans use in assessing knowledgeability – in addition to background and displays of knowledge – concerns an individual's interaction with others in a group. The students in the form 5 class, for example, asked whether the person took a prominent role in discussions. Did others seem to accept what he or she said? Did they defer to the individual? Perceptively, the students noted that it was far less certain that a particular individual was knowledgeable if he or she discussed matters with only a limited number of people. The real test came when many people were present for a discussion, when the individual opened himself up to criticism from numerous peers.

Related to this criteria, Pukapukans often deduce that something is true if no disputes arise among the parties involved in discussing an issue. One morning while talking with a man in his thirties, for example, I raised the question of how he knew that the patrilineages (*po*), matrimoieties (*wua*), and *Akatawa* actually worked in the past as people today claimed they did. That, he replied, was easy. When modern Pukapukans revived these organizations (see Chapter 5), each one turned out properly. There had been no disputes among the parties involved. Molingi enunciated the same perspective during a lengthy interview regarding the island's traditional social organization. I asked her why she believed that in former times women controlled taro swamps (*loto-uwi*) and men the "dry" land and coconut trees (*lungaa-wenua ma naa niu*). She replied, "They did not like to fight about rights to swamps in the olden days; fights did not erupt over such issues. That is why I believe it to be so." The point of these remarks is that social harmony often implicitly suggests validity. Or to phrase it another way, truth resides in the consensus of the community (cf. Errington 1984:107; Levin 1978a:5–6; Silverman 1971:322). One might note that, again, research supports this perspective. Data suggest that groups may collectively possess better recall than single individuals (see, e.g., Bernard et al. 1984:510).

In examining how Pukapukans assess a person's competency in matters of tradition, we have discussed several reasonable and, in some cases, rather astute criteria for assessing knowledgeability. But these criteria have shortcomings, and it is important for readers to realize what they are. One problem concerns the fact that people do not always recognize the same authorities. The form 5 schoolchildren resolved (with some limited exceptions) the argument regarding Vakayala's testicles because most children accepted Molingi as the authority on the matter. But what would have happened if more children had seriously challenged

Molingi's competence or someone like Petelo had disagreed with her?
Incidents such as the following frequently occurred on the atoll during
my stay. (This anecdote was told to me by the Australian teacher.)

One day after school, two form 5 schoolboys had a dispute over the
legendary character Lingutaemoa (see Beaglehole ms. b). The first asserted
that Lingutaemoa was a man, the second that Lingutaemoa was a woman.
They argued back and forth for a while without coming to any resolution.
    The next day, when they saw each other again, they continued their
argument, but this time, each of them had checked with people they viewed
as recognized authorities on traditional matters. The first boy had discussed
the question with his father – someone he trusted because several people had
asserted that his father was knowledgeable about such things. The second boy
had discussed it with his 'mother' – whom he felt was knowledgeable because
she had lived with one of the Beagleholes' now-deceased informants.
    Yet, again, nothing was resolved. The two knowledgeable sources
disagreed. The first boy's father said that Lingutaemoa was a man; the
second boy's 'mother' claimed that Lingutaemoa was a woman.

Both boys cited authoritative sources in their argument, but since neither
boy accepted the other source as more knowledgeable than his own,
the issue could not be resolved. This is what also happened in the
discussion of *kula* and *kula pupuni*. No clear consensus developed because some participants refused to accept Petelo as the undisputed authority on the subject.
    It is in the face of such difficulties that group discussions become
particularly important. Because respected individuals can collectively
argue about an issue until a consensus develops, group discussions offer
the best hope for resolving various issues. Most Pukapukans agree on
this, but again there is a problem. How does one determine whether a
consensus exists? Some people may agree overtly – to be amicable –
while in fact covertly disagreeing. As emphasized in Chapter 2, Pukapukans live on a small coral atoll, and maintaining harmonious social
relations can be extremely important – far more crucial, in fact, than
winning a debate.
    Take the following illustration as a case in point. After interviewing
eighty people on a topic, I generally held small group meetings attended
by recognized authorities on the subject. During one meeting concerning
legends, the same type of status rivalry arose between Petelo and Kililua
as it had in the *kula moemoe* discussion and in the informal chanting
practice. But this time, after several initial comments, Kililua remained
silent. To most Pukapukans if an individual does not voice opinions to
the contrary in public meetings, the implication is that he or she concurs
with, or at least accepts, what others say. The next day I asked Kililua
why he had not said more, since I knew, from earlier conversations with

him, that he disagreed with several opinions expressed in the meeting.
(Our discussion occurred in the presence of three other people.)

Kililua noted how senile some of the older people had been last night. They
had not seemed to know very much; they had made numerous mistakes. In
voicing these criticisms, he kept his comments on a general level, never
mentioning anyone by name.

   When asked why he had not spoken up more often during the meeting, he
smiled. He replied that he had not wanted to interfere with the others. He
had been curious to see what they actually knew. He had been content
simply to observe their mistakes.

   Thus a problem can arise with group discussions. Having people come
together in a group may bring about some resolution or consensus –
especially if Pukapukans perceive the need for doing so. Everyone then
overtly agrees on the issues involved. But the resulting consensus may
be a false one. Underneath the surface, people may still disagree.

Relying on one's own impressions and experiences

It is in the face of such problems and Pukapukan concerns over status
that adults often rely on their own experiences and their own reasoning.
It is easier and less humiliating to do so. It also affirms their competence
as knowledgeable authorities. A significant number of people referred
to their own experiences – to what they had observed or indirectly heard
people say – in discussing the way they validated assertions about the
past. Here is a sample of people's comments:

The reason I am certain about the things I am telling you is because they are
things I saw with my own eyes . . . that is why I am telling you them because I
saw them . . . and learned about them. The things I did not see, I am
uncertain about. (Paani)

You have asked me several questions and I have told to you what knowledge
I have acquired during my lifetime. (A man in his midsixties)

   If we closely examine Pukapukans working through various problems,
we frequently see individuals reasoning things out on their own:

One day, after Yolo and I had heard Petelo, Molingi, and Kililua discuss the
matrilineal origin myth (see Beaglehole and Beaglehole 1938:221–4), I
listened to Yolo trying to resolve out loud certain ambiguities in the story.
He believed that the story was true – in the sense that it accurately portrayed
events that had occurred in the past. But he was confronted with a problem.
The story asserted that people had changed into animals. He doubted this
ever occurred.

   He reasoned that the change of humans into animals was really a matter of
figurative language. He suggested that perhaps the survivors of the storm
decided to commemorate the memory of their brethren who had drowned by
giving them special names. Since the survivors were physically small (in
relation to those who drowned) they called their deceased brethren by the
names of large sea creatures (such as whales and sharks). To commemorate

their own survival, they named additional groups after small land creatures (such as rats and birds).

Later, when I heard Yolo tell the story to some children, this is the explanation he offered for the transformation of humans into animals.

One afternoon, while sitting on the porch of Tukia's house, he and I discussed how Pukapukans go about determining a recognized authority. A portion of the conversation follows:

[If you wanted to find out who was knowledgeable about a particular subject, what would you do?] I would go and ask an old person who I thought might know certain things. I could tell just by testing him.

[How would you know which questions to ask and how would you know if the answers were correct?] By just asking him some of the old tales (*tala*) or names that I personally knew from the past. Some people you can ask them any name and they will tell you the story about the person. That means he is a knowledgeable person about the past.

[How do you know he is not just making it up?] Because I know about the names I ask him. Say, if it is the name of one of the people in one of the tales that I normally know, that everybody knows, if he tells me something different from what everybody else knows, then I know he does not know it, that he is not a very clever person, that he has little knowledge.

As many Pukapukans do, Tukia validates the corpus of a person's knowledge by the part he himself understands. The approach makes considerable sense, but a difficulty exists. If a person's account differs from what another individual already knows, does it necessarily represent ignorance? Could it not be knowledge the individual lacks?

In some cases this problem may be alleviated because several people repeat the same story. As one knowledgeable elder phrased it:

I am not really sure on this point, is it correct or is it false. But here is what makes me certain, when the third person tells me this, I become certain. If it is only one person, I am not really sure. (Yolo)

This was a point made by the form 5 class as well. If several people told you the same legend, most likely it was correct.

A person might also mention something that jogs your memory, stating something that you recall having heard a long time ago but recently had forgotten. I asked Petelo one day, for example, why he thought Molingi was knowledgeable. He said, "If I ask her about things that I have forgotten, she sets me right; she tells me them again. That is how I know."

Still, a problem exists. As D'Andrade (1974), Hunter (1964), E. Loftus (1979), and Yarmey (1979) caution, people's memories can be vague and fluid. Loftus and Loftus state:

A person often remembers only parts of . . . [certain] material, and . . . tends to construct other bits and pieces in order to have a coherent story. That is, given that a few facts are remembered, other facts are constructed that are consistent with what is remembered. (1976:118)

In my opinion, Pukapukans' memories in such cases are often vague enough to allow for a variety of interpretations. People remember experiences from the past in light of what seems plausible to them today.

Can I prove that all Pukapukans do this? No, I cannot. But a detailed analysis of a few Pukapukans' behavior leads me to believe that the phenomenon is fairly prevalent. The following examples illustrate the type of data that support this assertion.

The story of Wutu (see Beaglehole ms. b:1021–3) is as popular today as it was during the Beagleholes' fieldwork.[3] It involves a character who is captured by ghosts (or gods) and is carried off by them in a wooden bowl (*kumete*). The individual subsequently defecates in the bowl to such an extent that he fills it with feces. Finally, the feces splash all over the ghosts when the bowl falls (or is thrown) down. Stated in this form, the story could easily be recognized by both the Beagleholes' and my own informants.

But there are two serious complications. First, the ghosts sing a chant as they carry Wutu along in the bowl. The chant, though generally intelligible to the Beagleholes' informants, is now altered to such an extent that only a few parts can be understood by modern Pukapukans. Second, various important details have changed since the Beagleholes' time. Whereas the exact location of the story was unclear before, most people agree today that it occurred at Motu Ko. Whereas before, Wutu's fate was ambiguous, today everyone asserts that he escaped. Whereas before, the story vaguely implied that Wutu was being punished for some sort of sexual impropriety, today the ghost's desire for food explicitly motivated his capture.

I asked Paleula one day to tell me the story. He included the main elements noted above plus the fact that Wutu escaped. He knew parts of the chant but not what they meant. During the next several weeks, we together listened to several tapes of people telling me their versions of the story. One of the first stories he heard was that told by a man in his sixties. This version, Paleula said, was exactly how he had remembered the tale being told when he was young. Everything was correct – from Wutu being on Motu Ko, to the ghosts planning to eat Wutu, to all the words of the chant. The only thing the man had forgotten, Paleula noted, was the reason Wutu had been on Motu Ko in the first place.

But as Paleula listened to more and more versions, he became less sure that the man's version was the right one and that it was the version he had heard when he was young. There was a logical contradiction the man had not explained. If Wutu had been at Matawea on Motu Ko, how could he have escaped and run to the main island (Wale)? He would have had to run right past the ghosts to get there. It was a contradiction that occurred in many of the accounts. It did not make sense to him. (He recalled that the version he had heard when he was young had made sense.)

Eventually, Paleula decided that Kililua's version was the correct one because it explained what Wutu was doing on Motu Ko and how he ran back to Wale. (Kililua said Wutu had been staying at Matautu, not Matawea.) It was this version, Paleula came to believe, that he had probably heard as a child.

What about the chant? That, he admitted, really puzzled him. In comparing the different versions, he decided that Molingi's was the correct one because more of the words made sense to present-day Pukapukans. He vaguely remembered Molingi, in fact, telling him the chant this way when he was young.

A similar pattern occurred in the story of Malangaatiale. In an initial interview, Paani had little recollection of the tale. But when he heard one or two people's accounts, it all came back to him – until he began hearing the contradictions in the versions. Then, on the basis of what he remembered, he tried to reconstruct (what he viewed as) the correct one. After thinking about the various accounts, Paani decided that Petelo was correct on one issue because he provided a more detailed explanation than did several others. He decided that Molingi was correct on another matter because what Petelo said did not make sense to him. Few people did that today, so why, he mused aloud to me, would they have done it in the past?

One can see in both these cases that informants' vague memories allowed for various interpretations. Some interpretations might go beyond the pale of general acceptability – Wutu capturing the ghosts certainly would not be recognized as part of the story. But within limits, various interpretations were possible.

In relying on their own opinions, Pukapukans often extrapolate (as noted) from a limited corpus of data, about which they possess some knowledge, to a far broader corpus of data, about which they lack information. My field notes contain numerous examples of this process, but as the following case illustrates this technique also presents certain problems.

Most people believe that Yaalongo *kawa* (or 'strip of land') was at one time owned by a single apical ancestor (cf. Beaglehole and Beaglehole 1938:230). No living Pukapukan (whom I interviewed), however, could substantiate this assertion. Many could substantiate selected parts of it. Several people provided me with detailed genealogies showing that at one time various sections of Yaalongo did indeed belong to a single individual. Figures 2 and 3 illustrate such cases. On the basis of these kinds of data, people made deductions as to the whole organization of Yaalongo *kawa*.

There are good reasons for doing so. As already noted, it is difficult for Pukapukans to collect certain types of genealogies. Few people casually describe in public genealogies related to their land claims for fear that others may try to claim the land as well. As a result, many people's genealogical knowledge is limited. They mainly know about sections they themselves have a stake in or about others they have heard people discuss.

Moving from what Pukapukans assert about Yaalongo *kawa* to what I deduce from my own research, one can see the problems associated with generalizing from limited cases. My data show that perhaps only three-fifths of the land sections within what might be termed Yaalongo *kawa* (see Map 3) fit the asserted pattern.

Approximately one-fifth of the land and swamps in Yaalongo *kawa* can be traced to the apical ancestor Koulangi, but Koulangi is the reputed founder of Tokelau cemetery (*po*) in Yayi *kawa*, the strip of land abutting Yaalongo to the east. His position as the apical ancestor of land in Yaalongo *kawa* is problematic at best within the above construct. Perhaps Koulangi shared some kinship relationship with Tualei (the person who reputedly reconstituted Yaalongo patrilineage after a devastating hurricane struck the island roughly four hundred years ago). But if he did, nobody that I have ever talked to knows about it. Except for Toa's suggestion that some of Koulangi's ancestors lie buried under a frangipani tree in Walepia cemetery, Koulangi's ancestry is a complete mystery to everyone on the island. The relation among the sections representing the other fifth of the *kawa* is unclear at best. It is too ambiguous for Pukapukans or myself to make sense of in any coherent way that fits into the pattern of the *kawa*'s other sections.

My point is that problems exist in generalizing from a limited, non-random sample. In the above case, numerous examples beautifully illustrate Pukapukans' abstract formulation of the *kawa*'s organization, but there are too many anomalies to say that the pattern fits the *kawa* as a whole. Since most Pukapukans cannot collect all the data I obtained, they make reasonable deductions. From what they do know, they make inferences as to what the rest of the data must be like. (They presume that the unknown corresponds in some manner to the known.) It is, in my opinion, a very reasonable assumption. But on the basis of data I obtained, it turns out to be partially incorrect. Making reasonable deductions does not necessarily guarantee that the resulting conclusions are valid.

Pukapukan ways of knowing

Learning and validating styles in cultural context

Turning to more general points (as a way of summarizing themes discussed in Chapters 3 and 4), we can perceive two distinct tendencies in Pukapukan ways of knowing.[4] On the one hand, a hierarchical tendency emphasizes subordination to authority and imitation of it. On the other, a more egalitarian tendency stresses independence and personal experience. Pukapukans defer to those older and more knowledgeable than themselves. They observe and imitate their behavior. But at the same time they question the competence of these people, challenge them, and emphasize their own perspectives.

It is important to realize that these themes are not simply Pukapukan. They belong to a general Polynesian pattern. When I state that knowledge is used by Pukapukans in status rivalries with their peers, for example, R. Firth (personal communication 1984) notes that "this could [as well] be a description of Tikopia" (a Polynesian outlier in the Solomons). Both Marcus (1978,1989) and Shore (1982) comment on parallel themes for other Polynesian islands.

In Pukapuka, the egalitarian orientation clearly prevails over the hierarchical one. This is related, of course, to the fact that the island is a coral atoll. Pukapuka lacks the resources and hierarchies of higher Polynesian islands (see Sahlins 1958). Most adults freely assert their opinions at meetings, concurring or disagreeing with others as they see fit. Recall that Petelo openly debunked the explanation offered by the chairman of the 'Council of Important People' during the *kula moemoe* discussion. He chose to criticize the chairman, in fact, rather than two other speakers. In this context, knowledge does not derive simply from high-status individuals. It is negotiated between the audience and various speakers as they challenge and affirm one another's perspectives (cf. Duranti 1985).

Though status rivalries are extremely important on the atoll and play a role in most social interactions, one should not ignore the significance of cooperation or people's concern for social harmony. People rarely push their rivalries with one another to the point of permanently breaching social relations. Despite all the rhetoric, most conflicts tend to remain muted. Competition is not allowed to disrupt communitywide concerns.[5]

The fact that there are many opportunities to observe and practice basic skills means that formal instruction need not constitute the primary style of education. This is especially so given the atoll's limited specialization of skills. What the Beagleholes stated more than forty years ago holds true today: "The amount of specialization in Pukapukan economic life is small. Every man considers himself able to perform adequately most male duties, and every woman considers herself a good enough cook or mat platter" (1938:47). Given the repetitive nature of the daily cycle, children have a great deal of opportunity to observe and perfect various skills. And because the population is culturally homogeneous, there is not as great a need as there is in the United States for a formal educational structure to instill a common set of values.

Finally, the oral nature of the atoll's traditions allows for flexibility in the formulation and presentation of knowledge. Disputes and uncertainties abound regarding which is or is not the correct view. Since no absolute point of reference exists, except that agreed to by the community at large, Pukapukans often creatively transform ambiguities of the past into plausible accounts of the present.

On the organization of Pukapukan knowledge

How do Pukapukan ways of knowing affect their construction of the past? Elements of diversity, ambiguity, and creativity seem to play a far greater role in Pukapukan formulations than in anthropological accounts.[6] We can see this by reflecting on several points already made.

Pukapukan education focuses on informally observing and listening to others. Because people differ in what they often observe or hear, diverse accounts of the atoll's cultural traditions often develop. Lima's and Unu's lashings of the outrigger differed, for example, because they drew different conclusions regarding how Tengele did his lashing underneath a joint. One made a diagonal before going under the bottom piece; the other did not. If Tengele had specifically instructed them or if they had watched more closely (rather than being concerned about not feeling too subordinate), this might not have occurred. Also, because adults ask questions indirectly, they do not always find out exactly what they want to know. They have to infer for themselves the meaning of someone's comment or where its significance lies. The fact that Pukapukan status rivalries pervade public discussions means that no real group consensus may develop on matters of tradition. Petelo, Kililua, and Vave, we noted, all came away with differing opinions regarding the meanings of *kula* and *kula pupuni*. The prevalence of diversity in Pukapuka should not be seen as something anomalous. A variety of social scientists, working from a diverse set of perspectives – from psychology (e.g., Cavalli-Sforza, Feldman, Chen, and Dornbusch 1982), from folklore (e.g., Finnegan 1977; Lord 1960), and from anthropology (e.g., Brunton 1980; Hays 1976; Mathews 1983; Wallace 1961) – emphasize the same point. Diversity is a significant element in the organization of cultural knowledge.

Still, this does not mean that there are no constraints on diversity. Because learning occurs within situationally relevant contexts, the number of interpretations people might make is limited. Such words as *wua* and *paapaa* are meaningful only within specified contexts. The meaning of *wua* depends on the context of the sentence. That of *paapaa* is more dependent on the age of the speaker. People often learn about a place in the process of going there, or children learn a fish name as they hear the fish being talked about.

Through repetition, experiences that may be poorly grasped initially become better understood over time. Lima did not learn to hew an outrigger from the single occasion he did it before working with Tengele. As the examples regarding the chants and dance practices illustrate, people learn these things with time, with practice. Repetition also enables people to grasp common themes underlying apparent diversity. Children often hear different versions of the same legend on separate occasions, but because common elements arise each time they hear it, they learn what different versions have in common, what the legend's basic form is.

Ridicule and challenges put limits on what constitutes publicly acceptable variation. People do not want to seem ignorant or foolish in public, so within reason, they often give the same sorts of answers. Throughout the discussion of *kula* and *kula pupuni* there was a common thread with slight variations. No one presented a totally different account. There might have been others at the feast who had different opinions, but they preferred not to say anything in public. The example of Toa illustrates that people may know each other for years and never broach a topic of common interest. And we saw in the first chapter that people may espouse one opinion in private and concur with a different one in a public group.

It is important to remember that many Pukapukans are uncertain or unclear about a variety of traditional matters. They do not know the exact number of food-sharing units formerly existing in Yato, why the Ngake cemetery of Ovete has a tie to a Yato patrilineage, or what the precise meaning of *kula pupuni* is. Only gradually, through time, do they reach some kind of resolution in such matters – if they reach one at all. Paleula provided me with a hypothetical example of this point:

Perhaps someone comes and says, "Hey, so and so got a telegram stating that so and so died in Rarotonga." A Pukapukan died in Rarotonga. He did not clarify the details about how this happened and so on. He does not know. He does not ascertain all these things (*e ye papu meitaki*) to you. Then after that, some other person comes and asks you, "Is this true that so and so died?" You say to him, "I am uncertain (*kei*). I do not know but so and so told me that this person had died." I do not really know. Perhaps he died, perhaps not . . . I wait until I am certain (*papu*). You heard it a long time before, but you are not sure if it is true or not.

But a long time after, you will discover that what was said was true. Likewise, a long time after you will discover that it was just a bunch of lies (*ni pikikaanga wua*). That is the way it goes.

People often create their own accounts from what they hear or observe. We saw this with Yolo, Paleula, and Paani in their interpretations of myths. As Yolo confided to me one day, "In some cases where there are mistakes [or misinterpretations], I just throw those parts away."

Take the case of Tai as an illustration of this creativity. I interviewed Tai before and after he assisted me in a survey dealing with Pukapukan myths:

His initial interview indicated that he possessed a rather limited knowledge of the Wutu story. Later, after we had listened to more than thirty informants tell us the story, I asked Tai one evening what he thought of the versions we had heard together. He noted that people told a variety of accounts regarding where the ghosts intended to carry Wutu. He felt, however, that the majority of the people agreed with what he viewed as the correct version – that the ghosts were carrying Wutu to a place called Te Aumaloa. This surprised me considerably. I recalled no one ever telling the story this way. In discussing the matter with him, he did not mention specific individuals by name, but he conveyed the clear impression that many people told the legend in such a manner. The version he suggested made considerable sense, but when I checked over the accounts we had heard together, none of them mentioned the ghosts carrying Wutu to Te Aumaloa.

In spite of what he said, Tai had constructed – either consciously or unconsciously – his own version of the story and clothed it in an authoritative rhetoric.

Maina's case is similar. I interviewed Maina as I had Tai, before and after he assisted me in a survey:

Maina felt that he had done much better in the postsurvey interview identifying Pukapukan material artifacts than in the presurvey one. I asked him why. He explained that he had initially felt unsure of several answers. When he listened carefully, however, to what various recognized authorities (such as Petelo, Molingi, and Kililua) said in their interviews and compared their accounts, he noted that they were all identical. He knew, as a result, that they must be correct. All this makes good sense, but although in some ways the accounts Maina mentioned did overlap, they did not overlap completely – a point that was readily evident from comparing their protocols. Nor were all the answers Maina gave identical with the answers of these authorities.

Maina, too, had created his own account and clothed it in an authoritative rhetoric.

Creativity exists in public performances as well as in private or semi-private reflections. Pukapukans put on plays about their native traditions – both for enjoyment and to instruct the young in their island's past. Before the first play rehearsal began for the legend of Malotini in 1979, Vave, the director, outlined the main plot. He mentioned briefly that Malotini had gotten in trouble and had been killed after coming back from fishing. With each rehearsal thereafter, the play took on more color. Whereas there had initially been ambiguity about what trouble he had gotten into, his lechery with married women gradually became more and more prominent because it made the play humorous. Whereas initially Vave claimed that Malotini had been out fishing by himself, it was later decided that he had been with a *tanganga* (or age-mate fishing group) because someone remembered the term and more people could be included in the play.

The point I want to emphasize is one that many scholars have made: People creatively synthesize materials in formulating their accounts of the past (see, e.g., Burke 1978; Finnegan 1977; Irvine 1978; Linnekin 1983, 1985). As Lord states, "The picture that emerges is not really one of conflict between preserver of tradition and creative artist; it is rather one of the preservation of tradition by the constant re-creation of it" (1960:29).[7]

Pragmatic, dynamic aspects of Pukapukan knowledge. It is one thing to state that Pukapukan traditional knowledge contains significant elements of diversity, ambiguity, and creativity. It is another to find a suitable perspective from which to describe them. Scribner makes an important point in discussing how social scientists represent knowledge.

There is debate whether knowledge is best represented as a semantic network (Anderson 1976), a script (Schank and Abelson 1977), or a categorical structure (Rosch 1975). Other researchers study how knowledge is used in intellectual tasks; for example, in speech understanding (Reddy and Newell 1974) or story comprehension (Stein and Glenn 1979). Still others try to characterize the mental models underlying complex behavior, such as in ... chess-playing (Chase and Simon 1973). These approaches to the study of knowledge have many accomplishments to their credit. But the dominant image they present of the human knower resembles closely that of a computer: This knower is an intelligent system with a storehouse of knowledge and a set of programs, performing tasks in isolation. The knower neither interacts with other people nor engages in transactions with the environment. The question we are addressing here – how knowers use their knowledge to get about the world and accomplish things – fails to arise as a central theoretical question (1985:199).

Anthropological analyses of the past two decades, particularly those associated with ethnoscience and formal semantic analysis, have had to face this issue. Hutchins comments, "It seems that the search for representations of what people know, as exemplified by the ethnoscience tradition in anthropology, got into trouble largely because it ignored the processes of how people go about knowing" (1980:11). Quinn and Holland (1987:14) observe, "Formal semantic analysis did not uncover the cultural models that individuals invoked for the performance of ... naturally-occurring cognitive tasks ... but gave only such partial and selective glimpses of those models as had come to be embedded in the lexical structure." Clement (1982), Crick (1982a), and Frake (1977) make similar remarks.

Pukapukan knowledge is not simply an abstract body of facts. It is shaped by use, by contextual and pragmatic considerations. People's assertions, for example, are often context specific. This may not be readily apparent when we listen to Pukapukans talk. In the abstract, absolute statements abound. People often talk as if context and use were not relevant factors in either the formulation or the presentation of knowledge. Many Pukapukans believe as a matter of principle that people should not adjust their views to contingencies of the moment; it connotes a certain weakness of character. But as Shore notes about Samoa, "The apparently absolute judgements made are absolute only in relation to their contexts. What is lacking is a privileged moral viewpoint outside any social context" (1982:191).

Looking at how people use their knowledge to convey certain impressions, we can perceive this context-specific quality. During a survey in June 1978, for example, I asked an informant in Yato if, since he lacked a radio of his own, he listened to someone else's:

He said no. He added that he was not really interested in such things. About a year later, I again asked him the same question and got the same answer. The second time he commented, "Whose radio would I listen to anyway?" When I explored this comment a little further it unintentionally took on the implication that he did not listen to the radio because he lacked friends. Well then, it turned out that he did listen to a radio after all. He even provided me with a list of friends' houses at which he listened.

Another informant strongly emphasized that ancestral ghosts punished Pukapukans who improperly changed their designated burial locations. The informant knew this, he said, because it had happened to two individuals, whom he named. Later, in discussing a matter related to Christian doctrine, he added that whereas some believed in ghosts he did not.

Such statements, taken out of context, seem contradictory. One cannot both listen and not listen to the radio, believe and not believe in ghosts, at the same time. Yet they are much less contradictory when we examine the contexts in which each statement was made. In both cases, the individuals were conveying a sense of their own competence and status within the community. As the contexts in which they affirmed this competence changed, so did their assertions. Take the case of ghostly retribution, for example. The individual's assertion about ghosts is a common one, well supported by a majority of the atoll's population. Few would disagree with it. But in discussing Christianity, which denigrates a belief in ghosts, he asserts a different position – one that emphasizes his status as a Christian.

The Pukapukan tendency to focus on context-specific aspects of knowledge fits with a much broader Polynesian orientation. Among Polynesians, Shore notes, there is a general tendency to define "entities in terms of their relationship to a local context rather than in terms of intrinsic features" (n.d.). Seen from afar, this tendency may appear to stand in sharp contrast to one we view as our own. Yet we, too, possess a similar tendency, though our rhetoric tends to obscure that fact. Politicians, for example, frequently adjust what they say to suit different audiences; so do salesmen. For both, it is part of being effective in their jobs. Anthropologists, too, often display a sensitivity to context. Comments made to one audience may not be made to another. Opinions espoused in private may differ from those asserted in public. The difference here is that we are well aware of the contexts in which these statements are made and live with them on a day-to-day basis. They are implicit in our understanding of what people say – whereas the contexts are not implicit to us when we listen to Pukapukans. Though there may be differences of degree between Polynesians and Westerners, for both of us contextual considerations shape the way we present knowledge to others.

It is important to realize that Pukapukans do not simply respond passively to situations. They actively redefine contexts (or relevant aspects of them) in their discussions. They manipulate them to their advantage. Take the following illustration as a case in point. At a Loto village meeting in July 1980, the question came up as to when the men would replace the women in guarding the public reserve (Motu Uta). According to village law, male and female *pule* alternately guard the reserve for six months of each year (cf. Beaglehole and Beaglehole 1938:36; Hecht 1976:22). At first the discussion leaned toward letting the men take over right away, but then the village secretary noted that, because of the transition from the *Akatawa* back to the village system, the women had guarded the reserve only since March, not January.

A man stood up and stated that what the secretary had said was true – the women had not as yet finished their six months of duty. In spite of what the women had tried to imply, careful analysis of the situation proved otherwise. He thought the best thing to do was to follow the village laws. Since the law specified six months for the women, they should do it for six months. When they had fulfilled their obligations, the men would gladly take over.

A woman stood up and addressed, as she phrased it, a point of clarification to the whole audience. She said she was not talking about anything very hard. Guard duty was, in fact, simple and often fun. The village law said six months and six months had passed since the New Year. Consequently the men should take over. That was the law and it should be followed.

The conversation went on like this for some time. No one disagreed about the village law or how long the women had been guarding the reserve. What they disagreed about was which facts were relevant to the issue. Different people emphasized different ones depending on the position they wished to support.

The fluid, dynamic character of Pukapukan knowledge claims can also be seen in Pukapukan traditions. If we simply listen to what people affirm in the abstract, the unchanging character of these traditions seems obvious. Traditional knowledge, Pukapukans assert, is drawn from the past. Such assertions have a social value, of course. They affirm the continuity, the enduring quality, of Pukapukan knowledge. The present community, its beliefs and organization, are grounded in tradition. "In Polynesian history," Shore notes, "the past and present are not so much sequential chapters in a linear plot, as they are organically linked aspects of a continuum" (n.d.). The assertions also stress the importance of one's predecessors. Ancestors constitute the sources, the roots, of present-day knowledge (cf. Feinberg 1978).

But when we examine specific facts and see how people use and transmit them through time in particular contexts, it is clear that ideas about the past are often changing. While some conceptions are being brought onto center stage through cultural revivals (as we shall see in Chapter 5), other conceptions of the past are dying out. Take the matrimoieties as a case in point. In 1934–5 several people indicated that matrilineages traditionally owned taro swamps. In 1978–81, only Molingi and Apela espoused that opinion (to my knowledge). Even in the brief time between Hecht's and my own fieldwork, I noted that conceptions of the matrimoieties had changed.

The point I want to stress here is that Pukapukan knowledge affirmations have a dynamic, pragmatic quality. It is not enough to analyze knowledge claims in the abstract. They must be examined in terms of actual *use* – in changing contexts as well as through time (cf. Dougherty and Keller 1982).[8]

Pukapukan cognitive styles[9]

The most striking impression I have regarding Pukapukan cognitive styles is that the contexts in which Pukapukans acquire knowledge closely correspond to and overlap with the contexts in which it is used. People learn about canoe building while building canoes. They learn the names of places by going to those places. Little need exists for moving beyond the immediate contexts in which one learns and uses knowledge to develop additional cognitive skills applicable to a broad array of contexts.

This observation fits with recent studies regarding the limited cross-context applicability of cognitive skills. In the case of literacy, for example, learning to write does not lead to an entirely new way of thinking or remembering (especially if the functions of literacy within the broader culture are limited). From their study of literacy among the Liberian Vai, Scribner and Cole report, "Instead of generalized changes in cognitive ability, we found localized changes in cognitive skills manifested in relatively esoteric experimental settings" (1981:234). Or as Scribner succinctly phrases it, "*What* you [cognitively] learn is bound up with what you have to do" (1985:203).

The impression I have is that Pukapukans operate quite comfortably, and often with a certain finesse, in the normal contexts of their everyday lives. They can relate abstract constructs to concrete facts with a skill and humor that both Pukapukans and anthropologists can appreciate. In this respect, I find Levy's description of Tahitians equally appropriate to Pukapukans: "The thinking of people . . . is *embedded* in its contexts and operates, often wisely and intelligently, within them, but does not challenge the context itself" (1973:269).

What Pukapukans lack is experience in stepping outside their normal everyday contexts. They possess what Scribner terms an "empirical bias" (1977:490). They appeal to concrete examples and particular circumstances, to "real world knowledge and experience" (1977:490) in making decisions and resolving problems. Scribner's research in Mexico and Liberia suggests

that traditional people can and do engage in valid deductive reasoning on verbal logic problems, provided they put brackets about what they know to be true and confine their reasoning to the terms of the problems. More often than not, traditional villagers fail to do just that, under conditions in which educated subjects almost always do just that. It appears characteristic for villagers to approach informally "as a matter of course." a task that [Western-educated] students approach formally "as a matter of course." (Scribner 1977:494)

Though I do not wish to lump Mexicans, Liberians, and Pukapukans into one broad category of "traditional," my observations suggest that Pukapukans are hesitant to lay aside and/or place at a distance the contexts they know and handle so well. This was, in a way, the point that Tukia raised with me. Pukapukan children, he indicated, were too absorbed with certain matters relating to their everyday concerns – with genealogical status and the social effects of behavior. They did not question the broader contexts within which they operated.

One example of this general point involves citing the actual names of informants. In Borofsky (1982), I tried to disguise informants' identities by using names taken from Pukapukans who had participated in the Beagleholes' research. Pukapukans who read the dissertation found such disguises disconcerting and disorienting. The dissertation, some noted, implied that informants who were known to have died before my study actually took part in it. Consequently, on the recommendation of several informants, I have used people's real names in this book (except where it might prove particularly embarrassing).

My point is that the contexts within which Pukapukans acquire knowledge help to shape this knowledge. Various details must still be worked out, for this is an area of ongoing debate in cognitive psychology. It may be, as Scribner (personal communication 1985) suggests, that a crucial variable in this regard is the diversity of contexts within which particular skills are periodically practiced. Others, such as Berland (1982), Lave (in press), and Shweder and Bourne (1982), focus on different possibilities. But whatever the case, one point is clear. Many of the processes described above – relating to acquisition, validation, and utilization – play important roles in the construction and reconstruction of Pukapukan knowledge.

5

Making history

Returning now to the *Akatawa*, it is important to realize that its revival in 1976 was not an isolated incident. It belonged to a set of revivals occurring on the atoll in the 1970s. Placing the 1976 revival within this broader context brings us to a better understanding of how and why the *Akatawa* developed when it did.

Reviving the past within the present

Reviving the traditional matrilineal organization

The story really begins in 1974. In that year the 'Council of Important People' (the Kau Wowolo) temporarily revived the island's traditional matrimoieties (or *wua*). Minute Number 10 of its 1974 meeting provides the best record of what happened:

> The meeting . . . has decided to have some entertainment (*tamataola*) between the (Wua) Kati and the Wua Lulu. So the generation of young adults (*maapu*) of today can know about this traditional form of organization. This is the form the games (*talekaleka*) will take – cricket for the men and the women. . . . The cricket games between the two *wua* will take place the 27th of February to the 28th of February, 1974.

Numerous sources confirm that Pukapuka once possessed a matrilineal form of organization. In 1904, Hutchin indicated that "the people reckon their descent from the mother's side" (1904:174). The Beagleholes and Hecht describe the atoll's matrilineal organization at some length. And other anthropologists who visited the island – Beckett (1964:417), MacGregor (1935:18), and Vayda (1959:128) – all mention the atoll's matrilineality in passing.

How did the matrilineal organization operate in former times? As

131

described in Chapter 2, the Beagleholes and Hecht agree on certain points. There were two overarching matrimoieties: Wua Kati and Wua Lulu. Each of these was divided into smaller matrilineal units, called *momo*, *keinanga*, or *manga*, which the Beagleholes refer to as lineages or sublineages. The matrilineal units formed the basis for a variety of activities – including sport competitions and life-crisis events – which, as Hecht (1976b:5) suggests, were rituals of unilineal identity. The oldest male or female member of the matrilineal group (the *wakatauila* or *wakalulu*) acted as a gift giver for certain feasts, represented the matrilineage at interlineage meetings, and arranged sporting contests.

As the 'Council of Important People's' minutes make clear, the council did not revive the matrilineal organization in toto, nor did it revive aspects of it for a long period of time. The Wua Lulu and the Wua Kati merely competed against each other in cricket for two days. Why did the council revive the matrilineal organization at all?

One day, while talking with Lavalua, the chairman of the 'Council of Important People,' I inquired about the reasons for the council's decision. His answer was simple. "We wanted to revive these traditional things." Another council member added, "We established these things such as the matrimoieties at the present time so that our children of today will know about them."

An outsider, interestingly, played a role in this decision. The chairman went on to note, "The question was that we had to revive the traditions of our island . . . when the anthropologist Julia, Julia Hecht, was here, we talked about it too – that part of our traditions should be revived." A conversation with Hecht, in 1982, indicated that she also felt her research affected the council's decision but in a less significant way than implied above. From her perspective, she had been mainly asking questions about the atoll's past. She had not specifically recommended reviving it.

The head of the 'Council of Important People' commented:

Yes, Julia and I talked about this, but it was not only her. She advised me to revive such things. But also myself, I wanted the traditions of this island to be revived. . . . Because of what I had gained from the older people in my village. . . . That is how I got the idea for this. When it came to our meeting, it was raised. And we all supported it.

Turning to a broader perspective – beyond what various individuals directly indicated – I believe that other factors also motivated the revival. The first has to do with the 'Council of Important People' itself. By reviving the past, the council was taking a more active role in island affairs. Technically, what it did was well within its jurisdiction, but for approximately two decades such authority had lain dormant. In breathing new life into old powers, the council was giving itself a new vitality (and also greater stature to its relatively new chairman).

Other factors made the reviving of past traditions a valued act. The nature of Pukapuka's economic resources, the form of its traditional social organization, and its linguistic and cultural differences from other islands in the Cooks all tend to encourage the conservation and perpetuation of the island's traditions. Manihiki and Penrhyn, two other atolls in the northern Cooks, grow pearl shell in their lagoons and often derive a considerable income from this operation. Pukapuka cannot do so because its lagoon has a muddy bottom. Pukapuka, however, possesses extensive taro swamps, which allow for a degree of self-sufficiency in diet. Manihiki and Penrhyn, lacking such swamps, are far more dependent on imported foodstuffs.

In comparing Pukapuka with Rakahanga, another atoll in the northern Cooks, Vayda observes that differences in traditional organization affected each atoll's response to Western commercialism. Whereas the latter became increasingly more involved in Western economy, the former was less radically affected:

The achievement of success in trading in Rakahanga implied a very general renunciation of customary procedures, which were sanctioned primarily by kinship claims and allegiances. It was this kind of renunciation that was unnecessary in Pukapuka, where the customary procedures were different. Commercialism begot more commercialism in Rakahanga, but it did not appear to do so in Pukapuka. (1959:136)

Moreover, when Pukapukans try to enter the modern Western economic system, they often find themselves at a relative disadvantage. In Western-oriented Rarotonga,

regular employment is not easily obtained and even in casual work the Pukapukan is at a disadvantage, having a reputation for laziness and awkwardness which may be attributed to his inexperience in plantation work and, indeed, any work routine. (Beckett 1964:428)

Being culturally distinct from most other Cook Islanders (Hecht 1978:11) and speaking an "incomprehensible" dialect (Beckett 1964:428), Pukapukans often find it difficult to assimilate into the national, Western-oriented economy and culture.

As a result, whereas other northern atolls – such as Manihiki, Penrhyn, and Rakahanga – are increasingly drawn into the modern Western economic system, Pukapuka is comparatively less so. Pukapukans, partially limited in their ability to assimilate into the Western economic system and possessing greater self-sufficiency, often focus on preserving their traditions (cf. Hobsbawm and Ranger 1983:4–7; Silverman 1971:132).

Other factors also probably played a role in the revival. No off-island powers, for example, restricted the island's revivalistic activity – in contrast to the prohibition of Melanesian cargo cults by colonial powers. Given its limited duration and nondisruptive nature, officials in Rarotonga did not view it as a threat to the national government's power (or programs).[1] The revival of the matrilineal organization also fit into the island's concern with alternative modes of organizing people and property. In emphasizing non-village-based alignments, it strengthened crosscutting ties and dampened intergroup conflict. Finally, the revival can be seen as part of a broader Pacific-wide movement toward decolonization. Reviving indigenous traditions affirmed a sense of cultural independence (cf. Keesing and Tonkinson 1982).[2]

The main difference between the matrimoiety pattern revived in 1974 and the traditional form of matrilineal social organization, described by the Beagleholes and Hecht, concerns the matrimoieties' internal organization. By 1974, the matrilineal units no longer had a clear group of leaders. There were no designated representatives who could provide, in this egalitarian-oriented culture, the authority and direction for organizing competitions. As a result, the 'Council of Important People,' not the matrimoieties, made the critical decisions regarding the cricket games.

Reviving the matrimoiety organization was not really something new. A similar revival had occurred, in fact, two decades before. "Matrilineal moiety affiliations," Vayda writes, "were said by one informant to have been the basis . . . for island-wide sports competitions held as recently as 1954" (1959:128). (Vayda did his fieldwork in 1957.) Hecht, in our informal conversation in 1982, indicated that Pukapukans remembered previous matrimoiety revivals occurring in the 1930s and in the 1950s.

One might ponder why the 'Council of Important People' in 1974 chose to revive the matrimoieties rather than the patrilineages or some other form of traditional social organization. I asked the chairman about this. "It just came into our minds to start it. We did not choose . . . well like this, we did not say we have to choose this first. But in our meeting it was just raised." This is the same impression that another person at the meeting had. "We did not set it all out in an orderly manner (*akapapa*) that we would learn about the *wua* first." But then he went on to add, "Perhaps we began with the *wua* because that was the earliest way [or work, *angaanga*]."

No one I talked to ever gave more than a vague, general opinion as to why people chose the matrimoieties. Nor did anyone seem particularly interested in explaining how and why the revival came about in the first place – beyond the fact that it was to teach the younger generation about the past. (This seemed to be an issue that interested me far more than them.) Yet we can observe, following the comments of Hecht and Vayda, that a similar revival had occurred in the recent past. In reviving the matrimoieties, the councilors were, to some extent, also perpetuating a tradition.

The 'Council of Important People's' efforts were clearly successful in one sense. The younger generation learned who belonged where in the matrimoiety organization. Rather than being told in words about the matrimoieties, they experienced them in operation. They learned through observation and participation.

But certain difficulties arose with the revival that made its continuation beyond the two-day period problematic at best. People became better acquainted with the past, but at the cost of certain social alignments within the present. As one informant explained:

People disliked (*veliveli*) staying by matrimoieties. With matrimoieties, my wife is a Wua Lulu. I am a [Wua] Kati. Consequently, when the Kati gather together, I go with the Kati. When the Wua Lulu gathers together, my wife goes with the Wua Lulu. I get angry. Perhaps... my wife is going off with some man. She thinks the same thing – perhaps I am getting to be friendly (*pili*) to some of the women.

Many other people made similar comments. Hecht noted the same thing. The matrimoiety revival, she recalled, generated a number of social tensions.

But these problems, in a sense, were only the tip of the iceberg. Whatever the matrimoieties' economic effectiveness in times past, given the atoll's current organization they did not constitute viable economic units in 1974. The matrimoieties lacked the organization and authority to regulate the island's resources. The matrimoieties, for example, had no authority over the public reserves and the production of copra. As Akima, the Island Council's chairman, pointed out, continuing the matrimoieties would have posed a threat to people's incomes. It would have disrupted copra production.

To summarize, the matrilineal organization Pukapukans revived in 1974 closely resembled the traditional one described by the Beagleholes and Hecht, but the revival caused certain disruptions. It was one thing to revive the past. It was quite another to make the past work in the present, given that the two now differed in significant ways. The matrimoiety revival did, however, emphasize an important point for Pukapukans, in spite of its brief duration and even with the problems it generated. It stressed that present-day alignments were not the only form of social organization. Pukapukans, in reviving the past, helped put the present in perspective.

Reviving the traditional patrilineal organization

Early in 1975, at its next annual meeting, the 'Council of Important People' revived another form of traditional social organization, this time for approximately one week. The best record of what transpired comes from the council's minutes:

There will be some games (*talekaleka*) on the land and in the ocean. First will be still-canoe fishing (*yikakai*). When that is done, cricket will be played. To round it off [or sweeten things up, *akamalie*], there will be *mako* chanting in the evening.

The organization of the cricket will be in terms of burial places (*tanumanga*). Ngake – Muliwutu and Maatanga, Loto – Tilotilowia and Tua, Yato – Yamaunga and Yaalongo. Three teams will, therefore, play cricket.

For the organization of the fishing, there will be four teams. The Aronga Nunui [the Rarotongan word for the 'Council of Important People'], Ngake, Loto, Yato. Each team will have eleven members.

What the 'Council of Important People' did in 1975 was to revive the traditional patrilineal organization. Maatanga, Muliwutu, Tilotilowia, Tua, Yamaunga, and Yaalongo are names of the traditional patrilineages (*po*) and their affiliated cemeteries (*po*). *Tanumanga* is simply the Rarotongan word for cemetery. (The 'Council of Important People's' minutes are customarily written in Rarotongan.) Substantial data confirm that Pukapuka traditionally possessed a patrilineal organization. Beckett (1964:417), Gill (1912:123), and Vayda (1959:128) all refer to it in passing. The Beagleholes and Hecht provide detailed descriptions.

Though the exact number of patrilineages (versus subpatrilineages) in former times remains unclear, the above six along with Yayi constitute the main ones cited in the Beagleholes' ethnography (1938:229). Each patrilineage controlled certain strips of land (*kawa*) that its members resided on and used. Members generally belonged to the village within whose boundaries they resided. In addition, each patrilineage possessed two distinct groupings: one involving people who shared a designated burial site (*po*) and the other involving those who shared a group of house sites (*yoolonga*). Membership in one did not completely overlap with the other as a result of adoption and patrilocal postmarital residence (i.e., wives moved to their husbands' residence on marriage). As the Beagleholes note, "The Yolongo [*sic*] group . . . exclude[s] blood members of the family who are adopted elsewhere and are not in residence with the patrilocal group, but . . . include[s] non-blood members who reside with the patrilocal group through marriage, or through adoption" (Beaglehole ms. a under "Organizations for Food Division and Games, etc. Yolongo"). The Beagleholes add that the *yoolonga*, not the *po*, formed the basis for patrilineal food divisions and sporting contests. Finally, each patrilineage had a chief (*aliki*) or subchief (*langatila*) who

Returning home from fishing

involved himself in patrilineal affairs as well as islandwide matters. The modern 'Council of Important People' (Kau Wowolo) constitutes a continuation of earlier councils held by the island's chiefs (*wakapononga a te wui aliki*).

What the 'Council of Important People' revived in 1975, in other words, was something that clearly had existed in the past, but the modern revival differed from the traditional patrilineal organization in an important respect. As just noted, competitions were formerly based on localized patrilineal groupings (*yoolonga*), not on designated burial sites (*po*). The 'Council of Important People's' minutes clearly state that the 1975 games were to be organized by burial sites. Interestingly, the difference between localized patrilineal groupings (*yoolonga*) and "burial categories" (to use Hecht's term) escapes most Pukapukans today. My own investigations suggest that Pukapukans frequently confuse the two (or give the distinction between them a somewhat different emphasis). People, for instance, referred to the 1975 competitions by both names, *po* and *yoolonga*. Such confusion is quite understandable, in my opinion. Only the *po*, as a burial category, operates with any force today. Localized groupings are now based on cognatic kinship and village residence.

There is one other difference between the 1975 revival and the earlier patrilineal organization described by the Beagleholes and Hecht. The 'Council of Important People' seemed to have become caught up in the competitive spirit, for it too decided to compete as a team in the fishing contest. Nothing in any of the available anthropological reports indicates that patrilineal groupings had ever before competed against the 'Council of Important People.'[3]

The 1975 patrilineal revival thus represented a more radical departure than the matrimoieties from the traditional social organization described by the Beagleholes and Hecht. Competitions were based on burial categories (*po*), not localized groupings (*yoolonga*). Burial categories and the 'Council of Important People' competed against each other. Only in terms of the leadership necessary to organize the games could one say that the 1975 revival more closely approached the traditional form of social organization. Unlike the matrimoieties, the patrilineages possessed the leadership and authority to form themselves into sporting teams. The 'Council of Important People' was a continuation of the earlier chiefly meetings.

As in 1974, the younger generation was able to see firsthand an aspect of their traditional social organization. People who simply belonged to a category, in terms of sharing a common burial site, temporarily became an active group as they competed together in various sporting contests. People learned about the past by participating in an aspect of it.

But reviving the patrilineal form of organization also created problems. An informant explains a situation I heard many people express concern about:

It was the same with the *yoolonga* as with the *wua* (or 'matrimoieties'). My wife and I, we are all right. We are both buried in Yato village, in the cemeteries of Yato. So we go together because we belong to the same *yoolonga*.

But some other people, like Kavai. Kavai belongs to the *yoolonga* of Ngake. Militoa, his wife, belongs to the *yoolonga* of Yato. If people gather according to *yoolonga*, Kavai goes to Ngake, Militoa goes to Yato. Militoa thinks, "Ooh, Kavai will befriend the people of his *yoolonga*," because they will be together in the evenings – without her. "He will leave me."

That is the same with Waletini. His wife Naunau belongs to the *yoolonga* of Ngake. Waletini belongs to the *yoolonga* of Loto. Naunau thinks, "Waletini may leave me. Perhaps he will go off with the women of the *yoolonga* of Loto."

Again, these social tensions represent the tip of the iceberg. Continuing the patrilineal organization would have caused conflicts with existing arrangements for regulating and distributing the island's economic resources. It would have necessitated significantly changing the present system of food-sharing as well as village membership.

Thus the matrimoieties and the patrilineages – the two forms of traditional social organization best known by both Pukapukans and anthropologists alike up to 1976 – encountered the same basic problem. Reviving traditional forms of social organization created new social alignments. This served the valuable purpose of allowing young people to place present-day arrangements within a broader historical perspective. But the revived forms also created tensions. They were impractical as semipermanent structures given the island's modern social organization.

Reviving the Akatawa

It was within this context that, at its next annual meeting, the 'Council of Important People' revived the *Akatawa* organization – the only form of traditional social organization for which no corroborating anthropological or historical data exist. Various anthropologists with whom I have discussed the matter asked what exactly happened in 1976. How did the *Akatawa* come about? That is not fully clear. I interviewed five people who attended the meeting. All of them stated that they supported the *Akatawa*'s revival, and all agreed that the council revived the *Akatawa* in order to teach younger people about the island's traditions. But none of them indicated that they themselves had initiated the proposal. Each person I talked to vaguely suggested that someone else had proposed the idea of reviving the *Akatawa*. The chairman, for example, indicated that perhaps it was Yala's suggestion. According to the chairman, Yala had experienced the *Akatawa* in his youth and consequently knew all about it. "When it happened long ago," the chairman noted, these "old people were still alive; they saw it." But Yala did not recall having experienced it in his youth nor, he added, had he proposed the idea at the meeting. When I questioned him about the topic, he vaguely responded that possibly Apela had suggested the idea. And so it went, each person vaguely indicating, when I inquired, that someone else had proposed the idea. From my observations, people did not seem particularly concerned about the specific details of how the *Akatawa* came about. (Who actually proposed the *Akatawa* was an idea that seemed to interest me far more than the council members I interviewed.)

As a result, the best record I have of the meeting again comes from the council's written minutes. Number 8 for 1976 reads:

We have decided to hold certain games (*talekaleka*) this year, when the meeting is over. There are to be two types of games — cricket for both men and women and still-canoe fishing (*yikakai*) for the men. This is the way they will be organized, it will be done by *Akatawa* — that is, there will be two groupings (*lulu lua*). Ngake village with all the sections of Tawa Ngake of the village Loto. Yato village and all the sections of Tawa Lalo of the village Loto. There are, therefore, two *tawa* [or 'sides'], which will be called Tawa Ngake and Tawa Lalo.

Staying like this will last for two weeks.... The first week, in regard to what we have said, will be the week of February 12th. Following directly after that will be the second week. In the first week, on a Wednesday, the men will play cricket. On Thursday, the women will play cricket. On Friday, there will be still-canoe fishing (*yikakai*). On Saturday, singing will occur.

For the second of the weeks, the teams that lost can rechallenge (*imulanga*). If the Tawa Lalo lost at cricket, then the second week they can rechallenge Tawa Ngake again. The same goes for the fishing. Everything will be brought to a close on Friday of this week with a picnic. The *Akatawa* will go to the two reserves (*motu*) – Tawa Lalo to Motu Kotawa, Tawa Ngake to Motu Ko.

In contrast to the two previous revivals, few frictions arose with this new form of social organization. At least at first, everyone seemed in favor of it. The chairman of the 'Council of Important People' explained, "When we tried the *Akatawa*, we set a limit of two weeks ... we tried to limit the time to two weeks. But when they got into it, the people liked it." Due to popular pressure, the council extended the *Akatawa*'s duration. Initially they extended it into 1979, later into 1980.

Pukapukans expressed various reasons for their satisfaction with the *Akatawa* organization. One reason involved access to more diverse resources:

It was nice because we shared various food together. The group called Tawa Lalo would go to Tawa Lalo in Motu Uta. They would eat the coconuts, the taro of Tawa Lalo in Motu Uta. When that was finished, they would go to Motu Kotawa; the people of Loto village would go, too. If we stayed in villages, Loto would not go to Motu Kotawa [because it was Yato village's reserve].

But in staying by *Akatawa*, they would go to Motu Kotawa; they would eat various types of foods found mainly there – birds like the bobby (*takupu*), the noddy tern (*ngongo*), the black tern (*lakia*), and also papayas. That is why people liked it. (A man in his seventies)

Several cricket players mentioned another reason to me. After the first match between the two sides, the losers rechallenged and defeated the winners. A man in his early fifties stated, "We wanted to challenge each other again so we would know which was the stronger side. Then we kept on going at it." The chairman of the 'Council of Important People' commented, "I think that is one reason the people liked this system. Because we could compete between two sides in . . . games – such as cricket, volley ball, fishing."

Others suggested that it was something new, something different to try. They did not add, but one can infer they meant, that it was something new that worked well – something that did *not* generate new social frictions.

Reflections on a process

The *Akatawa*'s revival illustrates, in a very palpable way, the creative, dynamic nature of Pukapukan traditional knowledge. Before 1976, the *Akatawa* must not have been well known or must have been perceived as having little traditional significance. How else can one explain why no Pukapukans elaborated on it for various anthropologists – even though Pukapukans actively participated in recording the island's traditions? Only Hecht recalls ever having heard anything about splitting the island in half, and as noted in Chapter 1, that was in a nebulous form that did not make much sense. When I conducted my research, from 1977 to 1981, the situation was radically different. Many people told me about previous *Akatawa*. Some validated their assertions with personal experiences. The *Akatawa* was an important part of Pukapukan tradition.

What brought about this change, I believe, was the historical circumstances surrounding the *Akatawa*'s revival in 1976. A few individuals' private (and probably vague) conceptions were drawn into the public realm and supported by both the 'Council of Important People' and the populace at large. Calling into question beliefs about earlier *Akatawa* after the revival began became a questioning of the authority and competency of these groups. Simply by working without major problems, the *Akatawa* also gained a measure of authenticity. As people experienced the *Akatawa* from 1976 onward, as they publicly discussed it, as they reflected on its possible historical antecedents, marginal or vaguely formulated views regarding past *Akatawa* spread into the public domain and became crystallized, enunciated, and accepted. A meaningful new tradition developed.

What makes changes such as this intriguing is that the final results may not always be foreseen. The changes may take on a momentum of their own. This occurred with the *Akatawa*. A marginal or vaguely formulated belief became the basis for "reviving" a form of social organization for two weeks. But then people liked it. They extended it. As described elsewhere (Borofsky 1982:225–8), the *Akatawa* almost permanently supplanted the three-village system as the central pillar of the atoll's social organization. And even when it did not, it still altered people's perceptions of the former matrimoiety organization.

A parallel process occurred among the Micronesian Bikinians when forced to resettle on another island (Kiste 1974, personal communication 1985). Their chief established a new land division based on traditional residence and land-use rights. But the division had unforeseen consequences in the new context. It altered Bikinian conceptions of land tenure, and it created new tensions. Sahlins characterizes the process well in his study of Hawaii (1981, 1985). "The reproduction of a structure [can become] its transformation" (1981:8). An idea, drawn from the past, can interact with new events and forces in unforeseen ways that can transform both it and the culture at large (see also Silverman 1971).

Preserving the past through change

Looking at Pukapuka's cultural revivals broadly, one can see an increasing movement away from the traditional forms of social organization described by the Beagleholes and Hecht. The 1974 matrimoieties needed the 'Council of Important People' to establish them. The 1975 patrilineages confused the distinction between patrilocal groupings (*yoolonga*) and patrilineal cemeteries (*po*). And the 1976 *Akatawa* lacks historical corroboration by outside sources. The irony in this situation, if one wants to call it irony, is that in reviving the past, in preserving past traditions by making them come alive again, Pukapukans were really altering them.

Pukapukans, I would argue, have not been alone in doing so. In helping to preserve the atoll's traditions, Western anthropologists have also, in a sense, altered them. In writing them down for posterity, they have depicted Pukapukan traditions as more uniform and static than they really are. The process has worked in more subtle ways as well. The Beagleholes, for instance, stimulated the production of plays concerning traditional Pukapukan myths and legends. When the Beagleholes visited the atoll in 1934–5, Pukapukans were performing biblical plays every May. But as Ernest Beaglehole recounts:

One morning early in April Makirai was idling round the house. I heard him mumbling something about going to a deacons' meeting to decide about "the May."
   "What plays will the deacons decide on?" I asked him casually.
   He pushed back his hat and scratched his head in doubt: "Oh, . . . plays about the Bible, David and Goliath and Joseph and his coat, and the rest, I suppose. We do those every year."
   Now I am not prejudiced unduly against stories just because they are Biblical, but I looked ahead and visualized us sitting all day in the hot sun, perhaps for more than two days, and I felt that it needed something more than David and Goliath to keep interest alive. So I put it to Makirai: Why not play for a change old Pukapukan stories, the story of Malotini for example, or the Eight Men of Ngake, or the Slaughter of the Yayake people? Everyone knew these stories – we had talked about them many times with large groups of informants; and besides, the acting of them would help us to remember them more vividly when we came to write them down. Makirai promised to make the suggestion, but I doubted his ability to persuade the missionary of the value of reviving heathen stories. From his account that evening, however, it seemed that the suggestion had been enthusiastically received. Ve[e]ti, Talainga and Eliu and others had rallied a *bloc* and carried the voting. They were all keenly interested in the future second book of Pukapuka [i.e., ms. b] and the more vivid our descriptions the more pleased they would be. Each village thereupon decided to present two old Pukapukan legends on May Day, and great was the hurrying back and fro before conflicting claims to this story and that were arbitrated and final choices achieved. (1944:174)

These native legends are still performed today (along with the biblical tales). The date has been changed to the Cook Islands Congregational Church's Gospel Day, and the performances are not always annual affairs. But still, they occur.

   In the process of acting as anthropological adviser to the Wellington Hospital Research Unit during his stay on Pukapuka in 1964, Jeremy Beckett collected a series of Pukapukan genealogies (see Hecht 1976a:iii). These he understandably took with him because they were part of his research. But after Beckett left, the government resident agent during this period, Tipuia Tiro, began collecting similar genealogies to assist in settling land disputes. Today his book constitutes one of the most comprehensive collections of Pukapukan genealogies. From talking to Tipuia Tiro, it is clear that Beckett's research stimulated his own work. It is difficult to state how many others were also influenced by Beckett (and Tipuia), but I do know there were some. Akima, for example, mentioned one day that this was the reason for his own sizable genealogical collection.

Hecht, as noted, played a role in stimulating the 1974 matrimoiety revival. I assisted several teachers in the writing of a Pukapukan-English dictionary (Mataola et al. 1981). I also financed two competitions – a chanting contest among the youth clubs and a string figure contest among the villages.

Many of these changes brought about by outside anthropologists have been instrumental in preserving valued aspects of Pukapukan traditional knowledge. From the plays, for example, Pukapukans learn a great deal about their traditional legends. The 1974 and 1975 revivals helped a whole new generation of Pukapukans to better understand the operation of past forms of social organization. And the various competitions I sponsored offered a new avenue for more formalized instruction.[4]

But the traditional knowledge that is being preserved is also being altered. By recording traditions in books, we, as outside anthropologists, are helping to make the knowledge less fluid and diverse than it in fact is. By encouraging public competitions and displays, we are helping to alter the informal patterns of education. In assisting in the preservation of Pukapukan traditional knowledge, we are helping to transform it into a more static, uniform body of data. But if there is irony in the fact that, in preserving traditional knowledge, both Pukapukans and anthropologists are altering it, there is greater irony in another fact. Pukapukans and anthropologists often succeed to a certain degree in their preservation efforts. Both preserve important aspects of traditional Pukapukan knowledge – in spite of the alterations they make in it.

Today Pukapuka is often considered the most traditional island in the Cook Islands and is probably one of the most traditional atolls in all of Polynesia. Not only do Pukapukans carry on many of their past customs, but they revive, as we have seen, certain ones that are dying out. For anthropologists, Pukapuka is one of the most thoroughly studied traditionally oriented atolls in the South Pacific. Six professionally trained anthropologists conducted research on the island between 1934 and 1981. They have written numerous publications regarding it. (Pukapukans and social scientists alike cite these anthropologists today as authorities on Pukapukan customs.)

Thus Pukapukan traditions, in being preserved, are being altered. But in being altered, they are also being preserved. The past is being made meaningful to those upholding it in the present. Perhaps Pukapukans and anthropologists preserve a past that never was, but they preserve it in a way that is meaningful to present-day audiences.

The process, I would argue, is a general one. Firth (1967:305, personal communication 1984), for example, indicates that a similar process occurred in Tikopia. When the pagan chiefs sought to perpetuate the traditional four-unit ritual structure (after the defection of a chief to Christianity), they created an innovation – splitting a clan in two – to maintain their traditions. In island Melanesia, Tonkinson writes, people "have frequently . . . [sought] to 're-invent' lost *kastom* – to reconstruct elements of a largely forgotten and distant past in order to satisfy what they perceive to be the demands of contemporary . . . ideology" (in Keesing and Tonkinson 1982:304). Or as Lindstrom puts it, people seek "to read the present in terms of the past by writing the past in terms of the present" (1982:317). Burke (1978) and Hobsbawm and Ranger (1983) show that Europeans have been involved in the same process – not just for decades, but for centuries.

Traditional knowledge must continually adjust to changing circumstances, must continually adapt, so as not to die out (or become buried away in some archive). What is at stake is a pragmatic rather than correspondent sense of truth – meaningfulness to the living rather than precise accuracy to the past.

Part of what is involved, then, with the *Akatawa* disagreement is that both Pukapukans *and* anthropologists have altered the island's traditions. Anthropologists have overstructured them by emphasizing their uniformity and stasis. Pukapukans have given them new meanings in the process of learning and validating them. The difficulty is not that they have both changed these traditions. As we have just noted, traditions are continually changing. The difficulty is that they have changed them in *different* ways – in responding to different contexts and different audiences.

Constructing traditions: Parallels and differences

This is only part of the problem regarding the *Akatawa*. There is another aspect of the differing accounts: Also at issue is the nature of the dialogue or interaction between indigenous informants and Western anthropologists.

The preceding chapters indicate that definite similarities exist between the ways Pukapukans and anthropologists gather information about the past. In collecting data, for example, Pukapukans and anthropologists alike observe adults, listen to group discussions, and participate in activities. They share many of the same criteria for deciding who is or is not knowledgeable about the island's traditions. Both look to older people who knew the atoll in earlier times. (Anthropologists' concern with historical reconstruction dovetails with the Polynesian emphasis on genealogical seniority and on elders as a source of knowledge.) Both place considerable emphasis on group interaction and the seeming consensus that arises out of it. For both, knowledge of old chants and legends is important. Both emphasize an informant's ability to explicate material in a coherent manner.

In validating the assertions of others, Pukapukans and anthropologists alike emphasize the indigenous perspective; they rely on individuals who have had limited exposure to Western ways. Though not always stating so, they frequently evaluate remarks in terms of what they themselves already know – from their own experiences or from what they have heard (or read).

Both anthropologists and Pukapukans see in the present aspects of the past. The Beagleholes, Hecht, Yolo, and Paleula all used their knowledge of the present to make deductions about former times. For the Pukapukans this represents an affirmation of continuity. (Sahlins, 1983:528, phrases the related New Zealand Maori perspective as ontogeny recapitulating cosmogony.) For the anthropologist, the present provides a means of reconstructing earlier, more "pristine" times. Both anthropologists and Pukapukans deemphasize diversity in describing Pukapukan traditions. The anthropologists' concern with simplifying matters for Western audiences fits well with individual Pukapukan affirmations that their particular views constitute the correct ones. For Pukapukans it involves an assertion of status.

Along with these apparent similarities are also subtle, but important differences. In collecting data, for example, Pukapukans tend to be less direct than anthropologists. They concern themselves far more with subtleties of personal relations and the contexts of interaction. Anthropologists, with their interviews, censuses, and maps, collect their data in a more systematic, straightforward manner than Pukapukans. They also do it in a far shorter period of time. Though aware that status rivalries exist, anthropologists tend (as outsiders) not to be as involved in them. Also, anthropologists are often less attuned to the ambiguities regarding how seniority merges into senility and less concerned with how challenges and counterchallenges constitute a means of self-affirmation. Though both Pukapukans and anthropologists fit new information into what they already know, they usually know different things to begin with, so their conclusions are frequently different. Both emphasize the native perspective – but which natives and how many? Pukapukans lay stress on their own individual perspectives. Anthropologists seek a broader accounting of what Pukapukans, in general, know.

Through three examples, we can see how these differences affect the knowledge both groups construct of the Pukapukan past. Each example explores a facet of the anthropologist-informant dialogue.

The issue of closure in group discussions

Chapters 3 and 4 indicate that Pukapukans often argue back and forth in group discussions without coming to a clear consensus. Each participant displays his or her knowledge, contradicting one person's position or clarifying and confirming another's. More than the validity of specific assertions is at stake – so are issues of competence and social standing. Unless some overriding community need exists for group closure, many issues regarding traditional knowledge are left ambiguous or unresolved in public. (The discussion of *kula* and *kula pupuni* is a case in point.) To do otherwise goes against the atoll's egalitarian orientation. It publicly implies that some people can impose their knowledge on others, that some people's answers are superior to their peers'. The closure that usually results tends to occur at an individual level – as each person privately reflects on the information presented. We can see this process at work in a group discussion among several teachers:

An argument arose among certain teachers one afternoon as we worked on the Pukapukan-English dictionary. At stake was whether the word *taavilinga*, or 'keyhole,' was traditional Pukapukan (and should be included in the dictionary) or was Rarotongan (and should not). One teacher asserted that it was Pukapukan and used the following sentence to prove his point: *Aulaka koe e peeni i te taavilinga o te ngutupaa naa*, 'Do not paint the keyhole of that door.'

A second teacher questioned this argument. He stated that the real Pukapukan word for keyhole was *pu vili*. The first teacher scoffed at the suggestion. Other islands, he asserted, did not use the word *taavilinga* for keyhole, only Pukapuka.

A third teacher got into the argument. He stated that he had heard numerous people use the word *taavilinga* in everyday speech. Certainly *taavilinga* was a much more common word for keyhole than *pu vili*. But the second teacher insisted that *pu vili* was clearer – it referred to the hole (*pu*) into which the key (*vili*) was put. The third teacher countered that *taavilinga* referred to the place where the key was turned (*taavili*).

The discussion went on and on like this with various teachers adding their own comments. The teachers never developed any consensus or resolution of the issue. I finally suggested that we go on to another word since our time together was limited.

Though all these teachers expressed an interest in writing a dictionary (by what they said and did), they still spent numerous hours wrangling over small words like this. If there was no clear pressure from me to come to a consensus, they often left the issue publicly unresolved.

Such ambiguity was unsatisfactory for my purposes. I was responsible for checking translations and coordinating various parts of the dictionary – for making it comprehensible to non-Pukapukans. A decision had to be made regarding *taavilinga* – should it be included or not? To leave the issue with no clear group consensus left me in doubt regarding what action to take. I could say that people disagreed on this and numerous other words. I could simply record every disagreement the teachers had. But that would complicate our task to the extent that we might never finish the dictionary (even during my forty-one-month stay). It would also make the dictionary something it was never intended to be – a record of certain teachers' disagreements (cf. Lindstrom 1983).

Most teachers seemed to realize (by what they told me) that we needed some sort of consensus on words like these; otherwise, they would spend all their time together arguing. But they usually left it to me to bring about a resolution. At times when one of them tried to do so, someone else injected a slightly different opinion. For certain words, it became too much trouble for the teachers to develop a group consensus. No one wanted to defer to anyone else.

As an outsider I was not as caught up in these status rivalries over traditional knowledge. The fact that I was ignorant of such things explained what I was doing in Pukapuka in the first place and why I asked all sorts of questions. When I interjected a comment into the above discussion everyone ignored me. I was not even worth competing with. Thus I could bring about a consensus.

But who is to say that what was agreed upon was correct? For years Pukapukans have been speaking a mixture of Pukapukan and Rarotongan (see, e.g., Beaglehole and Beaglehole 1938:6). Today, opinions abound on which words of the spoken language are Pukapukan and which Rarotongan. The teachers' diverse set of opinions probably expresses the current situation far better than the consensus I encouraged to "preserve" the language in written form (cf. Babadzan 1985).

Part of the situation, of course, results from the contexts in which we operate. I was one anthropologist among many Pukapukans. (If there had been one Pukapukan among several anthropologists, presumably the dictionary would have turned out differently.) And one should not overemphasize either the debates or the discrepancies between our two orientations. Certainly the teachers agreed on many words without argument. At times they also brought about group closure on their own. I could, and did, note the existence of diverse opinions (as the above example shows).

Still we often approached the issue of writing the dictionary from different perspectives. I at times created something that was not necessarily there. Though appreciating the diversity and fluidity of traditional Pukapukan knowledge, I tended to create a consensus of opinion because my primary aim was to record certain Pukapukan traditions and explicate them to people in my own culture. The Pukapukans, while appreciating the need for consensus in order to record knowledge, focused on affirming their social worth through status rivalries. Diverse opinions rather than uniform agreement, consequently, arose out of their conversations.

Pukapukans and I, in other words, drew different conclusions from the same group discussions. True, we both listened to the same points, but because we faced different problems, we came away with different accounts and syntheses. Pukapukans emphasized their own opinions; I, a group consensus partially of my own making.

Descriptions of change

One of the interesting aspects of the *Akatawa*'s revival is the fact that no one assumed credit for suggesting it to the 'Council of Important People.' Though the matter intrigued me, I was never able to ferret out exactly what happened at the key 1976 meeting – beyond the council's general support for the revival and what the council's minutes indicate. Pukapukans downplayed the role of specific individuals in making the decision. They focused on the group's consensus and described the event in vague generalities.

In 1980 I attended another critical meeting at which I did observe the council in action. At issue was whether to terminate the *Akatawa* and return to living in three villages. Let me briefly describe the event as I saw it. Initially, a few people, most of whom favored extending the *Akatawa*, dominated the discussion. Then a lull developed in the conversation. After a while, Lauvai, who had generally been quiet up to this time, spoke. Lauvai said that he personally saw many benefits to the *Akatawa* organization, some of which he listed. But at last year's meeting, he noted, the council had tentatively decided to terminate the *Akatawa* this coming year and that was what it should do. He himself, Lauvai stated in a voice deep with emotion, had promised a close relative not to support the extension of the *Akatawa*. Out of respect for what he had promised his relative and out of respect for what the council had promised the people last year, Lauvai felt the island should return to the village system – regardless of their personal feelings to the contrary. The manner in which the speech was delivered and the nature of the remarks seemed to galvanize the opposition. Several other people then came out in favor of terminating the *Akatawa*. From my reading of the situation, Lauvai's speech was an important factor in tipping the balance toward returning to the village form of organization. The flow of the conversation from then on ran mostly in favor of the *Akatawa*'s termination.

But did Pukapukans agree with my assessment of how the meeting went? Not really. Most council members stressed the consensual nature of the decision and how they had all participated in it. They again downplayed the role of individuals in bringing about change. Pukapukans, in other words, were emphasizing a different sense of historical process than I was. For them, these meetings did not involve some "heroic history" (in Sahlins's 1983 terms) in which individual actors directed events. Rather, their descriptions embodied an orientation very much in line with their own egalitarian perspective. Everyone supported the common good. Terminating the *Akatawa* involved a community effort.

This does not mean that Pukapukans did not grasp that people expressed divergent opinions at the meeting. Nor does it mean that they misperceived how individuals sought to influence one another before the crucial vote. They clearly were aware of both issues. Nor does it imply that all past events in the atoll's history derived from group consensus. (One need only remember Apakuka's role in helping to terminate Ngake's involvement in an earlier *Akatawa*.) But Pukapukans did seem to be emphasizing a different sense of historical process than I was – one oriented toward the community rather than the individual. As the atoll's legends indicate, a few individuals may cause disruptions (or even dramatic changes) through their willfulness, but positive changes often derive from a communal effort, from people working together. As both Lévi-Strauss (1966) and Sahlins (1983) indicate, different cultural groups describe change differently (see also Mannheim 1953:74–164).

Asking questions regarding the Akatawa's date and duration

A variety of scientific studies indicate that recall of past events is rarely completely accurate (see, e.g., Bernard, Killworth, Kronenfeld, and Sailer 1984; D'Andrade 1974; E. Loftus 1979; Loftus and Loftus 1976; Yarmey 1979). According to Hunter, "There are omissions, transpositions, and additions resulting from interpretation, from the individual's making the account conform to his standards of intelligibility" (1964:183). Anthropologists and sociologists, the Loftuses warn us, may

query people about their past in the course of studying some particular problem of interest. : . . [But] it is important to realize that the statements made during such interviews may not be particularly accurate as reports of prior events. The contents of an interview may not reflect a person's earlier experiences and attitudes so much as his or her current picture of the past. (Loftus and Loftus 1980:419)

Long-term-memory research thus suggests that individual recollections regarding former *Akatawa* may not be exact. The *Akatawa* recalled by the seven informants may have taken place before the 1914 hurricane or could have lasted for a shorter period of time, such as for a number of days (as the 1974 and 1975 revivals did). Either way, the event quite conceivably could have gone unrecorded in various historical documents of the time.

In my opinion, the group consensus regarding the former *Akatawa*'s date and duration derives from the interaction of two factors. First, it results from my probing for specific dates and a specific duration. I wanted to make people's vague recollections more precise because the 1976 revival struck me as an important phenomenon. I wanted to collect as many details as possible about its antecedents. Yet asking for dates and numbers probably placed an unrealistic burden on various informants' memories. As Vansina (1980:268, 276) notes, numbers are difficult to recall, particularly if they are rarely used in connection with an event, particularly, I might add, if they refer to something that happened sixty years earlier.

Still, and this is the second factor, people had to answer my questions. Their reputations were at stake. Pukapukans had to demonstrate their knowledge, both to their peers and to me (a outsider who sought to record their past). If they could not answer my questions – questions that apparently few Pukapukans asked each other – then implicitly they possessed less knowledge than they claimed or the *Akatawa*'s precedents were somewhat murky. Petelo's and Molingi's ability to answer my questions in a coherent manner in front of their peers affirmed their reputations as experts in such matters. Others perhaps had different views regarding the earlier *Akatawa*'s date and duration, but if so, they were unwilling to get drawn into a series of challenges and counter-challenges with individuals of Petelo's and Molingi's stature. (Their not raising challenges implied that a general consensus existed.)

What Petelo and Molingi provided, in answering my questions, was probably less a set of remembered facts than an explanatory form for validating knowledge. It was a style of explanation – a typification of the facts in which "a particular set of events could be narratively ordered and meaningfully understood" (Schieffelin 1982:23). It involved making an account conform with a certain sense of intelligibility. There are clear reasons for claiming that the *Akatawa* occurred in the 1914–15 period. It fits with what Pukapukans already knew about hurricanes and how the atoll coped with them. Hunter indicates, in summarizing literature on memory research, that a person often appears to organize

characteristics together into an arrangement which seems plausible. In doing this, [he] is governed by his general notions regarding what is likely and what is unlikely. . . . He seems to aim throughout at arranging his recalled characteristics into a story which is as coherent and reasonable as he can make it, even if this means discarding some features, exaggerating the importance of others, and rearranging their sequence. (1964:158)[5]

The specific date and duration of the former *Akatawa* probably derive, in other words, from knowledgeable Pukapukans trying to respond to my questions. To put it more bluntly, part of the reason for the differing accounts regarding the *Akatawa* stems from my being too curious. I asked too many questions.

The explanation is simple enough perhaps. But how else was I supposed to proceed – if not by being curious, if not by asking questions? Quiet observation is an important data-collecting technique, but to rely on that alone would have been extremely limiting. Remember that Molingi suggested the Beagleholes never found out about the *Akatawa* because they did not ask enough questions. As far as I know, the Beagleholes, Hecht, Vayda, and Beckett all asked questions. How could one understand Pukapukan traditions without asking questions? Even adult Pukapukans at times ask questions.

I accept that I asked for a great deal of information that influenced (and overstructured) the answers people gave me. Barth (1975:226), Keesing (1982:43), M. McArthur (1971:185), and Rabinow (1977:132–3), all make the same point regarding their own research. This is, ultimately, part of the nature of fieldwork, one of the results of the dialogue between indigenous informants and Western anthropologists. To record Pukapukan traditions, anthropologists must ask questions, but in asking questions they at times create traditions that do not exist. Distortions arise in the very way fieldwork proceeds. Nonetheless, such biases need not negate the value of anthropological accounts, as the following section indicates.

Anthropological ways of knowing

Throughout this book reference has periodically been made to certain anthropological ways of knowing the atoll's traditions. In this final section, I reflect back on what we have learned regarding the limitations and strengths of these approaches in a more general sense.

Chapter 2 makes clear the problem with individual ethnographies. They offer partial accounts and perspectives. Though the various accounts of Pukapukan social organization have been good – I would say that the Beagleholes' and Hecht's ethnographies have been very good – a much better sense of the atoll's social organization developed from the compilation of our various accounts. Adding one perspective on top of another, we perceive Pukapukan social organization with a greater sense of depth, with a greater appreciation for the processes and ambiguities involved. The corporate nature of the matri- and patrilineal groups, the significance of cognatic descent, the presence of earlier *Akatawa* all become increasingly more complex and subtle matters as a result of our collective efforts. Individual ethnographies establish framework for discussion; they delineate issues to consider. As Chapter 2 suggests, individual ethnographies provide a foundation for others to build on, but only on rare occasions are they definitive works in themselves.[6]

One may raise questions regarding the ordered coherence of anthropological descriptions. Pukapukan knowledge, we have seen, possesses a dynamic, pragmatic quality, a sensitivity to contexts that one cannot always put neat boxes around. The Beagleholes' census, Hecht's cultural analysis, and my generalizations all attempt to make sense of Pukapukan social organization in ways that outsiders can appreciate. I think they generally succeeed in this goal, but in each case, there are loose ends. The descriptions ignore important elements of diversity. They impose an order on the subtle and complex processes at work.[7]

Finally, questions exist in respect to a stated goal of ethnography: "grasp[ing] the native's point of view... realiz[ing] *his* vision of *his* world" (Malinowski 1961:25). Anthropological constructions are generally not produced for the individuals studied. (Many of them know a certain amount of the material already.)'They are produced for Western audiences (see Marcus and Cushman 1982). To what degree, we then must ask ourselves, can ethnographic accounts properly represent indigenous perspectives – and still be read by others? This, I noted, was the problem behind the *Akatawa*. It was also the problem regarding the writing of the dictionary. Anthropological constructions are developed in different contexts and directed toward different audiences than Pukapukan constructions.

Many of these problems are not new, of course. Over the years, a variety of peope have dealt with them. Well before the recent Freeman-Mad controversy (Brady 1983; Freeman 1983; M. Mead 1928) – or even before the Redfield-Lewis disagreement regarding Tepoztlan (Lewis 1951:428–40, 1953; Redfield 1930, 1953:155–7, 1960:132–48) – anthropologists were aware that different fieldworkers studying in the same locate often formulated their ethnographic understandings in different ways (see, e.g., Bennett 1946; Fortune 1939; M. Mead 1935). Likewise, more than forty years ago Sapir noted that "Two Crows, a perfeoctly good and authoritiative [Omaha informant], could presume to rule out of court the very existence of a custom or attitude or belief vouched for by some other [informant], equally good and authoritative" (Sapir 1938:7–8).

But it is also true that these issues have gained prominence in recent times. The growing accumulation of ethnographic data has made it increasingly obvious that these problems are part and parcel of anthropology. They are not anomalies. What Fox (1985:xii) describes as "the perception of malaise" or Bentley (1984:170) "the widely heralded 'crisis' " within anthropology involves, as Levy observes, an increasing critical "self-conscious[ness] about our received paradigms and . . . to some degree about our data" (1984:85–6). In piling these problems on top of one another, this book allows one to see *en clair* the issues involved. One can perceive in detail – in regard to specific ethnographers and specific informants – how and why they exist in the forms they do.

But one can see more than the limitations of anthropology. The ethnographic detail that makes these limitations so clear also emphasizes anthropology's real strengths. Though not objective in an absolute sense, anthropology does possess a degree of objectivity that makes it more than simply another folk model or "local" form of knowledge. At its core, anthropology involves comparison, the analysis of cultural differences and similarities. By the nature of its research, anthropology opens itself to a dialogue with other people possessing different insights and perspectives on the same situation.[8] Anthropological accounts make ideas considered self-evident in one culture subject to doubt, subject to comparison with alternative styles common in the other. Anthropology is still embedded in contexts, but it is relatively freer of these contexts because it continually opens itself to a diversity of perspectives that challenge its own.[9]

That has occurred here. Clearly I possess biases. But I was able to move beyond some of them in drawing comparisons between Pukapukan and anthropological constructions of the atoll's past. And I was able to use these comparisons, as I am doing now, to reflect back more generally on anthropological ways of knowing.

Ethnographic disagreements and divergent perspectives, we have seen, often bring anthropological biases to the fore. Differences between the Beagleholes' and Hecht's account of the atoll illuminated factors behind their separate constructions. And differing accounts by anthropologists and Pukapukans of the *Akatawa* has led, as we see here, to reflections on the construction of ethnographies.

Though this limited degree of objectivity lacks a correspondent sense of truth, it does prove of value in important respects. First, anthropological knowledge is frequently cumulative. As different fieldworkers return to the same site, they keep enlarging our vision of the culture. Hecht's analysis built on the Beagleholes'. Mine, coming later, built on both of theirs. Though differences exist, the collective result provides a richer, deeper understanding of Pukapukan culture than any one account would alone.

The accumulation of anthropological material leads to an increasing sophistication in our tools of analysis. The earlier patrilineal framework has given way to a more subtle appreciation of the flexible principles underlying Polynesian social organization. And a concern with the complexities and subtleties of informant knowledge claims is now replacing the previous focus on cultural stasis and homogeneity.

Anthropology, moreover, establishes bridges of cross-cultural understanding. Through ethnographic accounts one gains a better understanding of other people's perspectives in relation to one's own. This, I noted, is what happened in respect to the *Akatawa*. But ethnographic accounts also do more. They help indigenous populations reach a deeper understanding of themselves and their traditions – not necessarily because they agree with all that is stated about themselves in enthnographies but because ethnographies provide a form of understanding that is ultimately complementary to their own. That is why the Beagleholes' *Ethnology of Pukapuka* is a valued book on the atoll and that is why, perhaps, Tukia noted in respect to my dissertation (Borofsky 1982), "I did not find anything that you have written that may have caused embarrassment. . . . Instead, I am very grateful and happy to [have] someone . . . come to Pukapuka and write a permanent record of our disappearing . . . tradition."

The anthropological concern with understanding others as a means of understanding ourselves, of placing our own and others' traditions in broader perspective, is as relevant today, I believe, as when the Beagleholes first set foot on the atoll or Malinowski first described Trobriand *kula* exchanges. As Scholte phrases it, "The comparative understanding of others contributes to self-awareness" (1973:448; note also Ricoeur 1980).

Thus one can see that anthropological ways of knowing, despite their limitations, constitute a movement toward greater cultural understanding. This understanding develops not from a single ethnography but over time. Through a dialogue with others possessing different constructions and perspectives, we move beyond the complacency of our own constructions toward increased knowledge.

On this note, the book draws to a close. In traditional anthropological fashion, I have tried to show how a specific ethnographic study sheds light on broader issues – in this case, on different people's ways of knowing, of constructing, tradition. But though we approach the end, the need for dialogue continues. Important issues remain to be resolved regarding the strengths and limitations of anthropological ways of knowing. Handling them, however, will require more than abstract discussion. We must return to the basics of ethnography – looking not just at our specific disagreements but at the reasons for their existence, at the processes and contexts creating them. Then our different perspectives will help illuminate not only the cultures we study but aspects of our own discipline (and culture) as well.

Appendix
Regarding land disputes

Ko naa papaanga i loto te puka nei, e wolo te konga na maua mai ai, penei koi ai naa konga e ye maleka loa te kau na taaikua i loto. Kaaleka laa, ko naa papaanga tenei na talaina mai kiaku, kaale ai i leila ko te tika tikaai tenei. No leila aulaka lava naa papaanga nei e wakaliloina wai mea kimi pekapeka wenua, me kole, wai papaanga tano tikaai no te pilianga o naa koputangata.

Ko naa kootinga (me kole naa kena) i lunga o naa maapu i loto te puka nei, ko ye tano tikaai. Te tayi, ko aku penupenu vaito na milimili ai au, e wolo tikaai te takayala ka maua mai, i naa toe taime ka talea te laungaula tapuae takayala. Te lua, no te mea e wolo te tangata naa tuukeke a latou tala mainga i naa kootinga, no leila mea ai loa au i aku kootinga i taku manatunga. No leila, aulaka lava na maapu i loto te puka nei e wakaliloina wai mea kimi pekapeka wenua, me kole, wai mea tika tikaai no naa kootinga o naa wenua.

Although some individuals may wish to use genealogies and maps in this book to clarify questions regarding Pukapukan land ownership, they should realize that because of the contexts in which these data were collected, they are not appropriate for resolving land disputes on the island today.

157

Notes

Preface

1   Further details regarding the fieldwork are provided in Borofsky (1982:xiv-xx).

2   I selected a stratified random sample of seventy individuals: ten Pukapukan ten year olds, ten roughly twenty year olds, ten roughly thirty year olds, ten roughly forty year olds, ten roughly fifty year olds, and twenty who were more than sixty-three years of age. (The term roughly refers to the fact that I had to include people slightly older and slightly younger when there were not enough individuals of the specified age.) In each group, half were men, half women (except in two surveys regarding fishing knowledge). In addition, I included the ten people viewed by Pukapukans as most knowledgeable in traditional affairs. Since these individuals were all more than sixty-three years of age, the elderly group actually consisted of thirty people; but only twenty were selected randomly. Although the elderly population on the atoll was initially sixty-nine in my census, when I excluded people who (1) had died between the census and the undertaking of various surveys, (2) were too sick to be interviewed, (3) were obviously senile, and (4) had left the island for one reason or another, the survey population was never more than fifty-six and decreased throughout the research. Thus the elderly nonrandom sample of thirty constituted 54 percent of the elderly population examinable on the island.

3   The sex and approximate age of the named informants cited in the texts are as follows: Akima (male, 51), Apela (male, 78), Kililua (male, 64), Lavalua (male, 39), Lemuna (female, 67), Limapeni (male, 22), Maina (male, 46), Molingi (female, 77), Ngalau (male, 78), Nimeti (male, 72 years), Paani (male, 72), Paleula (male, 49), Petelo (male, 75), Poyila (male, 57), Taavini (female, 66), Tai (male, 17), Tengele (male, 46), Toa (male, 62), Tukia (male, 32), Unu (male, 21), Vave (male, 65), Viliamu (male, 43), Walemaki (male, 88), Yala (male, 70), Yingonge (male, 40), and Yolo (male, 65). The ages are as of March 1978. Names not listed here, such as Taputu and Lama, are fictitious.

4   See, e.g., Brady (1983), Clifford and Marcus (1986), Hamelink (1983),

Keesing and Tonkinson (1982), Kuper (1983), Levy (1984), Malinowski (1967), Marcus and Cushman (1982), Marcus and Fischer (1986), Rabinow (1977), Rabinow and Sullivan (1979), and Wayne (Malinowska) (1985). My understanding of the broader context within which these ideas developed draws much from a discussion with Greg Dening on the subject.

5 To facilitate readers' analysis of the data, I have noted in the main text a rough estimate of the frequency with which various remarks and/or incidents occurred during fieldwork.

1 Differing accounts of the past

1 See E. Beaglehole (1937b, 1944), E. Beaglehole and P. Beaglehole (1938, 1939, 1941, ms. a, ms. b), Beckett (1964), Cook Islands Census of Population and Housing (1977), Davies (1956a, 1956b), Department of Health (n.d.), F. Frisbie (1948), J. Frisbie (1959), R. Frisbie (1928a, 1928b, 1929a, 1929b, 1929c, 1930, 1935, 1939), Gill (1912), Hecht (1976a, 1976b, 1977, 1978, 1981, 1985), Hutchin (1904), Mataola et al. (1981), New Zealand Meteorological Service (n.d.), I. Prior (1971, 1974), I. Prior et al. (1966, 1981), Shapiro (1942), Tiro (n.d.), Turner (1978), Vayda (1957, 1958, 1959), as well as considerable manuscript material located in the Government Archives, Rarotonga and the Government Office, Pukapuka.

2 My description of *waka* does not include various linguistic subtleties. Readers can gain an idea of these from examining Biggs's (1969:83–4) description of the New Zealand Maori cognate *whaka*. Most Pukapukans readily understood what the term *Wakatawa* meant. It was simply that they never seemed to use it, just as we do not use the words *thou* and *dost*.

3 On the basis of a discussion with Dr. George Pararas-Carayannis (personal communication 1985), director of the International Tsunami Information Center in Hawaii, it appears that the devastation was not caused by a seismic, or tidal, wave as reported by the Beagleholes. The Beagleholes describe the event as "thunder was pounding, lightning was striking, the wind was blowing from all directions" (1938:386). According to Dr. Pararas-Carayannis, this description fits a hurricane, not a tidal wave.

2 Pukapukan social organization

1 At the time I conducted a census in 1980, there were 137 households on the island. Of these, 123 easily fit within the viripatri-uxorimatrilocal distinctions discussed in the text. Another nine possessed dual classifications because each spouse asserted a different connection to the household site. For these nine cases I recorded both connections and then gave each one-half a point. (For example, if the husband explained current residence on the basis of viripatrilocal ties and his wife on the basis of uxorimatrilocal ties, each of these categories received an 0.5 score. In summarizing the results, I rounded off each category's scores to the nearest whole integer.) Two households fit into a miscellaneous category (e.g., one household head was a friend of a relative of the owner). Three possessed house sites because of their occupations: the chief administrative officer and the doctor lived in government housing; the Seventh Day Adventist minister lived in housing provided by his congregation.

Based on the above, eighty-eight households (or 64 percent of 137) fit within some virilocal or patrilocal category: 26 percent involved viripatri-locality, 20 percent virimatrilocality, 3 percent virilocality (with no further details available regarding form of virilocality), and 16 percent patrilocality (with no details regarding form of patrilocality). (These add up to 65 percent because I rounded integers off to the nearest whole percent.)

Forty-four households (or 32 percent of 137) fit within some uxorilocal or matrilocal category: 14 percent involved uxoripatrilocality, 9 percent uxorimatrilocality, and 9 percent matrilocality (with no further details available regarding the form of matrilocality).

2 Of the forty households within the geographical confines of Ngake village, two households belong to other village organizations. One household belongs to Loto's village organization, the other to Yato's.

3 Village boundaries within the lagoon are ambiguous today (cf. Beaglehole and Beaglehole 1938:32). The small islet at the far left, called the Toka, is an uninhabited shifting sand bar. It is dangerous to land at except in calm weather.

4 The Pukapukan word *wuaanga* was used significantly less often than the Rarotongan term *koputangata* in 1977–81 to discuss the constructs examined here. According to Mataola et al. (1981), *wuaanga* refers to (1) a nuclear family and (2) consanguineal relatives. For a slightly different perspective on *wuaanga*, see Hecht (1976a:86–7, 1981:76).

5 *Cultural construct*, in this book, constitutes a rhetorical means of conceptualizing and discussing past events as well as framing and legitimizing present ones. It involves a set of linked concepts that guide and inform, rather than determine, people's actions.

I prefer the use of the term *cultural construct* to *model* or *schema* for two reasons. First, both *model* and *schema* have been used in a number of ways by a variety of authors. Howe comments, "The term 'model' is all too often used indiscriminately to refer to any one of the following: plan, programme, template, collective representation, set of ideas, culture, and so forth" (in Holy and Struhlik 1983:92). Quinn and Holland note, "The reader should beware . . . of the differing and conflicting uses of 'model' . . . as is typical of new theoretical endeavors, this one has not yet gotten its terminology under control" (1987:25). *Schema* has similar problems, as a reading of Casson (1983), Hutchins (1980), and Tyler (1978) makes clear.

In addition, *model* implies, I believe, a broader degree of coherence, of order and meaning, than *construct*. Constructs may well fit together into meaningful clusters, as we see below. But they might not. Their integration into broader patterns is something to be determined, not presumed.

My perspective here owes much to discussions with Dorothy Holland and Edwin Hutchins, though, in fairness to them, it should be noted that our positions are not exactly the same.

6 Hecht also discusses some of these constructs, though she phrases her discussion in slightly different terms. See Hecht (1977:196; 1981:71) for the seniority construct, (1976a:38ff.; 1977:186ff.) for the gender construct, and (1977:185) for the apical ancestor (*pu mua*) construct. For an interesting parallel to the ambiguities surrounding the "sloughing off" process of relatives, see Silverman (1971:309).

7 Interesting parallels to this construct exist in the *tamatane/tamafafine* distinction of the Tokelaus and Samoa. See Huntsman (1971) and Shore (1982:93).

8   In cases in which an older person was in the process of transmitting her rights and/or allowing close relatives to temporarily use her sections in 1977–81, the older person alone is shown in the genealogy, since, technically speaking, the older person still controlled the rights to that section. To give readers a sense of how the "sloughing off" process works, all five of Kitewu's children are included. However, only individuals directly involved in the transmission process are listed among succeeding generations for simplicity and clarity in diagraming the genealogy.

9   As in Figure 1, I have included the first-generation children of key ancestors to provide a sense of how the "sloughing off" process works. Again, for clarity, I have listed among succeeding generations only individuals directly involved in the transmission process.

10   For clarifying details, see note 9. This genealogy involves part of the same *koputangata* as cited in Figure 2. Two stewards (*tiaki*) jointly supervise sections 2 and 3 together.

11   *Tawa* boundaries outside the reserves (*motu*) and in the lagoon are unclear.

12   These figures were calculated by (1) taking the two boat trips recorded by Turner (1978:19) for imported foodstuffs, (2) dividing the amount of food-stuffs in half (to get the approximate amount per trip), (3) multiplying that figure by 5 (the number of ship visits in 1978), and (4) rounding the amount off to the nearest 100 (given that the figures are tentative at best). The 1978 figures, I suspect, may be inflated somewhat. Wide variations exist between trips depending on what supplies are available in Rarotonga at the time of a boat's departure. Still, the figures give a rough idea of the degree to which modern Pukapukans import food.

13   The data are (1) the association of patrilineal groupings with strips of land in all village reserves, (2) the association of the same patrilineal groupings with strips of land (running from lagoon to the ocean) outside the reserve, (3) the relation of present-day food-sharing units to *yoolonga* groupings, (4) the earlier localization of village membership cited by the Beagleholes, and (5) the greater significance of patrilineal games in previous times. For supporting material see Hecht (1976a:22, 60–3; 1977:184ff.). Additional materials exist in government records (located in the Government Office, Pukapuka) as well as in the Beagleholes' field notes (ms. a).

14   For a fuller discussion of how anthropologists have sought to distinguish themselves intellectually from other Westerners living in foreign locales as well as how they have sought to enhance their respectability by affirming scientific perspectives, readers may consult Harris (1968), Kuper (1983), Langham (1981), Leaf (1979), Stocking (1968), Ulin (1984), and Voget (1973).

15   Readers should consult the following sources and their references: Colson (1985), Ebihara (1985), Eggan (1968), Ellen (1984), Harris (1968), Kuper (1983), Leaf (1979), Lowie (1937), and Stocking (1983b).

16   Rudmin (n.d.) provides a valuable analysis of Ernest Beaglehole's contributions to cross-cultural psychology.

17   Although several other matrilineal swamps might have been chosen in examining this point, Puwatu is a particularly significant case. Because most of the swamp's cultivators fall within the Beagleholes' census for Yato, their matrilineal affiliations can be precisely determined. Also, Puwatu was not included in a 1939 islandwide redivision of taro swamps (of *te au wua wowolo*), which could confuse reconstruction of the swamp's cultivators in 1934–5.

Map 5 contains a slight bias in favor of plots belonging to the Kava submatrilineage. Regarding the case of an elderly man who almost certainly had his plots cultivated by others (presumably his daughters and daughter-in-law), I listed the taro plots under his matrilineal affiliation, Kava. (I suspect Pukapukans would have done likewise.)

Readers should also note that *kawa* (or strips of the swamp) 1 through 9 constitute the swamp's central core. Both end sections of the swamp include new plots that have been excavated in the past several decades. Since I am not sure precisely when individual plots were dug, I have included all of them in both Map 5 and Figure 1 (to be on the safe side). This addition does not significantly affect the genealogical information depicted in Figure 1 nor the conclusions drawn from it.

One cannot be absolutely certain that the reconstructions in Figures 1 and 2 (as well as Maps 5 and 6) are accurate in every respect because, as noted in the text, people who are temporarily given land (as an act of friendship) sometimes take it over and establish their own genealogical connections to the relevant apical ancestor. However, I believe the reconstructions to be *at least* 85 percent accurate and see no reason to doubt the conclusions regarding them in the text. I believe they are solidly supported by the existing data.

18   Given that Awale, like Puwatu, was not redivided in 1939 and that many of its cultivators fall within the Beagleholes' census, a reasonably unbiased reconstruction can be made both of the swamp's cultivators in 1934–5 and of each cultivator's patrilineal affiliation.

In the cases in which cultivators fell outside the Beagleholes' census (i.e., those residing in Loto), present-day informants' retrospective accounts were used to determine patrilineal affiliation. (This involved asking an adult where his or her parents were buried – a readily known fact rarely subject to distortion or inaccuracy.) Readers should note that the names and categorization of patrilineages have changed somewhat since 1934–5. Wherever discrepancies exist in terminology, I have used the modern term. (This bias, in my opinion, is a minor one at best since the different names still refer to the same location.)

19   Adoption requires such consent. Full and closed cemeteries are rather specialized or modern exceptions to the general rule.

20   To a certain degree – depending on how one defines the term (see, e.g., Lévi-Strauss 1960, 1963a, 1963b; Maybury-Lewis 1960, 1967) – the *Akatawa* might be viewed as an example of dual organization and seen as paralleling the bipartite grouping of the matrimoieties. Certainly the *Akatawa* divides the island into two groups that compete against one another. But this duality is based on village food-sharing units rather than matrilineal descent, and it lacks some of the abstract oppositions occurring with other dual organizations (see, e.g., Maybury-Lewis 1967) or the dualistic principles related to gender (male/female) and power (sacred/secular) that Shore (n.d.) insightfully discusses with regard to Polynesia at large.

Without denying that the *Akatawa* might be considered a form of dual organization, I believe its major significance lies in constituting an alternative to the predominant village organization as a means of organizing people and property.

21   See Agar (1982), Bleicher (1980), and Gadamer (1975a, 1975b) for an elaboration of this theme.

3 Acquiring traditional knowledge

1   In addition to the specific references cited throughout this chapter, I found the following helpful in formulating my analysis of learning and cultural transmission on Pukapuka; interested readers may wish to consult these for elaboration of and comparison with themes developed in the text: Barth (1975), Bateson (1972), Berland (1982), Best (1974), Brenner (1985), Burke (1978), Cavalli-Sforza, Feldman, Chen, and Dornbusch (1982), Du Bois (1960), Fortes (1938), Funnell and Smith (1981), Gearing (1973), Gearing and Sangree (1979), Heider (1976), Holland (1984), Horton and Finnegan (1973), Irvine (1978), Keesing (1982), Kimball and Burnett (1973), Lave (1980, 1982, in press), Levin (1978b), Lord (1960), M. Mead (1928), Middleton (1970), Raum (1938), Reed and Lave (1979), Salmond (1982), Scribner and Cole (1981), Shore (n.d.), Shweder and LeVine (1984), Silverman (1971), and Williams (1958).

2   This idea derives from discussions with Alan Howard.

3   The ideas in this paragraph owe much to a discussion with Judith Huntsman on the subject.

4   For interested readers, the following is additional information regarding Pukapukan concepts of knowing. The English word *knowledge* can be translated by two Pukapukan words: *kite* and *wanewane*. In the sentence, *Kaae kite loa o te peepee i te mea lelei ma te mea kino*, 'A baby has no knowledge of good and evil,' *kite* has the same implication as in the text – that knowledge comes from visual experience. *Wanewane* is more closely related to skill and intelligence: *E tangata wai wanewane ia Ngutu e te wowou vaka*, 'Ngutu possesses considerable knowledge regarding the making of canoes.'

As a descriptive, the related English word *knowing* might best be translated as *maawutu*. *E tangata maawutu ia Petelo*, 'Petelo is a knowing (or clever) person.' *Knowing*, in a more verbal sense, would be either *iloa* or *kitea*: *Ko ye iloa loa e wea te vaia ka tupu ai*, 'There is no way of knowing when it will happen.' *Na kave wua koe i toku vaka ma te ye aku kitea*, 'You took my canoe without my knowing about it.'

The word *maalama* connotes understanding in the sense that something has become clear. *E kiai te tamaiti ia na maalama tikaai e wea te talatala a te puapii na mea kia ana*, 'The boy did not really understand (or it was not really clear to the boy) what the teacher said to him.' The related word *maalamalama* refers to a window (in the sense of something that lets in light), clear (as in clear sky), and transparent (in the sense of something that can be seen through). *Maawutu* and *iloa* also connote understanding as we use it in English: *E wolo te maawutu o te wolomatua i te Puka Tapu*, 'The pastor shows considerable understanding of the Bible.' *Ko ye au iloa la e tuulanga kino toku mea*, 'You don't understand what a difficult position I am in.'

Insight, in the sense of ability to understand, would fall within the scope of *maalama*. *Wanewane* conveys the sense of insight as intellectual ability: *Koi to wanewane wua e maua ai ia koe e te alu i naa yanga waingataa naa*, 'You have to use your insight to be able to do those difficult tasks.'

Learning in Pukapukan is *wakamau*: *Ko wakamau te kau taane e lua mako woou*, 'The group of men are learning two new chants.' As will be noted later in the chapter, some Pukapukans also perceive *apii* as connoting learning. Forgetting is *ngalopoaina* or *ye manatua*: *Iaku ko ngalopoaina wua loa e te wulu i oku nio i te motaeyao*, 'I keep forgetting to brush my teeth in the morning.' *Ye manatua* connotes more a sense of having something from one's mind or be set aside (as to have forgotten a grudge): *Ko ye aku manatua loa e ka wo te wii taane yii ika i te po nei*, 'I keep forgetting that all the men will be going fishing tonight.'

Further information on Pukapukan vocabulary can be found in Mataola et al. (1981).

5 This is an exception to the general rule of not providing other Pukapukans with detailed genealogies that might threaten one's own land claims (see Chapters 2 and 4). It derives from the nature of the relationship between the two individuals and from the genealogies requested.

4 Validating traditional knowledge

1 Awale is also sometimes viewed as a major cemetery, though few people are buried there today.

2 In addition to the references cited below in the text, I found the following material helpful in formulating may analysis of Pukapukan validating procedures; interested readers may wish to consult these for elaboration of and comparison with themes developed in this chapter: Brown and Roberts (1980), Evans-Pritchard (1937), Horton and Finnegan (1973), Hutchins (1980), Irvine (1978), Keesing (1982), Keesing and Tonkinson (1982), Koskinen (1968), Lave (1985, 1988), Levy (1973), Lindstrom (1984), Rubinstein (1981), and Shore (1982, n.d.).

3 In the Beagleholes' manuscript the main character is called Kutu, not Wutu, as he is today. This slight change raises a very interesting question. The Rarotongan word for lice is *kutu*, whereas the Pukapukan word is *wutu*. It is possible that the name became "Pukapukanized" from what was perceived to be a Rarotongan form.

4 This idea was first suggested to me by Bradd Shore.

5 Although one should not overemphasize Pukapukan concerns with status rivalry, it is also important not to ignore them. Various researchers (e.g., Graves and Graves 1978; Thomas 1975, 1978) have rightfully emphasized the cooperative aspects of Polynesian learning, but little has been said to date regarding its competitive aspects. (Ritchie and Ritchie state, in discussing research on Polynesian learning styles, "It sometimes seems . . . that researchers are more interested in cooperation than are Polynesians," 1989:127–8.) In Pukapuka, status rivalries are a pervasive part of the learning process. They motivate people to learn; they add a certain zest to the educational experience.

6 J. Huntsman (personal communication 1985) suggests that one might distinguish between two general types of knowledge among Pukapukans: esoteric and practical. While noting that some categories, such as land disputes, bridge this distinction, she suggests that the types of ambiguities dealt with here probably exist more in areas of esoteric knowledge than in areas of practical knowledge. I would agree. In a later paper, I hope to explore this subject further.

Readers should be cautioned, however, that the matter is not a simple one. Pukapukans appear to disagree on a variety of matters related to everyday life – for example, cooking recipes, kinship terms, and identifications of fish (both live and photographed). Where disagreement merges with ambiguity, where practical knowledge merges with esoteric knowledge is not always easy to delineate.

In his book on Kwaio religion, Keesing (1982:208) makes a related distinction between operational and interpretative knowledge – between possessing a "detailed step-by-step knowledge of how to conduct a rite" and "a coherent understanding of the symbolic grammar of which it is an expression." Keesing observes: "Some Kwaio individuals command very broad knowledge, both open and esoteric, have a commitment to systematic understanding (if not ultimate explanation), and have access to deep symbolic structures. The majority know less than they could, apparently understand only superficial layers of symbolism, and assume a pragmatic approach to the spirits they seek to live with in harmony, not understand." (1982:5)

7   The following are additional references regarding the diversity, fluidity, and creativity of traditional knowledge: Barnes (1984), Barth (1975), Bilmes (1975, 1976), Brickler (1975), Brown and Roberts (1980), Crick (1982b), Errington (1984), Furbee and Benfer (1983), Howard (1979), Keesing (1982), Keesing and Tonkinson (1982), Kiste (1974), Lewis (1980), Lindstrom (1982), Pelto and Pelto (1975), Radin (1957), Rubinstein (1981), Salisbury (1984), Sanjek (1977), Scribner (1985), Shweder and LeVine (1984), Silverman (1971, 1977), and Weller (1984b).

8   My concern with the dynamic quality of Pukapukan knowledge claims should not be viewed as slighting the importance of structural patterns. As Shore (1982) emphasizes, such patterns can underlie both diversity and change. We have seen that here, especially in the past three chapters. Still, in dealing with structural patterns, caution is in order. We must be clear regarding who has created what. Are the structures based on the anthropologist's analysis, various informants' assertions, or ecological factors? Are they simply meant to be tools of analysis or do they imply some deeper cognitive organization that orders and predicts experience? Combining different senses of structure, without being sensitive to the dynamics involved in the production of each, can be misleading, as we saw in Chapter 2. Too often anthropologists assume the existence of coherent structures without precisely delineating the level at which they occur or the way they came about. It becomes easy under such circumstances to fall prey to tautological thinking – discovering coherent structures because we presume they exist. As Brunton (1980) emphasizes, this can generate a sense of "misconstrued order."

R. Levy (personal communication 1985) and G. Marcus (personal communication 1985) suggest, in a related theme, that the process of acculturation may generate ordered, self-conscious accounts by informants. With Westernization, informants begin consciously to formulate a sense of tradition, explaining to themselves and others their distinctive cultural identity (cf. Howard 1979). Levy points out that these structured, self-conscious forms of knowledge may falsely support our own intellectual conception of how cultures work, especially in regard to oversimplifying processes of diversity and change.

9   Though a great deal has been written about non-Western patterns of thought, one must approach this topic with a certain amount of caution. Crick comments that "much anthropological work about 'modes of thought' is vague so that one scarcely knows what authors are talking about let alone how to test their propositions" (1982b:290). Also, though anthropologists

have functioned effectively as critics of laboratory experiments, rarely have they matched in their analyses the sophisticated experimental techniques developed by cross-cultural psychologists in the field (see, e.g., Scribner and Cole 1981).

References on the subject, besides those cited in the text, that aided the formulation of my analysis are Best (1974), Brenner (1985), Cole (1977), Crick (1982b), Duranti (1985), Errington (1984), Goody (1977), Goody and Watt (1963), Hallpike (1979), Hollis and Lukes (1982), Hutchins (1980), Horton and Finnegan (1973), Laboratory of Comparative Human Cognition (1978, 1979), Lave (1980, 1985), Murtaugh (1985), Sahlins (1976), Scribner and Cole (1973, 1981), Sharp, Cole, and Lave (1979), Shore (n.d.), Shweder (1977, 1979–80), Shweder and LeVine (1984), and Wilson (1970).

5 Making history

1   Andrew Arno originally suggested this idea to me.
2   In contrast to cargo cults, these cultural revivals constitute affirmations of solidarity the Western powers, still exerting considerable control in the area, could often understand and accept since they are related to their own histories as nations (cf. Keesing and Tonkinson 1982:298).
3   The paid government workers played a set of cricket matches against the villages in August and September of 1972. These matches may have acted as a model or basis for the 'Council of Important People's' decision to compete against the three patrilineal groupings.

J. Hecht (personal communications 1985, 1986) mentioned, in regard to the *Akatawa* revival (see later in the text), that the government workers called themselves the "Eastern Territories," because the government offices exist on the eastern side of the island. Since Hecht had only recently arrived on the island, she did not recollect (nor was certain) that an indigenous Pukapukan term was used in addition to "Eastern Territories" to describe the government team. But if it were, she and I concur that Tawa Ngake would be a reasonable translation. According to Lakulaku Eliu, the reputed originator of the phrase, the "Western Territories" referred to the three villages and the churches.

To what degree, if any, this stimulated the formation of the *Akatawa* is uncertain at best. Certainly no Pukapukan ever mentioned this as a factor to me, and the opposition between "Eastern" and "Western" territories involved different units than those established under the *Akatawa*.
4   In practicing for the competitions I sponsored, older people instructed others, at times quite formally, in the required skills.
5   Similarly, Bernard, Killworth, Kronenfeld, and Sailer (1984:508) indicate, "Informants respond to questions by reporting cultural norms, or 'what goes with what,' rather than dredging up actual events [or] circumstances." See also D'Andrade (1974) and Shweder and D'Andrade (1980).
6   Such cautiousness is particularly important since, as Crick notes, "the number of articles published . . . which give rise to protracted debate is small. In this sense, ethnographic meanings become knowledge through an ab-

sence of comment" (1982a:29–30). Describing one's biases, as has recently become popular, does not really resolve the problem. It only presumes that anthropologists understand all of their biases – a dubious assumption at best (see, e.g., Magnarella 1983).

7 Pertinent references regarding the styles by which anthropologists over-structure the fluidity and diversity of cultural knowledge, and the reasons they do so, are Agar (1982), Barth (1975), Brunton (1980), Burke (1978), Crick (1982a), Finnegan (1977), France (1969), Hobsbawm and Ranger (1983), Howard (1979), Howe (1984), Keesing (1982), Keesing and Tonkinson (1982), Leaf (1979), Lord (1960), Marcus and Cushman (1982), Mathews (1983), Pelto and Pelto (1975), Rabinow (1977), Shweder and LeVine (1984), Silverman (1971), Stocking (1983b), Wagner (1981), and Wolf (1982).

8 Pertinent references regarding the dialogical nature of anthropological re-search are Agar (1982), Barth (1975), Bleicher (1980), Boon (1982), Brown and Roberts (1980), Burke (1978), Clifford (1980, 1982, 1983a, 1983b), Clifford and Marcus (1986), Crapanzano (1977), Crick (1982a, 1982b), Dening (1980), Dumont (1978), Dwyer (1982), Ellen (1984), Fabian (1983), Finnegan (1977), Gadamer (1975a, 1975b), Gartrell (1979), Horton and Finnegan (1973), Keesing (1982), Keesing and Tonkinson (1982), Larcom (1982), Levy (1984), Linnekin (1983), Marcus and Cushman (1982), Marcus and Fischer (1986), Parkin (1982), Rabinow (1977), Ranger (1983), Salmond (1982), Scholte (1973), Silverman (1971), Stocking (1983b), and Wagner (1981). I found material by Dening, Clifford, Marcus, and Gadamer particularly valuable in formulating my own perspective.

9 The ideas embodied in this paragraph owe much to a discussion with Robert Levy.

Bibliography

Agar, Michael
    1982   Toward an Ethnographic Language. *American Anthropologist* 84:779–95.
Alkire, William
    1968   Porpoises and Taro. *Ethnology* 7:280–9.
Ammar, Hamed
    1970   The Aims and Methods of Socialization in Silwa. In *From Child to Adult*. John Middleton, ed., pp. 226–49. Austin: University of Texas Press.
Anderson, John R.
    1976   *Language, Memory, and Thought*. Hillsdale, NJ: Erlbaum.
Appadurai, Arjun
    1981   The Past as a Scarce Resource. *Man* 16:201–19.
Arno, Andrew
    1985   Structural Communication and Control Communication: An Interactionist Perspective on Legal and Customary Procedures for Conflict Management. *American Anthropologist* 87:40–55.
Asad, T., ed.
    1973   *Anthropology and the Colonial Encounter*. New York: Humanities Press.
Babadzan, Alain
    1985   From Oral to Written: The *Puta Tupuna* of Rurutu. In *Transformations of Polynesian Culture*. Antony Hooper and Judith Huntsman, eds., pp. 177–93. Auckland: The Polynesian Society.
Baddeley, Josephine
    1978   Rarotongan Society: The Creation of Tradition. Doctoral dissertation. University of Auckland, Department of Anthropology.
Barnes, R. H.
    1984   *Two Crows Denies It: A History of Controversy in Omaha Sociology*. Lincoln: University of Nebraska Press.
Barnes, S. H.
    1968   Paradigms, Scientific and Social. *Man* 1:94–102.

Barrau, Jacques
  1965   L'Humide et le Sec: An Essay on Ethnological Adaptation to
             Contrastive Environments in the Indo-Pacific Area. *Journal of
             the Polynesian Society* 74:329–46.
Barth, Fredrik
  1975   *Ritual and Knowledge among the Baktaman of New Guinea*. New
             Haven, CT: Yale University Press.
Bartlett, Frederic
  1932   *Remembering: A Study in Experimental and Social Psychology.*
             New York: Macmillan.
Bateson, Gregory
  1972   The Logical Categories of Learning and Communication. In *Steps to
             an Ecology of Mind*. pp. 279–308. New York: Ballantine Books.
Bauer, Dan, and John Hinnant
  1980   Normal and Revolutionary Divination: A Kuhnian Approach to
             African Traditional Thought. In *Explorations in African Systems
             of Thought*. Ivan Karp and Charles Bird, eds., pp. 213–36.
             Bloomington: Indiana University Press.
Beaglehole, Ernest
  1932   *Property: A Study in Social Psychology*. London: George Allen
             and Unwin.
  1937a   Cultural Peaks in Polynesia. *Man* 37(176):138–40.
  1937b   Emotional Release in a Polynesian Community. *Journal of Ab-
             normal and Social Psychology* 32:319–28.
  1937c   *Notes on Hopi Economic Life*. Yale University Publications in
             Anthropology, 15. New Haven, CT: Yale University Press.
  1944   *Islands of Danger*. Wellington: Progressive.
Beaglehole, Ernest, and Pearl Beaglehole
  1938   *Ethnology of Pukapuka*. Bernice P. Bishop Museum Bulletin
             150. Honolulu: Bernice P. Bishop Museum.
  1939   Brief Pukapukan Case History. *Journal of the Polynesian Society*
             48:135–43.
  1941   Personality Development in Pukapukan Children. In *Language,
             Culture and Personality*. L. Spier, A. Hallowell, and S. Newman,
             eds., pp. 282–98. Menasha, WI: Sapir Memorial Publication Fund.
  ms. a   Field Notes. Manuscript in the Bernice P. Bishop Museum Li-
             brary. Honolulu, Hawaii.
  ms. b   Myths, Stories and Chants from Pukapuka. Manuscript in the
             Bernice P. Bishop Museum Library. Honolulu, Hawaii.
Beaglehole, J. C.
  1966   *The Exploration of the Pacific*. Stanford, CA: Stanford Univer-
             sity Press.
Beaglehole, Pearl
  1935   Census Data from Two Hopi Villages. *American Anthropologist*
             37:41–54.
Beckett, Jeremy
  1964   Social Change in Pukapuka. *Journal of the Polynesian Society*
             73:411–30.
Bennett, John
  1946   The Interpretation of Pueblo Culture: A Question of Values.
             Southwestern Journal of Anthropology 2:361–74.

Bentley, G. Carter
1984   On Anthropological Epistemology: Praxis and Critique. *Reviews in Anthropology* 11:170–84.
Berger, Peter, and Thomas Luckmann
1966   *The Social Construction of Reality: A Treatise in the Sociology of Knowledge.* New York: Doubleday.
Berland, Joseph
1982   *No Five Fingers Are Alike: Cognitive Amplifiers in Social Context.* Cambridge, MA: Harvard University Press.
Bernard, Russell, Peter Killworth, David Kronenfeld, and Lee Sailer
1984   The Problem of Informant Accuracy: The Validity of Retrospective Data. *Annual Review of Anthropology* 13:495–517.
Best, Elsdon
1974   *The Maori School of Learning: Its Objects, Methods, and Ceremonial.* Wellington, New Zealand: Shearer, Government Printer.
Biggs, Bruce
1969   *Let's Learn Maori: A Guide to the Study of the Maori Language.* Wellington, New Zealand: Reed.
Bilmes, Jack
1975   Misinformation in Verbal Accounts: Some Fundamental Considerations. *Man* 10:60–71.
1976   Rules and Rhetoric: Negotiating the Social Order in a Thai Village. *Journal of Anthropological Research* 32:44–57.
Bleicher, Josef
1980   *Contemporary Hermeneutics: Hermeneutics as Method, Philosophy and Critique.* London: Routledge and Kegan Paul.
Bloch, Maurice
1977   The Past and the Present in the Present. *Man* 12:278–92.
Blount, Ben
1975   Agreeing to Agree on Genealogy: A Luo Sociology of Knowledge. In *Sociocultural Dimensions of Language Use.* M. Sanches and B. Blount, eds., pp. 117–35. New York: Academic Press.
Boggs, Stephen
1972   The Meaning of Questions and Narratives to Hawaiian Children. In *Functions of Language in the Classroom.* Courtney Cazden, Vera John, and Dell Hymes, eds., pp. 299–327. New York: Teachers College Press.
Bohannan, Laura
1952   A Genealogical Charter. *Africa* 22:301–15.
1954   *Return to Laughter.* New York: Harper Bros. (Published under the pseudonym Elenore Smith Bowen.)
Boon, James
1982   *Other Tribes, Other Scribes: Symbolic Anthropology in the Comparative Study of Cultures, Histories, Religions, and Texts.* New York: Cambridge University Press.
Borofsky, Robert
1982   Making History: The Creation of Traditional Knowledge on Pukapuka, A Polynesian Atoll. Doctoral dissertation. University of Hawaii, Department of Anthropology.

Brady, Ivan, ed.
1983   Speaking in the Name of the Real: Freeman and Mead on Samoa. *American Anthropologist* 85:908–46.
Brenner, Mary
1985   The Practice of Arithmetic in Liberian Schools. In *The Social Organization of Knowledge and Practice: A Symposium. Anthropology and Education Quarterly* 16:177–86.
Brickler, Victoria; ed.
1975   Intra-Cultural Variation. Special Issue. *American Ethnologist*, 2(1).
Brown, Ann, and Lucia French
1979   Commentary. In *Education and Cognitive Development: The Evidence from Experimental Research*. Monographs of the Society for Research in Child Development. Serial No. 178, Vol. 44(1–2):101–9.
Brown, Kenneth, and Michael Roberts, eds.
1980   Using Oral Sources: Vansina and Beyond. *Social Analysis*, No. 4.
Brunton, Ron
1980   Misconstrued Order in Melanesian Religion. *Man* 15:112–28.
Buck, Peter (See Te Rangi Hiroa)
Burke, Peter
1978   *Popular Culture in Early Modern Europe*. London: Temple Smith.
Burrows, Edwin
1939   Breed and Border in Polynesia. *American Anthropologist* 41:1–21.
Carmack, Robert
1972   Ethnohistory: A Review of Its Development, Definitions, Methods, and Aims. *Annual Review of Anthropology* 1:227–46.
Casson, Ronald
1981   *Language, Culture and Cognition: Anthropological Perspectives*. New York: Macmillan.
1983   Schemata in Cognitive Anthropology. *Annual Review of Anthropology* 12:429–62.
Cavalli-Sforza, L., M. Feldman, K. Chen, and S. Dornbusch
1982   Theory and Observation in Cultural Transmission. *Science* 218:19–27.
Chase, W. G., and W. H. Simon
1973   Perception in Chess. *Cognitive Psychology* 4:55–81.
Chung, Sandra
1978   *Case Marking and Grammatical Relations in Polynesian*. Austin: University of Texas Press.
Clanchy, M. T.
1979   *From Memory to Written Record: England, 1066–1307*. Cambridge, MA: Harvard University Press.
Clement, Dorothy
1982   Samoan Folk Knowledge of Mental Disorders. In *Cultural Conceptions of Mental Health and Therapy*. A. J. Marsella and G. M. White, eds., pp. 193–214. Dordrecht, Holland: Reidel.

Clifford, James
    1980   Fieldwork, Reciprocity, and the Making of Ethnographic Texts:
                The Example of Maurice Leenhardt. *Man* 15:518–32.
    1982   *Person and Myth: Maurice Leenhardt in the Melanesian World.*
                Berkeley: University of California Press.
    1983a   On Ethnographic Authority. *Representations* 1:118–46.
    1983b   Power and Dialogue in Ethnography: Marcel Griaule's Initiation. In
                Observers Observed: Essays on Ethnographic Fieldwork. George
                Stocking, ed., pp. 121–56. Madison: University of Wisconsin Press.
Clifford, James, and George Marcus
    1986   *Writing Cultures: The Poetics and Politics of Ethnography.*
                Berkeley: University of California Press.
Cole, Michael
    1977   An Ethnographic Psychology of Cognition. In *Thinking: Read-
                ings in Cognitive Science.* P. Johnson-Laird and P. Wason, eds.,
                pp. 468–82. New York: Cambridge University Press.
Cole, Michael, and John Gay
    1972   Culture and Memory. *American Anthropologist* 74:1066–84.
Cole, Michael, John Gay, Joseph Glick, and Donald Sharp
    1971   *The Cultural Context of Learning and Thinking.* New York: Basic
                Books.
Cole, Michael, and Sylvia Scribner
    1974   *Culture and Thought: A Psychological Introduction.* New York:
                Wiley.
Colson, Elizabeth
    1985   Defining American Ethnology. In *Social Contexts of American
                Ethnology, 1840–1984: 1984 Proceedings of the American Eth-
                nological Society.* June Helm, ed., pp. 177–84. Washington, DC:
                American Anthropological Association.
Condliffe, J. B.
    1971   *Te Rangi Hiroa: The Life of Sir Peter Buck.* Christchurch, New
                Zealand: Whitcombe and Tombs.
Connelly, John
    1979   Hopi Social Organization. In *Handbook of North American In-
                dians*, Vol. 9. A. Ortiz, vol. ed., pp. 539–53. Washington, DC:
                Smithsonian Institution.
Cook Islands Census of Population and Housing, 1976
    1977   Rarotonga: Government of the Cook Islands.
Crapanzano, Vincent
    1977   On the Writing of Ethnography. *Dialectical Anthropology*
                2(1):69–73.
Crick, Malcolm
    1982a   Anthropological Field Research, Meaning Creation and Knowl-
                edge Construction. In *Semantic Anthropology.* David Parkin,
                ed., pp. 15–37. New York: Academic Press.
    1982b   Anthropology of Knowledge. *Annual Review of Anthropology*
                11:287–313.
Crocombe, R. G.
    1964   *Land Tenure in the Cook Islands.* New York: Oxford University
                Press.

1967   From Ascendancy to Dependency. *Journal of Pacific History*
              2:97–111.
D'Andrade, Roy
1974   Memory and the Assessment of Behavior. In *Measurement in
              the Social Sciences*. H. Blalock, ed., pp. 159–86. Chicago:
              Aldine.
Davies, G. N.
1956a   Dental Conditions Among Polynesians of Pukapuka (Danger
              Island): I. General Background and the Prevalence of Maloc-
              colusion. *Journal of Dental Research* 35:115–31.
1956b   Dental Conditions Among the Polynesians of Pukapuka (Danger
              Island): II. The Prevalence of Periodontal Disease. *Journal of
              Dental Research* 35:734–41.
Dening, Greg
1980   *Islands and Beaches: Discourse on a Silent Land: Marquesas
              1774–1880*. Honolulu: University of Hawaii Press.
Department of Health
n.d.   *Survey of Medical and Environmental Conditions of Inhabitants
              of a South Sea Island Atoll: Pukapuka 1951*. Wellington, New
              Zealand: Department of Health.
Dewey, John
1948   *Reconstruction in Philosophy*. Boston: Beacon Press.
Dougherty, Janet, and Charles Keller
1982   Taskonomy: A Practical Approach to Knowledge Structures.
              American Ethnologist 9:763–74.
Douglas, Mary, ed.
1973   *Rules and Meanings: The Anthropology of Everyday Knowledge*.
              Baltimore: Penguin Books.
Du Bois, Cora
1960   *The People of Alor*, Vol. I. Minneapolis: University of Minnesota
              Press.
Dumont, Jean-Paul
1978   *The Headman and I: Ambiguity and Ambivalence in the Field-
              working Experience*. Austin: University of Texas Press.
Duranti, Alessandro
1985   Famous Theories and Local Theories: The Samoans and Witt-
              genstein. *Quarterly Newsletter of the Laboratory of Comparative
              Human Cognition* 7:46–51.
Dwyer, Kevin
1982   *Moroccan Dialogues: Anthropology in Question*. Baltimore,
              MD: Johns Hopkins University Press.
Earle, James
1967   James, William. In *The Encyclopedia of Philosophy*, 4:240–9.
              New York: Macmillan.
Ebihara, May
1985   American Ethnology in the 1930s: Contexts and Currents. In
              *Social Contexts of American Ethnology, 1840–1984: 1984 Pro-
              ceedings of the American Ethnological Society*. June Helm, ed.,
              pp. 101–21. Washington, DC: American Anthropological
              Association.

174   *Bibliography*

Eggan, Fred
1968   One Hundred Years of Ethnology and Social Anthropology. In
            One Hundred Years of Anthropology. J. O. Brew, ed., pp. 119–
            49. Cambridge, MA: Harvard University Press.
Ellen, R. F.
1984   *Ethnographic Research: A Guide to General Conduct.* New York:
            Academic Press.
Errington, Frederick
1984   *Manners and Meaning in West Sumatra: The Social Context of
            Consciousness.* New Haven, CT: Yale University Press.
Evans-Pritchard, E. E.
1937   *Witchcraft, Oracles, and Magic Among the Azande.* Oxford:
            Clarendon Press.
Ezorsky, Gertrude
1967   Pragmatic Theory of Truth. In *The Encyclopedia of Philosophy*
            6:427–30. New York: Macmillan.
Fabian, Joannes
1983   *Time and the Other: How Anthropology Makes Its Object.* New
            York: Columbia University Press.
Feinberg, Richard
1978   Anutan Ethnoepistemology: The Roots of "Knowledge" on a
            Polynesian Outlier. Paper prepared for the annual meetings of
            the Association for Social Anthropology in Oceania, 1978.
Finnegan, Ruth
1977   *Oral Poetry: Its Nature, Significance, and Social Context.* New
            York: Cambridge University Press.
Firth, Raymond
1936   *We the Tikopia.* London: Allen and Unwin.
1957   A Note on Descent Groups in Polynesia. *Man* 57:4–8.
1961   *History and Traditions of Tikopia.* Wellington, New Zealand:
            The Polynesian Society.
1963   Bilateral Descent Groups: An Operational Viewpoint. In *Studies
            in Kinship and Marriage.* I. Shapera, ed. Occasional Paper no.
            16, pp. 22–37. London: Royal Anthropological Institute of Great
            Britain and Ireland.
1967   *The Work of the Gods.* London: The Athlone Press.
1970   *Rank and Religion in Tikopia: A Study in Polynesian Paganism
            and Conversion to Christianity.* Boston: Beacon Press.
Fortes, Meyer
1938   Social and Psychological Aspects of Education in Taleland.
            Africa 11 (4, supplement). Reprinted in *From Child to Adult.*
            John Middleton, ed., pp. 14–74. Austin: University of Texas
            Press.
Fortune, Reo
1939   Arapesh Warfare. *American Anthropologist* 41:22–41.
Foster, George, Thayer Scudder, Elizabeth Colson, and Robert Kemper, eds.
1979   *Long-Term Field Research in Social Anthropology.* New York:
            Academic Press.
Foucault, Michel
1965   *Madness and Civilization.* New York: Random House.
1972   *The Archeology of Knowledge.* A. M. Sheridan-Smith, trans.

New York: Pantheon Books.

Fox, Richard
1985   *Lions of the Punjab: Culture in the Making*. Berkeley: University
of California Press.

Frake, Charles
1977   Plying Frames Can Be Dangerous: Some Reflections on Methodology in Cognitive Anthropology. *Quarterly Newsletter of the
Institute for Comparative Human Development*. Reprinted in
Language, Culture, and Cognition. Ronald Casson, ed., pp. 366–
77. New York: Macmillan.

France, Peter
1969   *The Charter of the Land: Custom and Colonization in Fiji*. New
York: Oxford University Press.

Freeman, Derek
1983   *Margaret Mead and Samoa: The Making and Unmaking of an
Anthropological Myth*. Cambridge, MA: Harvard University
Press.

Freilich, Morris
1977   Field Work: An Introduction. In *Marginal Natives at Work: Anthropologists in the Field*. M. Freilich, ed., pp. 1–37. Cambridge,
MA: Schenkman.

Frisbie, Florence
1948   *Miss Ulysses from Puka-Puka: The Autobiography of a South
Sea Trader's Daughter*. New York: Macmillan.

Frisbie, Johnny
1959   *The Frisbies of the South Seas*. New York: Doubleday.

Frisbie, Robert
1928a   At Home in Puka-Puka: Life on an Atoll. *Atlantic Monthly*
142(1):1–12.
1928b   Business as Usual. *Atlantic Monthly* 142(4):440–9.
1929a   Adventures in a Puka-Puka Library. *Atlantic Monthly*
143(2):172–9.
1929b   Puka-Puka Neighbors. *Atlantic Monthly* 144(2):186–95.
1929c   Magic Dances. *Atlantic Monthly* 144 (5):676–9.
1930   *The Book of Puka-Puka*. New York: Century.
1939   *Mr. Moonlight's Island*. New York: Farrar and Rhinehart.
1944   *The Island of Desire: The Story of a South Sea Trader*. New
York: Doubleday, Doran.

Funnell, Robert, and Richard Smith
1981   Search for a Theory of Cultural Transmission in an Anthropology
of Education: Notes on Spindler and Gearing. *Anthropology and
Education Quarterly* 12:275–300.

Furbee, Louanna, and Robert Benfer
1983   Cognitive and Geographical Maps: Study of Individual Variation
Among Tojolabal Mayans. *American Anthropologist* 85:305–34.

Gadamer, Hans-Georg
1975a   The Problem of Historical Consciousness. Universite Catholique
de Louvain, *Graduate Faculty Philosophy Journal* 5 (1). Reprinted in *Interpretive Social Science: A Reader*. Paul Rabinow
and William Sullivan, eds., pp. 103–60. Berkeley: University of
California Press.

1975b   *Truth and Method.* Garrett Barden and John Cumming, eds.
         New York: Seabury Press.
Gallimore, Ronald, Joan Boggs, and Cathie Jordan
1974   *Culture, Behavior, and Education: A Study of Hawaiian-Amer-
         icans.* Beverly Hills, CA: Sage.
Gallimore, Ronald, Stephen Boggs, and W. Scott MacDonald
1968   Education. In *Studies in a Hawaiian Community: Na Makamaka
         O Nanakuli.* R. Gallimore and A. Howard, eds., pp. 28–54.
         Pacific Anthropological Records, No. 1. Honolulu: Bernice P.
         Bishop Museum.
Gardner, P. M.
1976   Birds, Words and a Requiem for the Omniscient Informer.
         American Ethnologist 3:446–68.
Gartrell, Beverley
1979   Is Ethnography Possible? A Critique of *African Odyssey. Journal
         of Anthropological Research* 35:426–46.
Gearing, Frederick
1973   Anthropology and Education. In *Handbook of Social and Cul-
         tural Anthropology.* J. Honigmann, ed., pp. 1223–49. Chicago:
         Rand McNally.
Gearing, Frederick, and Lucinda Sangree
1979   *Toward a Cultural Theory of Education and Schooling.* New
         York: Mouton.
Geertz, Clifford
1973   *The Interpretation of Cultures.* New York: Basic Books.
1976   "From the Native's Point of View": On the Nature of Anthro-
         pological Understanding. In *Meaning in Anthropology.* Keith
         Basso and Henry Selby, eds., pp. 221–37. Albuquerque: Uni-
         versity of New Mexico Press. (Reprinted from *Bulletin of the
         American Academy of Arts and Sciences* 28 (1), 1974.)
Gill, William Wyatt
1862   South Seas Letters, Sydney, July 16, 1862: *London Missionary
         Society Records Relating to the South Seas 1796–1899.*
1876   *Life in the Southern Isles.* London: The Religious Tract Society.
1912   A Word About the Original Inhabitants of Pukapuka Island.
         Journal of the Polynesian Society 21:122–4.
Gilson, Richard
1980   *The Cook Islands 1820–1950.* Ron Crocombe, ed. Wellington,
         New Zealand: Victoria University Press.
Gladwin, Thomas
1970   *East Is a Big Bird: Navigation and Logic on Puluwat Atoll.* Cam-
         bridge, MA: Harvard University Press.
Goffman, Erving
1959   *The Presentation of Self in Everyday Life.* New York: Doubleday.
Goldman, Irving
1970   *Ancient Polynesian Society.* Chicago: University of Chicago
         Press.
Goodenough, Ward
1955   A Problem in Malayo-Polynesian Social Organization. *American
         Anthropologist* 57:71–83.

1961   Book review of *Social Structure in South East Asia*, edited by
            G. P. Murdock. *American Anthropologist* 63:1341–47.

Goody, Jack
1977   *The Domestication of the Savage Mind*. New York: Cambridge
            University Press.

Goody, Jack, and Ian Watt
1963   The Consequences of Literacy. *Comparative Studies in Society
            and History* 5:304–45.

Graves, Nancy, and Theodore Graves
1978   The Impact of Modernization on the Personality of a Polynesian
            People. *Human Organization* 37:115–35.

Greenfield, Patricia, and Jean Lave
1982   Cognitive Aspects of Informal Education. In *Cultural Perspec-
            tives on Child Development*. Daniel Wagner and Harold Steven-
            son, eds., pp. 181–207. San Francisco: Freeman.

Gruber, Jacob
1970   Ethnographic Salvage and the Shaping of Anthropology. *Amer-
            ican Anthropologist* 72:1289–99.

Gunson, Neil
1978   *Messengers of Grace: Evangelical Missionaries in the South Seas
            1797–1860*. New York: Oxford University Press.

Hallpike, C. R.
1979   *The Foundations of Primitive Thought*. New York: Oxford Uni-
            versity Press.

Hamelink, Cees
1983   *Cultural Autonomy in Global Communications: Planning Na-
            tional Information Policy*. New York: Longman.

Hansen, Judith
1982   From Background to Foreground: Toward an Anthropology of
            Learning. *Anthropology and Education Quarterly* 13:189–202.

Hanson, Allan
1979   Does God Have a Body? Truth, Reality and Cultural Relativism.
            Man 14:515–29.

Hanson, Allan, and Louise Hanson
1983   *Counterpoint in Maori Culture*. London: Routledge and Kegan
            Paul.

Harris, Marvin
1968   *The Rise of Anthropological Theory*. New York: Crowell.

Harwood, Frances
1976   Myth, Memory, and the Oral Tradition: Cicero in the Trobri-
            ands. *American Anthropologist* 78:783–96.

Hays, Terence
1976   An Empirical Method for the Identification of Covert Categories
            in Ethnobiology. *American Ethnologist* 3:489–507.

Hecht, Julia
1972   Pukapuka Kinship and Social Organization. Research Proposal
            Submitted to the National Science Foundation. Manuscript.
1976a   "Double Descent" and Cultural Symbolism in Pukapuka, North-
            ern Cook Islands. Doctoral dissertation. University of Chicago,
            Department of Anthropology.

1976b   "Double Descent" and Cultural Symbolism in Pukapuka, Northern Cook Islands. Dissertation abstract. Submitted to the National Science Foundation. Manuscript.

1977   The Culture of Gender in Pukapuka: Male, Female and the *Mayakitanga* 'Sacred Maid.' *Journal of the Polynesian Society* 86:183–206.

1978   "Let's Go to Pukapuka": The Home Island and Homes Away from Home. Revised version of paper presented at the annual meetings of the Association for Social Anthropology in Oceania, 1977.

1981   The Cultural Contexts of Siblingship in Pukapuka. In *Siblingship in Oceania*. Mac Marshall, ed., pp. 53–77. Ann Arbor: University of Michigan Press.

1985   Physical and Social Boundaries in Pukapukan Theories of Disease. In *Healing Practices in the South Pacific*. Claire Parsons, ed., pp. 144–57. Laie, Hawaii: The Institute of Polynesian Studies.

Heider, Karl
1976   Dani Children's Development of Competency in Social Structural Concepts. *Ethnology* 15:47–62.

1983   The Rashomon Effect in Ethnography: The Problem of Contradiction and Replicability. Paper prepared for the annual meetings of the Association of Social Anthropology in Oceania, 1984.

Hobsbawm, Eric, and Terence Ranger, eds.
1983   *The Invention of Tradition.* New York: Cambridge University Press.

Holland, Dorothy
1984   On the Generalization of Cultural Models Learned from Peers versus Teachers. Paper presented at the American Anthropological Association Meetings. 1984.

Holland, Dorothy, and Debra Skinner
1987   Prestige and Intimacy: The Folk Models Behind Americans' Talk About Gender Types. In *Cultural Models in Language and Thought*. Dorothy Holland and Naomi Quinn, eds. pp. 78–111. New York: Cambridge University Press.

Hollis, Martin, and Steven Lukes, eds.
1982   *Rationality and Relativism.* Cambridge: MIT Press.

Holy, Ladislav, and Milan Stuchlik
1983   The Structure of Folk Models: A CA Book Review. *Current Anthropology* 24:89–100.

Hooper, Antony
1981   *Why Tikopia Has Four Clans* (with comment by R. Firth). Occasional Paper No. 38. London: Royal Anthropological Institute of Great Britain and Ireland.

Hooper, Antony, and Judith Huntsman, eds.
1985   *Transformations of Polynesian Culture.* Auckland, New Zealand: The Polynesian Society.

Horton, Robin
1967   African Traditional Thought and Western Science. I: From Tradition to Science. II: The "Closed" and "Open" Predicaments. *Africa* 37:50–71, 155–87.

Horton, Robin, and Ruth Finnegan, eds.
  1973   *Modes of Thought: Essays on Thinking in Western and Non-Western Societies*. London: Faber and Faber.
Howard, Alan
  1970   *Learning to Be Rotuman*. New York: Teachers College Press.
  1972   Polynesian Social Stratification Revisited: Reflections on Castles Built of Sand (and a Few Bits of Coral). *American Anthropologist* 74:811–23.
  1973   Education in 'Aina Pumehana: The Hawaiian-American Student as Hero. In *Learning and Culture*. S. Kimball and J. Burnett, eds., pp. 115–30. Seattle: University of Washington Press.
  1974   *Ain't No Big Thing: Coping Strategies in a Hawaiian-American Community*. Honolulu: University of Hawaii Press.
  1979   Book review of *Rotuma: Split Island*, edited by Chris Plant. *Journal of the Polynesian Society* 88:354–5.
Howard, Alan, and John Kirkpatrick
  1989   Social Organization. In *Developments in Polynesian Ethnology*. Alan Howard and Robert Borofsky, eds. pp. 47–94. Honolulu: University of Hawaii Press.
Howe, K. R.
  1984   *Where the Waves Fall: A New South Sea Islands History from First Settlement to Colonial Rule*. Honolulu: University of Hawaii Press.
Hunn, Eugene
  1982   The Utilitarian Factor in Folk Biological Classification. *American Anthropologist* 84:830–47.
Hunter, Ian
  1964   *Memory*. Baltimore, MD: Penguin Books.
Huntsman, Judith
  1971   Concepts of Kinship and Categories of Kinsmen in the Tokelau Islands. *Journal of the Polynesian Society* 80:317–54.
Huntsman, Judith, and Antony Hooper
  1975   Male and Female in Tokelau Culture. *Journal of the Polynesian Society* 84:415–30.
Hutchin, J. J. K.
  1904   Traditions and Some Words of the Language of Danger or Pukapuka Island. *Journal of the Polynesian Society* 13:173–6.
Hutchins, Edwin
  1980   *Culture and Inference: A Trobriand Case Study*. Cambridge, MA: Harvard University Press.
Irvine, Judith
  1978   When Is Genealogy History? Wolof Genealogies in Comparative Perspective. *American Ethnologist* 5:651–74.
James, William
  1975   *Pragmatism*. Cambridge, MA: Harvard University Press.
Jameson, Frederic
  1981   *The Political Unconscious: Narrative as a Socially Symbolic Act*. Ithaca, NY: Cornell University Press.
Kaplan, David
  1974   The Anthropology of Authenticity: Everyman His Own Anthropologist. *American Anthropologist* 76:824–39.

Kay, Paul
1975   Synchronic Variability and Diachronic Change in Basic Color
            Terms. *Language in Society* 4:257–70.
Keesing, Roger
1970   Shrines, Ancestors, and Cognatic Descent: The Kwaio and Tal-
            lensi. *American Anthropologist* 72:755–75.
1974   Theories of Culture. *Annual Review of Anthropology* 3:73–97.
1982   *Kwaio Religion: The Living and the Dead in a Solomon Island
            Society.* New York: Columbia University Press.
Keesing, Roger, and Robert Tonkinson
1982   Reinventing Traditional Culture: The Politics of Kastom in Is-
            land Melanesia. *Mankind* 13(4).
Kimball, Solon, and Jacquetta Burnett
1973   *Learning and Culture.* Seattle: University of Washington Press.
Kirkpatrick, John
1983   *The Marquesan Notion of the Person.* Ann Arbor: UMI Research
            Press.
Kiste, Robert
1974   *The Bikinians: A Study in Forced Migration.* Menlo Park, CA:
            Cummings.
Kloosterman, Alphons
1976   *Discoverers of the Cook Islands and the Names They Gave.* Cook
            Islands Library and Museum, Bulletin 1. Rarotonga: Cook Is-
            lands Library and Museum.
Koskinen, Aarne
1968   **Kite: Polynesian Insights into Knowledge.* Helsinki: The Finnish
            Society for Missiolocy and Ecumenics.
Kuklick, Henrika
1983   The Sociology of Knowledge: Retrospect and Prospect. *Annual
            Review of Sociology* 9:287–310.
Kuper, Adam
1983   *Anthropology and Anthropologists: The Modern British School.*
            London: Routledge and Kegan Paul.
Laboratory of Comparative Human Cognition
1978   Cognition as a Residual Category in Anthropology. *Annual Re-
            view of Anthropology* 7:51–69.
1979   What's Cultural About Cross-Cultural Cognitive Psychology?
            Annual Review of Psychology 30:145–72.
Langham, Ian
1981   *The Building of British Social Anthropology: W. H. R. Rivers
            and His Cambridge Disciples in the Development of Kinship Stud-
            ies, 1898–1931.* Dordrecht, Holland: Reidel.
Larcom, Joan
1982   The Invention of Convention. *Mankind* 13(4):330–7.
Latour, B., and S. Woolgar
1979   *Laboratory Life: The Social Construction of Scientific Facts.* Bev-
            erly Hills, CA: Sage.
Lave, Jean
1975   Inter-Moiety-System Systems: A Structural Explanation of the
            Proliferation of Ramkokamekra Ceremonial Associations. Social
            Sciences Working Papers, 69a. University of California, Irvine,
            School of Social Sciences. Photocopy.

1980	Tailored Learning: Education and Cognitive Skills Among Tribal Craftsmen in West Africa. Manuscript.
1982	A Comparative Approach to Educational Forms and Learning Process. *Anthropology and Education Quarterly* 13:181–7.
1985	Introduction: Situationally-Specific Practice. In *The Social Organization of Knowledge and Practice: A Symposium. Anthropology and Education Quarterly* 16:171–6.
1988	*Cognition in Practice: Mind, Mathematics and Culture in Everyday Life*. New York: Cambridge University Press.

Lawrence, Peter
| 1971 | Statements About Religion: The Problem of Reliability. In *Anthropology in Oceania: Essays Presented to Ian Hogbin*. L. Hiatt and C. Jayawardena, eds., pp. 139–54. Sydney: Angus and Robertson. |

Leaf, Murray
| 1979 | *Man, Mind, and Science: A History of Anthropology*. New York: Columbia University Press. |

Levin, Paula
| 1978a | Questioning and Answering: A Cultural Analysis of Classroom Interrogative Encounters. Paper presented at the 76th Annual Meetings of the American Anthropological Association. |
| 1978b | Students and Teachers on Tubuai: A Cultural Analysis of Polynesian Classroom Interaction. Doctoral dissertation. University of California, San Diego, Department of Anthropology. |

Lévi-Strauss, Claude
1960	On Manipulated Sociological Models. *Bijdragen tot de Taal-, Land- en Volkenkunde* 116:17–44. Reprinted as *The Meaning and Use of the Notion of Model*. In *Structural Anthropology*, Vol. 2, pp. 71–81. New York: Basic Books.
1963a	Do Dual Organizations Exist? In *Structural Anthropology*, Vol. 1, pp. 132–63. New York: Basic Books.
1963b	Social Structures of Central and Eastern Brazil. In *Structural Anthropology*, Vol. 1, pp. 120–31. New York: Basic Books.
1966	*The Savage Mind*. Chicago: University of Chicago Press.

Levy, Robert
1972	Tahiti, Sin, and the Question of Integration Between Personality and Sociocultural Systems. In *The Psychoanalytic Study of Society*, Vol. 5. Warner Muensterberger and Sidney Axelrad, eds. Reprinted in *Culture and Personality: Contemporary Readings*. Robert LeVine, ed., pp. 287–306. Chicago: Aldine.
1973	*Tahitians: Mind and Experience in the Society Islands*. Chicago: University of Chicago Press.
1984	Mead, Freeman, and Samoa: The Problem of Seeing Things as They Are. *Ethos* 12:85–92.

Lewis, G.
| 1980 | *Day of Shining Red: An Essay on Understanding Ritual*. New York: Cambridge University Press. |

Lewis, Oscar
| 1951 | *Life in a Mexican Village: Tepoztlan Restudied*. Urbana: University of Illinois Press. |
| 1953 | Tepoztlan Restudied: A Critique of the Folk-Urban Concep- |

tualization of Social Change (with discussion by R. Beals). *Rural Sociology* 18:121–37.

Lindstrom, Lamont
  1982   Leftamap Kastom: The Political History of Tradition on Tanna (Vanuatu). *Mankind* 13(4):316–29.
  1983   The Politics of Dictionary Making on Tanna (Vanuatu). Paper presented at the 15th Pacific Science Congress, New Zealand.
  1984   Doctor, Lawyer, Wise Man, Priest: Big-Men and Knowledge in Melanesia. *Man* 19:291–309.

Linnekin, Joycelyn
  1983   Defining Tradition: Variations on the Hawaiian Identity. *American Ethnologist* 10:241–52.
  1985   *Children of the Land: Exchange and Status in a Hawaiian Community.* New Brunswick, NJ: Rutgers University Press.

Loftus, Elizabeth
  1979   *Eyewitness Testimony.* Cambridge, MA: Harvard University Press.
  1980   *Memory.* Reading, MA: Addison-Wesley.

Loftus, Elizabeth, and Geoffrey Loftus
  1980   On the Permanence of Stored Information in the Human Brain. *American Psychologist* 35:409–20.

Loftus, Geoffrey, and Elizabeth Loftus
  1976   *Human Memory: The Processing of Information.* Hillsdale, NJ: Erlbaum.

Lord, Albert
  1960   *The Singer of Tales.* Cambridge, MA: Harvard University Press.

Lovett, Richard
  1899   *The History of the London Missionary Society, 1795–1895.* 2 Vols. London: Henry Frowde.

Lowie, Robert
  1920   *Primitive Society.* New York: Boni and Liveright.
  1937   *The History of Ethnological Theory.* New York: Holt, Rhinehart and Winston.
  1942   *Studies in Plains Indian Folklore.* University of California Publications in American Archaeology and Ethnology, 40(1): 1–26.

Luomala, Katharine
  1974   Review article: Condliffe, J. B. *Te Rangi Hiroa: The Life of Sir Peter Buck. Journal of the Polynesian Society* 83:467–78.

MacGregor, Gordon
  1935   Notes on the Ethnology of Pukapuka. Bernice P. Bishop Museum Occasional Papers. Vol. 11, No. 6. Honolulu: Bernice P. Bishop Museum.

Magnarella, Paul
  1983   Book review of *Moroccan Dialogues: Anthropology in Question,* by K. Dwyer. *American Anthropologist* 85:981–2.

Malinowski, Bronislaw
  1961   *Argonauts of the Western Pacific.* New York: Dutton.
  1967   *A Diary in the Strict Sense of the Term.* New York: Harcourt, Brace, and World.

Mannheim, Karl
  1952   *Essays on the Sociology of Knowledge.* P. Kecskemeti, ed. Lon-

don: Routledge and Kegan Paul.
1953   *Essays on Sociology and Social Psychology.* P. Kecskemeti, ed. London: Routledge and Kegan Paul.

Marcus, George
1978   Status Rivalry in a Polynesian Steady-State Society. *Ethos* 6:242–69.
1989   Chieftainship. In *Developments in Polynesian Ethnology.* Alan Howard and Robert Borofsky, eds., pp. 175–209. Honolulu: University of Hawaii Press.

Marcus, George, and Dick Cushman
1982   Ethnographies as Texts. *Annual Review of Anthropology* 11:25–69.

Marcus, George, and Michael Fischer
1986   *Anthropology as Cultural Critique: An Experimental Moment in the Human Sciences.* Chicago: Chicago University Press.

Mason, Leonard
1959   Suprafamilial Authority and Economic Process in Micronesian Atolls. *Humanites, Cahiers de l'Institut de Science Economique Appliquee* 5(1):87–118. Reprinted in *Peoples and Cultures of the Pacific.* Andrew P. Vayda, ed., pp. 299–329. New York: Natural History Press.

Mataola, Tukia, Mataola Tutai, Robert Borofsky, Waleeu Wuatai, Walewoa Teingoa, Tuiva Kalowia, Ron Vetter, Tiaki Wuatai, Tautua Tautua, Lavalua Tutai, Penese Poyila, and Itaako Elisa
1981   Pukapukan-English Dictionary: A Preliminary Edition. Manuscript.

Mathews, Holly
1983   Context-Specific Variation in Humoral Classification. *American Anthropologist* 85:826–47.

Maude, H.
1968   *Of Islands and Men: Studies in Pacific History.* New York: Oxford University Press.

Mayberry-Lewis, David
1960   The Analysis of Dual Organizations: A Methodological Critique. *Bijdragen tot de Taal-, Land- en Volkenkunde* 116:17–44.
1967   *Akwe-Shavante Society.* Oxford: Clarendon Press.

McArthur, Margaret
1971   Men and Spirits in the Kunimaipa Valley. In *Anthropology in Oceania.* L. R. Hiatt and C. Jayawardena, eds., pp. 155–89. Sydney: Angus and Robertson.

McArthur, Norma
1968   *Island Populations of the Pacific.* Honolulu: University of Hawaii Press.

Mead, George Herbert
1929   *A Pragmatic Theory of Truth: Studies in the Nature of Truth.* University of California Publications in Philosophy 11:65–88.
1938   *The Philosophy of the Act.* Charles Morris, ed. Chicago: University of Chicago Press.

Mead, Margaret
1928   *Coming of Age in Samoa.* New York: Morrow.
1935   *Sex and Temperament in Three Primitive Societies.* New York: Morrow.

Merton, Robert
1968   *Social Theory and Social Structure*. New York: Free Press.
Middleton, John, ed.
1970   *From Child to Adult: Studies in the Anthropology of Education*.
          Austin: University of Texas Press.
Moore, George Edward
1953   *Some Main Problems of Philosophy*. New York: Macmillan.
Morphy, Howard, and Frances Morphy
1984   The 'Myths' of Ngalakan History: Ideology and Images of the
          Past in Northern Australia. *Man* 19:459–78.
Morrell, W. P.
1960   *Britain in the Pacific Islands*. Oxford: Clarendon Press.
Morris, Brian
1976   Whither the Savage Mind? Notes on the Natural Taxonomies of
          a Hunting and Gathering People. *Man* 11:542–57.
Munroe, Robert, and Ruth Munroe
1975   *Cross-Cultural Human Development*. Monterey, CA: Brooks/
          Cole.
Murtaugh, Michael
1985   The Practice of Arithmetic by American Grocery Shoppers. In
          *The Social Organization of Knowledge and Practice: A Sympo-
          sium. Anthropology and Education Quarterly* 16:186–92.
New Zealand Meteorological Service
n.d.   Untitled Weather Reports on Pukapuka, Cook Islands, 1930–
          1974. Manuscript.
Noricks, Jay
1983   Unrestricted Cognatic Descent and Corporateness on Niutao, a
          Polynesian Island of Tuvalu. *American Ethnologist* 10:571–84.
Ochs, Elinore
1982   Talking to Children in Western Samoa. *Language in Society*
          11:77–104.
Oliver, Douglas
1974   *Ancient Tahitian Society*. Honolulu: University Press of Hawaii.
Parkin, David
1982   Introduction. In *Semantic Anthropology*. David Parkin, ed.,
          pp. xi-li. New York: Academic Press.
Peel, J.
1984   Making History: The Past in the Ijesha Present. *Man* 19:111–32.
Pelto, Pertti, and Gretel Pelto
1975   Intra-Cultural Diversity: Some Theoretical Issues. *American
          Ethnologist* 2:1–18.
1978   *Anthropological Research: The Structure of Inquiry*. New York:
          Cambridge University Press.
Piaget, Jean
1966   Need and Significance of Cross-Cultural Studies in Genetic Psy-
          chology. *International Journal of Psychology* 1:3–13.
Prior, A. N.
1967   Correspondence Theory of Truth. In *The Encyclopedia of Phi-
          losophy* 2:223–32. New York: Macmillan.
Prior, Ian
1971   The Price of Civilization. *Nutrition Today* 6, 4:2–11.

1974   Cardiovascular Epidemiology in New Zealand and the Pacific. *New Zealand Medical Journal* 80:245–52.

Prior, Ian, Flora Davidson, Clare Salmond, and Z. Czochanska
1981   Cholesterol, Coconuts, and Diet on Polynesian Atolls: A Natural Experiment: The Pukapuka and Tokelau Island Studies. *American Journal of Clinical Nutrition* 34:1552–61.

Prior, Ian, H. Harvey, M. Neave, and Flora Davidson
1966   *The Health of Two Groups of Cook Island Maoris*. New Zealand Department of Health Special Report Series, No. 26. Wellington: Government Printer.

Quinn, Naomi and Dorothy Holland
1987   Culture and Cognition. In *Cultural Models in Language and Thought*. Dorothy Holland and Naomi Quinn, eds., pp. 3–40. New York: Cambridge University Press.

Rabinow, Paul
1977   *Reflections on Fieldwork in Morocco*. Berkeley: University of California Press.

Rabinow, Paul, and William Sullivan, eds.
1979   *Interpretive Social Science: A Reader*. Berkeley: University of California Press.

Radin, Paul
1957   *Primitive Man as a Philosopher*, rev. ed. New York: Dover.

Ranger, Terence
1983   The Invention of Tradition in Colonial Africa. In *The Invention of Tradition*. Eric Hobsbawm and Terence Ranger, eds., pp. 211–62. New York: Cambridge University Press.

Raum, Otto
1938   Some Aspects of Indigenous Education Among the Chaga. *Journal of the Royal Anthropological Institute* 68:209–21.

Reddy, R., and A. Newell
1974   Knowledge and Its Representation in a Speech Understanding System. In *Knowledge and Cognition*. L. W. Gregg, ed., pp. 253–85. Potomac, MD: Erblaum.

Redfield, Robert
1930   *Tepoztlan: A Mexican Village*. Chicago: University of Chicago Press.
1953   *The Primitive World and Its Transformations*. Ithaca, NY: Cornell University Press.
1960   *The Little Community and Peasant Society and Culture*. Chicago: University of Chicago Press.

Reed, H., and Jean Lave
1979   Arithmetic as a Tool for Investigating Relations Between Culture and Cognition. *American Ethnologist* 6:568–82.

Ricoeur, Paul
1980   Existence and Hermeneutics. In *Contemporary Hermeneutics*. Josef Bleicher, ed., pp. 236–56. London: Routledge and Kegan Paul.

Ritchie, James
1966   Obituary: Ernest Beaglehole, 1906–1965. *Journal of the Polynesian Society* 75:109–19.

Ritchie, Jane, and James Ritchie
1979   *Growing Up in Polynesia*. Sydney: George Allen and Unwin.

1989   Socialization and Psychological Development. In *Developments in Polynesian Ethnology*. Alan Howard and Robert Borofsky, eds., pp. 95–135. Honolulu: University of Hawaii Press.

Roberton, J. B.
1962   The Evaluation of Maori Tribal Tradition as History. *Journal of the Polynesian Society* 71:293–309.

Romanucci-Ross, Lola
1983   Alone and Adrift in Samoa: Early Mead Reconsidered. *Reviews in Anthropology* 10(3):85–92.

Rosaldo, Renato
1980   *Illongot Headhunting, 1883–1974: A Study in Society and History*. Stanford, CA: Stanford University Press.

Rosch, Eleanor
1975   Cognitive Representations of Semantic Categories. *Journal of Experimental Psychology: General* 104:192–233.

Rose, Michael, and Kimball Romney
1979   Cognitive Pluralism or Individual Differences: A Comparison of Alternative Models of American English Kin Terms. *American Ethnologist* 6:752–62.

Rubinstein, Robert
1981   Knowledge and Political Process on Malo. In *Vanuatu: Politics, Economics and Ritual in Island Melanesia*. Michael Allen, ed., pp. 135–72. New York: Academic Press.

Rudmin, Floyd
n.d.   Ernest Beaglehole. Manuscript.

Sahlins, Marshall
1958   *Social Stratification in Polynesia*. Seattle: University of Washington Press.
1976   *Culture and Practical Reason*. Chicago: University of Chicago Press.
1981   *Historical Metaphors and Mythical Realities*. Ann Arbor: University of Michigan Press.
1983   Other Times, Other Customs: The Anthropology of History. *American Anthropologist* 85:517–44.
1985   *Islands of History*. Chicago: University of Chicago Press.

Salisbury, Kevin
1984   Tradition and Change in the Music of Pukapuka, Cook Islands. *Pacific Arts Newsletter* 19:42–55.

Salmond, Anne
1982   Theoretical Landscapes: On a Cross-Cultural Conception of Knowledge. In *Semantic Anthropology*. David Parkin, ed., pp. 65–87. New York: Academic Press.

Sanjek, Roger
1977   Cognitive Maps of the Ethnic Domain in Urban Ghana: Reflections on Variability and Change. *American Ethnologist* 4:603–22.

Sapir, Edward
1938   Why Cultural Anthropology Needs the Psychiatrist. *Psychiatry* 1:7–12.

Savage, Stephen
1962   *A Dictionary of the Maori Language of Rarotonga*. Wellington, New Zealand: Department of Island Territories.

Schank, Roger, and R. P. Abelson
1977   *Scripts, Plans, Goals, and Understanding.* Hillsdale, NJ:
            Erlbaum.
Scheffler, Harold
1964   Descent Concepts and Descent Groups: The Maori Case. *Journal
            of the Polynesian Society* 73:126–33.
1966   Ancestor Worship in Anthropology: Or Observations on De-
            scent and Descent Groups. *Current Anthropology* 7:541–51.
Schieffelin, Edward
1982   The Retaliation of the Animals: On the Cultural Construction
            of the Past in Papua New Guinea. Manuscript.
Schneider, David
1968   *American Kinship: A Cultural Account.* Englewood Cliffs, NJ:
            Prentice-Hall.
1972   What Is Kinship All About? In *Kinship Studies in the Morgan
            Memorial Year.* P. Reinig, ed., pp. 32–63. Washington, DC:
            Anthropological Society of Washington.
1976   Notes Toward a Theory of Culture. In *Meaning in Anthropology.*
            Keith Basso and Henry Selby, eds., pp. 197–220. Albuquerque:
            University of New Mexico Press.
Scholte, Bob
1973   Toward a Reflexive and Critical Anthropology. In *Reinventing
            Anthropology.* Dell Hymes, ed., pp. 430–57. New York: Ran-
            dom House.
Scollon, Ron, and Suzanne Scollon
1981   *Narrative, Literacy and Face in Interethnic Communication.* Nor-
            wood, NJ: Ablex.
Scribner, Sylvia
1977   Modes of Thinking and Ways of Speaking: Culture and Logic
            Reconsidered. In *Thinking: Readings in Cognitive Science.* P.
            Johnson-Laird and P. Wason, eds., pp. 483–500. New York:
            Cambridge University Press.
1985   Knowledge at Work. In *The Social Organization of Knowledge
            and Practice: A Symposium. Anthropology of Education Quar-
            terly* 16:199–206.
Scribner, Sylvia, and Michael Cole
1973   Cognitive Consequences of Formal and Informal Education. *Sci-
            ence* 182:553–9.
1981   *The Psychology of Literacy.* Cambridge, MA: Harvard Univer-
            sity Press.
Shankman, Paul
1984   The Thick and the Thin: On the Interpretive Theoretical Pro-
            gram of Clifford Geertz (with CA Comment). *Current Anthro-
            pology* 25:261–79.
Shapiro, H.
1942   *The Anthropometry of Pukapuka.* Anthropological Papers of the
            American Museum of Natural History 38(Pt.3):143–69.
Sharp, Donald, Michael Cole, and Charles Lave
1979   *Education and Cognitive Development: The Evidence from Ex-
            perimental Research.* Monographs of the Society for Research in
            Child Development, Serial 178, Vol. 44(1–2).

Shils, Edward
1981   *Tradition*. Chicago: University of Chicago Press.
Shore, Bradd
1982   *Sala'ilua: A Samoan Mystery*. New York: Columbia University Press.
n.d.   Polynesian World Views: A Synthesis. Manuscript.
Shweder, Richard
1977   Likeness and Likelihood in Everyday Thought: Magical Thinking in Judgements About Personality (with comment). *Current Anthropology* 18:637–58.
1979–80   Rethinking Culture and Personality Theory, Parts I, II, and III. *Ethos* 7:255–311, 8:60–94.
Shweder, Richard, and Edmund Bourne
1982   Does the Concept of the Person Vary Cross-Culturally? In *Cultural Conceptions of Mental Health and Therapy*. A. Marsella and G. White, eds., pp. 97–137. Dordrecht, Holland: Reidel.
Shweder, Richard, and Roy D'Andrade
1980   The Systematic Distortion Hypothesis. In *Fallible Judgement in Behavior Research: New Directions for Methodology of Social and Behavioral Science*, No. 4. Richard Shweder, ed., pp. 37–58. San Francisco: Jossey-Bass.
Shweder, Richard, and Robert LeVine, eds.
1984   *Culture Theory: Essays on Mind, Self, and Emotion*. New York: Cambridge University Press.
Silverman, Martin
1971   *Disconcerting Issue: Meaning and Struggle in a Resettled Pacific Community*. Chicago: University of Chicago Press.
1977   Making Sense: A Study of a Banaban Meeting. In *Exiles and Migrants in Oceania*. Michael Lieber, ed., pp. 121–60. Honolulu: University of Hawaii Press.
Smith, John
1977   The Singer or the Song? A Reassessment of Lord's 'Oral Theory.' *Man* 12:141–53.
Southwald, Martin
1979   Religious Belief. *Man* 14:628–44.
Spindler, George, and Louise Spindler
1981   Comment on Funnel and Smith. *Anthropology and Education Quarterly* 12:300–3.
Stein, Nancy, and Christine Glenn
1979   An Analysis of Story Comprehension in Elementary School Children. In *New Directions in Discourse Processing*. Roy Freddle, ed., pp. 53–120. Norwood, NJ: Ablex.
Stocking, George
1968   *Race, Culture, and Evolution: Essays in the History of Anthropology*. New York: Free Press.
1983a   The Ethnographer's Magic: Fieldwork in British Anthropology from Tylor to Malinowski. In *Observers Observed: Essays on Ethnographic Fieldwork*. George Stocking, ed., pp. 70–120. Madison: University of Wisconsin Press.
Stocking, George, ed.
1983b   *Observers Observed: Essays on Ethnographic Fieldwork*. Madison: University of Wisconsin Press.

Strauss, Claudia
  1984   Beyond "Formal" versus "Informal" Education: Uses of Psy-
              chological Theory in Anthropological Research. *Ethos*
              12(3):195–222.
Swartz, Marc
  1982   Cultural Sharing and Cultural Theory: Some Findings of a Five-
              Society Study. *American Anthropologist* 84:314–38.
Te Rangi Hiroa (Peter H. Buck)
  1945   *An Introduction to Polynesian Anthropology*. Bernice P.
              Bishop Museum Bulletin 187. Honolulu: Bernice P. Bishop
              Museum.
Thayer, H. S.
  1967   Pragmatism. In *The Encyclopedia of Philosophy* 6:430–6. New
              York: Macmillan.
Thomas, David
  1975   Cooperation and Competition Among Polynesian and European
              Children. *Child Development* 46:948–53.
  1978   Cooperation and Competition Among Children in the Pacific
              Islands and New Zealand: The School as an Agent of Social
              Change. *Journal of Research and Development in Education*
              12(1):88–95.
Tiffany, Sharon
  1975   The Cognatic Descent Groups of Contemporary Samoa. *Man*
              10:430–47.
Tiro, Tipuia
  n.d.   Historical Notes and Genealogy. Manuscript. (Located at the
              Government Office, Pukapuka.)
Turner, Paul
  1978   *Report on My Visit to Pukapuka/Nassau/Palmerston*. Rarotonga:
              Ministry of Planning and External Affairs.
Tyler, Stephen
  1978   *The Said and the Unsaid: Mind, Meaning, and Culture*. New
              York: Academic Press.
Ulin, Robert
  1984   *Understanding Cultures: Perspectives in Anthropology and Social
              Theory*. Austin: University of Texas.
Vansina, Jan
  1978   *The Children of Woot: A History of the Kuba Peoples*. Madison:
              University of Wisconsin Press
  1980   Memory and Oral Tradition. In *The African Past Speaks: Essays
              on Oral Tradition and History*. Joseph Miller, ed., pp. 262–79.
              Hamden, CT: Archon Books.
Vayda, Andrew
  1957   Census of Yato Village *et al*. Manuscript.
  1958   The Pukapukans on Nassau Island. *Journal of the Polynesian
              Society* 67:256–65.
  1959   Native Traders in Two Polynesian Atolls. *Cahiers de l'Institut de
              Science Economique Appliquee* 5(1):119–37.
Vivian, J. C.
  1871–2   Journal. In *London Missionary Society Records: Journals South
              Seas 1796–1899*. (Box 11, Archives of the London Missionary
              Society.)

Voget, Fred
  1973   The History of Cultural Anthropology. In *Handbook of Social and Cultural Anthropology*. John Honigmann, ed., pp. 1–88. Chicago: Rand McNally.
Wagner, Roy
  1981   *The Invention of Culture*. Chicago: University of Chicago Press.
Wallace, Anthony
  1961   *Culture and Personality*. New York: Random House.
Wayne (Malinowska), Helena
  1985   Bronislaw Malinowski: The Influence of Various Women on His Life and Works. *American Ethnologist* 12:529–40.
Weiner, Annette
  1976   *Women of Value, Men of Renown: New Perspectives on Trobriand Exchange*. Austin: University of Texas Press.
Weller, Susan
  1984a   Consistency and Consensus among Informants: Disease Concepts in a Rural Mexican Village. *American Anthropologist* 86:966–75.
  1984b   Cross-Cultural Concepts of Illness: Variation and Validation. *American Anthropologist* 86:341–51.
White, Alan
  1967   Coherence Theory of Truth. In *The Encyclopedia of Philosophy* 2:130–3. New York: Macmillan.
White, Hayden
  1973   Metahistory: The Historical Imagination in Nineteenth-Century Europe. Baltimore, MD: Johns Hopkins University Press.
Williams, Thomas Rhys
  1958   The Structure of the Socialization Process in Papago Indian Society. *Social Forces* 36(3):251–6.
Wilson, Bryan, ed.
  1970   *Rationality*. New York: Harper and Row.
Wolf, Eric
  1982   *Europe and the People Without History*. Berkeley: University of California Press.
Wright, Peter
  1979   A Study in the Legitimisation of Knowledge: The 'Success' of Medicine and the 'Failure' of Astrology. In *On the Margins of Science: The Social Construction of Rejected Knowledge*. Sociological Review Monograph 27. Roy Wallis, ed., pp. 85–101. Keele, England: University of Keele.
Yarmey, Daniel
  1979   *The Psychology of Eyewitness Testimony*. New York: Free Press.
Znaniecki, Florian
  1940   *The Social Role of the Man of Knowledge*. New York: Columbia University Press.

Index

adoption, and burial site, 63, 67, 68, 136
age
  of brothers, and authority, 26
  as criteria for recognized authority, 111–12, 145
Akatawa (form of social organization), 72, 73
  dates of, 7, 8, 11, 16, 151, 152
  differences among, 8
  length of, 10, 11, 13, 16, 151, 152
  matrimoiety system paralleling, 69
  number of, 7, 8, 10
  occurrences of, prior to 1976 revival, 1, 6–8, 10–11, 13, 16, 141–2, 151
  origin myth of, 6, 8
  Pukapukan knowledge of, 1, 6–8, 10–11, 150–2
  reasons for, 10, 11
  revival of, *see Akatawa* revival (1976)
  similarities among, 8, 10–11
  termination of, 10, 11
  Westerners' lack of knowledge of, 1–2, 12–16, 139, 141, 152
  as word, 6–7
Akatawa revival (1976), 1, 23, 139–42
  changes occurring during, 14, 35–8, 72–3, 140, 142
  extensions of, 140, 142
  frictions arising from, 140
  individual decision making about, downplaying of, 139–40, 149
  reasons for, 139
  satisfaction with, 140–1
  termination of, 149
Akima
  on evaluating accuracy of statements, 110

genealogies collected by, 143
  as Island Council's chairman, 103, 135
  on matrimoiety revival, 135
  speech at feast, 103
Alaikongo, rejected as informant by Beagleholes, 58
ancestor, apical, see *pu mua*
ancestral ghosts, punishment by, for changing cemeteries, 63, 67, 126
anthropological research
  contexts of, xv–xvii, 40–1, 45–50, 59–62, 153, 154
  dialogical nature of, 145, 147–9, 150–2, 154, 155, 167n9
  as scientific, 46–7, 50
anthropologists
  sensitivity of, to context, 127
  ties of, to colonial regimes, 47
  traditions overstructured by, 2, 145, 148, 152, 165n8, 167n8
  traditions preserved and changed by, 132, 142–4
Apela
  on former *Akatawa*, 8, 10
  as knowledgeable about traditional matters, 7
  living through *Akatawa* in youth, 7
  on matrilineage ownership of taro swamps, 128
  and wrestling chants, 81, 96
apical ancestor, see *pu mua*
artifacts, *see* material culture
ascribed social positions, knowledge not based on, 112
Ato, *see* Yato

191

Printed in the United Kingdom
by Lightning Source UK Ltd.
9475800001B